WEST EUROPEAN COMMUNIST PARTIES
AFTER THE REVOLUTIONS OF 1989

Also by Martin J. Bull

CONTEMPORARY ITALY: A Research Guide

Also by Paul Heywood

MARXISM AND THE FAILURE OF ORGANISED
SOCIALISM IN SPAIN, 1879–1936

SPAIN'S NEXT FIVE YEARS: A Political Risk Analysis

West European Communist Parties after the Revolutions of 1989

Edited by

Martin J. Bull
Lecturer in Politics and Contemporary History
University of Salford

and

Paul Heywood
Senior Lecturer in Politics
University of Glasgow

St. Martin's Press

Selection and editorial matter © Martin J. Bull and
Paul Heywood 1994
Introduction © Paul Heywood 1994
Chapter 8 © Martin J. Bull 1994
Chapters 1–7 © The Macmillan Press Ltd 1994

First published in Great Britain 1994 by
THE MACMILLAN PRESS LTD
Houndmills, Basingstoke, Hampshire RG21 2XS
and London
Companies and representatives
throughout the world

A catalogue record for this book is available
from the British Library.

ISBN 0–333–57934–8

Printed in Great Britain by
Antony Rowe Ltd
Chippenham, Wiltshire

First published in the United States of America 1994 by
Scholarly and Reference Division,
ST. MARTIN'S PRESS, INC.,
175 Fifth Avenue,
New York, N.Y. 10010

ISBN 0–312–12268–3

Library of Congress Cataloging-in-Publication Data
West European communist parties after the revolutions of 1989 / edited
by Martin J. Bull and Paul Heywood.
p.   cm.
Includes bibliographical references and index.
ISBN 0–312–12268–3
1. Communist parties—Europe.   2. Communism—Europe.   3. Post-
communism—Europe.   I. Bull, Martin J.   II. Heywood, Paul.
HX239.W46 1994
324.1'75'90409049—dc20
                                        94–14211
                                        CIP

The loathsome mask has fallen, the man remains
Sceptreless, free, uncircumscribed, but man
Equal, unclassed, tribeless, and nationless,
Exempt from awe, worship, degree, the king
Over himself; just, gentle, wise: but man
Passionless? – no, yet free from guilt or pain,
Which were, for his will made or suffered them,
Nor yet exempt, though ruling them like slaves,
From chance, and death, and mutability,
The clogs of that which else might oversoar
The loftiest star of unascended heaven,
Pinnacled dim in the intense inane.

Percy Bysshe Shelley,
Prometheus Unbound, III.iii.193

Contents

List of Tables

List of Abbreviations

AGMs	Annual General Meetings
APU	*Aliança do Povo Unido* (United Peoples' Alliance) (Port.)
CC OO	*Comisiones Obreras* (Workers' Commissions) (Sp.)
CDS	*Centro Democrático y Social* (Social and Democratic Centre) (Sp.)
CDU	*Coligação Democrática Unitário* (Democratic Coalition) [comprising PCP, *Intervenção Democrática, Os Verdes-PEV*, and UDP] (Port.)
CDU	*Christlich-demokratische Union* (Christian Democratic Union) (Ger.)
CiU	*Convergència i Unió* (Convergence and Unity) (Sp.)
CGT	*Confédération Générale du Travail* (General Workers' Union) (Fr.)
CGTP	*Confederação Geral dos Trabalhadores Portugueses* (General Confederation of Portuguese Workers) (Port.)
CNAPD	Peace Movement (Belg.)
CPN	Communist Party of the Netherlands
CPGB	Communist Party of Great Britain
CPs	Communist Parties
CPSU	Communist Party of the Soviet Union
DC	*Democrazia Cristiana* (Christian Democracy) (It.)
DFU	*Deutsche Friedensunion* (German Peace Union)
DKP	*Deutsche Kommunistische Partei* (German Communist Party, from 1969)
DL	Democratic Left (Brit.)
DSU	*Deutsche Soziale Union* (German Social Union)
EC	European Community
EE	*Euskadiko Ezkerra* (Basque Left) (Sp.)

EMU	Economic and Monetary Union
EPK	*Euskadi Partit Komunista* (Basque Communist Party) (Sp.)
FDJ	*Freie Deutsche Jugend* (Free German Youth)
FGTB	*Fédération Générale du Travail de Belgique* (General Workers' Federation of Belgium)
FRG	Federal Republic of Germany
GDR	German Democratic Republic
IMF	International Monetary Fund
INES	*Instituto de Estudos Sociais* (Institute of Social Studies (Port.)
IU	*Izquierda Unida* (United Left) (Sp.)
KKE	*Kommunistikon Komma Ellados* (Greek Communist Party)
KPD	*Kommunistische Partei Deutschlands* (German Communist Party, until 1956)
MDP/CDE	*Movimento Democrático Português* (Portuguese Democratic Movement)
MFA	*Movimento das Forças Armadas* (Armed Forces Movement) (Port.)
MfS	*Ministerium für Staatssicherheit* (Ministry for State Security – the '*Stasi*') (Ger.)
MP	Member of Parliament
MT	*Marxism Today* (CPGB weekly)
NATO	North Atlantic Treaty Organisation
NUM	National Union of Mineworkers (Br.)
Pasoc	*Partido de Acción Socialista* (Socialist Action Party) (Sp.)
PCB	*Parti Communiste de Belgique* (Belgian Communist Party)
PCE	*Partido Comunista de España* (Spanish Communist Party)
PCE-mr	*Partido Comunista de España – marxista revolucionario* (Spanish Communist Party – Revolutionary Marxist; later PTE)
PCF	*Parti Communiste Français* (French Communist Party)
PCI	*Partito Comunista Italiano* (Italian Communist Party)

PCP	*Partido Comunista Português* (Portuguese Communist Party)
PCPE	*Partido Comunista de los Pueblos de España* (Communist Party of the Spanish People)
PDS	*Partei des Demokratischen Sozialismus* (Democratic Socialist Party, successor to East German SED) (Ger.)
PDS	*Partito Democratico della Sinistra* (Democratic Party of the Left) (It.)
PNV	*Partido Nacionalista Vasco* (Basque Nationalist Party) (Sp.)
POS-SAP	*Parti Ouvrier Socialiste* (Socialist Workers' Party; Trotskyist) (Belg.)
PP	*Partido Popular* (Peoples' Party) [prior to 1989 known variously as AP (*Alianza Popular*), CD (*Coalición Democrática*), CP (*Coalición Popular*)] (Sp.)
PPPS	People's Press Printing Society (Brit.)
PRD	*Partido Renovador Democrático* (Democratic Renewal Party) (Port.)
PS	*Parti Socialiste* (Socialist Party) (Fr.)
PSD	*Partido Social Democrata* (Social Democrat Party) (Port.)
PSI	*Partito Socialista Italiano* (Socialist Party)
PSOE	*Partido Socialista Obrero Español* (Spanish Socialist Workers' Party)
PSP	*Partido Socialista Português* (Socialist Party) (Port.)
PSUC	*Partido Socialista Unificado de Cataluña* (United Socialist Party of Cataluña) (Sp.)
PTB-PvdA	*Parti du Travail de Belgique* (Belgian Labour Party; Maoist)
PTE	*Partido de Trabajadores Españoles* (Spanish Workers' Party; originally PCE-mr)
SED	*Sozialistische Einheitspartei Deutschlands* (Socialist Unity Party of Germany; successor to PDS)
SKP	*Suomen Kommunistinen puolue* (Finnish Communist Party)

SPD	*Sozialdemokratische Partei Deutschlands* (Social Democratic Party of Germany)
UCD	*Unión de Centro Democrático* (Union of the Democratic Centre) (Sp.)
UDP	*União Democrática Popular* (Popular Democratic Union) (Port.)
UGT	*União Geral dos Trabalhadores* (General Workers' Union) (Port.)
UGT	*Unión General de Trabajadores* (General Workers' Union) (Sp.)
USA	United States of America
USSR	Union of the Soviet Socialist Republics
VKP	Swedish Commuinst Party
VVN	*Vereingung der Verfolgten des Naziregimes* (Association of those Persecuted by the Nazi Regime) (Ger.)
WECPs	West European Communist Parties
YCL	Young Communist League (Brit.)

Notes on the Contributors

Martin J. Bull is Lecturer in Politics and Contemporary History at the University of Salford. He is a specialist in comparative and Italian politics and is author of *Contemporary Italy: A Research Guide* (forthcoming).

Philip Daniels is Lecturer in Politics at the University of Newcastle upon Tyne. His main teaching and research interests are in the field of contemporary European politics. He has published widely on Italian politics.

Pascal Delwit is a political scientist at the Free University of Brussels, where he is also a member of the Institute of Sociology's research group on the history and sociology of communism. He is joint author of *L'Europe des communistes* (1992) and co-editor of *La gauche face aux mutations en Europe* (1993).

Nina Fishman teaches history, politics and industrial relations at the University of Westminster, Harrow Campus. She is the author of *The British Communist Party and the Trade Unions, 1933–45* (1994) and has also written on the politics of electoral reform, the nationalisation of coal in 1945–7 and the Communist Party and British miners. She is at present working on Communist participation in British unions in the Cold War.

Paul Heywood is Senior Lecturer in Politics at the University of Glasgow. He has published widely on modern Spain, and is author of *Marxism and the Failure of Organised Socialism in Spain, 1879–1936* (1990). He is currently completing a study of the Spanish political system, to be published by Macmillan.

Günter Minnerup teaches German politics and history at the University of Birmingham. He has written on East and West German politics, the 'German Question' and theories of nationalism, and is editor of *Debatte: Review of Contemporary German Affairs.*

Peter Morris is Senior Lecturer in Politics at the University of Nottingham. His publications include *Consensus Politics from Attlee to Thatcher* (with D. A. Kavanagh), a *Biographical Guide to French Political Leaders* (co-editor) and *French Politics Today.*

Maria Teresa Patrício is a Professor of Sociology at the Instituto Superior de Ciências do Trabalho e da Empresa in Lisbon. She has published extensively on Portuguese politics and society.

Alan David Stoleroff is Associate Professor at the Instituto Superior de Ciências do Trabalho e da Empresa in Lisbon. He has published widely on labour and trade union issues in Portugal and has directed a major research project on the Portuguese system of industrial relations.

Jean-Michel de Waele is a political scientist at the Free University of Brussels, where he is also a member of the Institute of Sociology's research group on the history and sociology of communism. He is joint author of *L'Europe des communistes* (1992) and co-editor of *La gauche face aux mutations en Europe* (1993).

Introduction: of Chance, and Death, and Mutability

Paul Heywood

In the late 1970s and early 1980s West European communist parties were the focus of considerable attention by political analysts. 'Eurocommunism', which generated a vast outpouring of academic literature, was widely seen as presaging the emergence of communist parties as key players on the West European political stage.[1] It arose in response to one of the central dilemmas facing the communist movement in the industrialised Western democracies: how were communist parties to win significant support whilst they remained so closely associated with the Soviet Union? By claiming independence from any Soviet lead and embracing the parliamentary road to socialism, the parties involved in the eurocommunist trend sought to offer an attractive and distinctive option on the left. In Italy, France and Spain in particular, communism in its new-look modern and moderate guise was expected to make major electoral advances – although, ironically, only the Portuguese and French Communist Parties, the former having rejected eurocommunism outright and the latter having renounced it after a brief flirtation, were to enjoy briefly the fruits of political power.[2]

In practice, the eurocommunist dream was soon shattered. Rather than advances for the communist left, the 1980s saw a resurgence of the radical right throughout much of Western Europe, boosted by the twin examples of Margaret Thatcher and Ronald Reagan. Even where the right was eclipsed, as in France, Spain and Greece, communist parties were condemned to a secondary role; moreover, ruling socialist parties soon found themselves obliged to adopt economic policies which seemed to derive their inspiration from the neo-liberal orthodoxy established in the leading Western powers. The rhetoric of individual choice and rights, brokered through the hegemony of the free market, appeared to render otiose the communists' continued belief in an interventionist and directive state. Communist parties came to be seen as an irrelevance in the Western world, their message increasingly out of tune with the prevailing *Zeitgeist.*

Moreover, even the very distinctiveness of communist parties was gradually being eroded. Rather than cadre parties whose members underwent regular ideological fitness tests, they became catch-all parties like any other, playing according to the rules of the democratic game. This process – which had its roots in the Italian *svolta* of Salerno in the mid-1940s when the PCI under Togliatti was transformed into a party of government with a mass base – reached its apogee with the adoption of eurocommunism. The November 1975 Rome declaration of the PCI and PCF, the fullest political statement of eurocommunist intent, accepted the 'lay nature and democratic functioning of the State', 'the plurality of political parties, ... the right to existence and activity of opposition parties, ... the free formation of majorities and minorities and the possibility of their alternating democratically', together with 'the existence, guarantee and development of democratic institutions fully representative of popular sovereignty and the free exercise of direct, proportional universal suffrage'.[3] In short, the embrace of the 'democratic road to socialism' entailed a series of measures which blurred the ontological distinction between communist parties and their erstwhile hated social-democratic reformist rivals.

Shorn of their revolutionary rhetoric, but still fatally associated with the Soviet Union and the 'real socialist' regimes of the Eastern bloc, communist parties in Western Europe became ever more marginal to mainstream politics. It was the advent to power of Mikhail Gorbachev, who became general-secretary of the CPSU in 1985, which rekindled interest in the West European communist parties. Not only did the

Soviet Union have for the first time a leader who was seen in the West as charismatic, but his adoption of *glasnost* and *perestroika* demanded a response from the CPSU's fraternal parties in Western Europe. Gorbachev's actions as Soviet leader appeared implicitly to endorse the main thrust of the by now largely forgotten eurocommunist experiment. His embrace of détente and disarmament, together with a relaxation of the Soviet Union's vigilance over the communist regimes of Eastern Europe, briefly promised a more harmonious 'new world order', built around Gorbachev's notion of a 'common European home'.

With hindsight, it is clear that the Soviet leader early on lost control of the momentous changes he had set in motion.[4] Rather than leading to the rehabilitation of communism, Gorbachev's reforms acted as the catalyst of its collapse. As events moved with bewildering speed in the late 1980s and early 1990s, West European communist parties were no less astonished than any other observers at the disintegration of the Soviet system. Indeed, in many instances communist leaders tried to assimilate the enormity of what they were witnessing in what appeared to be a stunned silence. It was left to others to pronounce on the fate of communism: obituaries were not long in arriving, often in the shape of somewhat triumphalist proclamations that the Cold War had been 'won' by the West. As early as 1988, Zbigniew Brzezinski was writing of the death of communism.[5]

However, just as the hopes associated with eurocommunism were exaggerated, so the easy assumption that communism in Western Europe is now finished may be premature. Certainly, communism as a world movement appears to have collapsed irrevocably. Yet, in spite of the rejection of communism in East-Central Europe and the disintegration of the Soviet empire, communist parties in Western Europe have not all crawled away to die. Some have transmuted, most notably the PCI. Others, such as the PCE in Spain, have tried to adapt whilst retaining their essential identity intact. Still others – the French and the Portuguese parties – have steadfastly sought to ignore the implications of events in the former Soviet Union, maintaining that Marxism and the communist ideal remain relevant.

This volume seeks to assess how various communist parties in Western Europe have been affected by, and how they have responded to, the collapse of their Soviet lodestar. It focuses on seven case-studies. The parties which were central to the emergence of eurocommunism – the PCI, PCF and PCE – form an obvious starting point for analysis: these had all established a significant communist presence in the European Community's three largest countries (prior to the re-unification of Germany). Their reaction to the collapse of communism therefore had a wider domestic resonance, affecting the politics of the left in general. As is demonstrated in the first three chapters, each party responded in a different manner to the challenges posed by events in the former communist bloc, with markedly different results. Whereas the PCF sought to carry on regardless and saw a sharp fall in support, the PCI relaunched itself as a non-communist party (PDS) in 1990 and appears to have reaped some benefit amidst the wreckage of Italian party politics following the dramatic corruption scandals of the early 1990s. In Spain, the PCE has retained its faith in communism, yet tried to present a more flexible public image via the *Izquierda Unida* (United Left) electoral coalition. Whilst the PCF appears doomed to adapt or die, the jury remains out on future prospects for the PDS and the PCE/IU.

Chapter 4 looks at the Portuguese Communist Party (PCP). In contrast to its Latin neighbours, the PCP had never dallied with eurocommunism. Under the inflexible leadership of Alvaro Cunhal, the Portuguese communists remained amongst the most steadfastly loyal of all European parties to Moscow. After initial enthusiasm for *perestroika*, the PCP's Extraordinary Congress of May 1990 explained the crisis in Eastern Europe and the Soviet Union in terms of 'errors' and 'deviations' from Leninism and reaffirmed its belief in democratic centralism and the 'Communist ideal'. The PCP supported the August 1991 coup in the Soviet Union and opposed Boris Yeltsin's post-coup reformist policies. Ultimately, however, even Cunhal was unable to resist calls for change from within his own party – especially as the PCP vote continued to fall – and he finally stood down as secretary-general in 1993. The party's future direction remains unclear.

In chapters 5 and 6 attention is devoted to communist parties which have not been key players in their domestic political environments, to see whether they adopted a different response to the events of 1989–91. Such parties have rarely been accorded academic attention, precisely because of their lack of political influence; they remain of interest, however, in a comparative study of communist party adaptation. Chapter 5 looks at the Belgian communist party and demonstrates how it also effectively tried to ignore the overthrow of communist regimes in Eastern Europe. Not faced with the responsibilities of power, the Belgian communist leadership saw the events of 1989 and 1991 as confirmation of the correctness of its political line. It is perhaps not surprising that the collapse of communism has had little impact on a party which was already in long-term historic decline.

In Britain, by contrast, the events of 1989 prompted extensive debate. As is shown in chapter 6, the CPGB followed the Italian lead and changed its name – but only after a long history of bitter internal divisions played out in the party's leading journals. Faced with both a funding crisis and steady loss of membership, the CPGB had lost organisational discipline long before the advent of Mikhail Gorbachev. The decline of Britain's heavy industry under the Conservative government of the early 1980s had undermined the CPGB's traditional base in the union movement, leaving it increasingly marginal in the one area where it could exert any political influence. Enthusiasm for *perestroika* was eventually followed to its logical conclusion, with the party's 'revisionists' rejecting their communist heritage and relaunching the movement as the 'Democratic Left' in late 1991.

Chapter 7 looks at Germany, a unique case of a party from the former communist bloc adapting to the conditions of an already established pluralist democracy. The reunification of Germany, inextricably connected to the demise of the Eastern bloc regimes, presented the communist parties of both the Federal and the former Democratic Republics with major challenges as to their future direction. The German experience represents a fascinating comparative perspective, bringing into stark relief the implications of the events of 1989 for both ruling and non-ruling communist parties. Ironically, the incorporation into German political life of the *Partei des Demokratischen Sozialismus* (PDS, the successor to the East German SED) may give communism – albeit under a new label – a greater presence in the expanded Federal Republic than had ever been achieved under the *Deutsche Kommunistische Partei* (DKP).

A concluding chapter offers an analytical overview of the transformation of the West European communist movement, laying emphasis on the various different approaches adopted in the face of the crisis posed by events of 1989–91. It is suggested that, whilst it would be foolhardy to proclaim the definitive collapse of communism in Western Europe, it is no longer possible to talk meaningfully of a 'family' of communist parties. Any individual party's prospects will depend in large measure on a number of *domestic* factors, some structural and others contingent.

The contributors – all of them experts on the politics of the left in their respective countries – were asked to focus on a number of specific issues. Although the chapters address broadly similar general themes, each analyses the specific historical context within which the various parties confronted the events of 1989–91, covering such issues as their prior relationship with Moscow, their domestic political influence, their organisational structure and their ideological development. Responses to *perestroika* and the subsequent collapse of communism after the August 1991 coup form the central focus of all the chapters, with particular emphasis on the impact of the changing shape of European politics. Authors were also asked to analyse how parties responded in terms of ideological identity (whether they abandoned Marxist and/or communist tenets), organisational structure (if they maintained democratic centralism) and membership (whether they were able to prevent militants leaving, or even recruit new members).

The answers to these questions naturally helped shape the parties' domestic position after the collapse of communism. The chapters therefore look at relations between communist parties and other forces on the left – notably socialist parties – to see whether they sought to build new alliances (either with socialist parties or with 'new social movements'), were subsumed by existing groups, or marginalised altogether. Naturally, any given party's response to crisis was largely determined by its internal divisions and balance of power, and the impact of the events of 1989–91 on leadership structures and organisational discipline forms another focus of analysis. Finally, each chapter attempts to assess the likely prospects for the parties in question.

The chapters in this volume represent a contribution to an area which has received scant attention within political science literature: political *party* transition, as opposed to regime transition. Communist parties in Western Europe have been in a state of turmoil since the end of the 1980s, but the debate over their future has shifted from one concerned with adaptation to avoid decline to one concerned with a much more fundamental party transition. The transformation of communist parties into other ideologically and ontologically distinct entities is of considerable political interest, suggesting a degree of adaptability and flexibility which runs counter to many received nostrums about communism. This is not to argue that *all* the parties analysed here have followed the transformative road. Nevertheless, the issue is now at the top of the political agenda even for those parties whose leaderships have so far resisted any moves towards 'transition', prompted in most cases by internal pressure. How these parties respond and adapt may have a bearing on the prospects of the European left in general.

The idea for this volume emerged from a two-panel session, chaired by the editors, on 'West European Communist Parties and the Revolutions of 1989' at the 1991 Political Studies Association Conference, University of Lancaster.

The result originally of independent initiatives by both
editors, the session was organised under the auspices of
the PSA specialist group on Politics and Society in
Mediterranean Europe (POSME), which is currently
chaired by Geoffrey Pridham and Paul Heywood. Professor
Pridham, who was the discussant at the Lancaster panels,
also offered valuable assistance via the Centre for
Mediterranean Studies, University of Bristol. Martin Bull
wishes to thank the British Academy for financial support
during the research and writing of parts of this book. Both
editors would also like to thank all those who attended the
original sessions, as well as Clare Andrews at Macmillan who
has proved more patient than we could have dared
anticipate.

NOTES

1.   See, for example, Roy Godson and Stephen Haseler (eds), '*Euro-
      Communism*' (Basingstoke: Macmillan, 1978); Morton A. Kaplan
      (ed.), *The Many Faces of Eurocommunism* (New York: The Free Press,
      1978); R. N. Tannahill, *The Communist Parties of Western Europe: A
      Comparative Study* (Westport, CT: Greenwood, 1978); Paolo Filo
      della Torre, Edward Mortimer and Jonathan Story (eds),
      Eurocommunism: Myth or Reality? (Harmondsworth: Penguin, 1979);
      G. R. Urban (ed.), *Communist Reformation* (London: Temple Smith,
      1979); D. E. Albright (ed.), *Communism and Political Systems in
      Western Europe* (Boulder, Col.: Westview Press, 1979); Carl Boggs
      and David Plotke (eds), *The Politics of Eurocommunism* (Basingstoke:
      Macmillan, 1980); David Childs (ed.), *The Changing Face of Western
      Communism* (London: Croom Helm, 1980); Keith Middlemas (ed.),
      Power and the Party (London: André Deutsch, 1980); G. Schwab (ed.),
      Eurocommunism: The Ideological and Political-Theoretical Foundations
      (Westport, CT: Greenwood, 1981); P. Lange and M. Vanicelli (eds),
      *The Communist Parties of Italy, France and Spain: Postwar Change and
      Continuity* (London: Allen & Unwin, 1981); Richard Kindersley
      (ed.), *In Search of Eurocommunism* (Basingstoke: Macmillan, 1981);
      Howard Machin (ed.), *National Communism in Western Europe: A
      Third Way to Socialism?* (London: Methuen, 1983); A. Kriegel, *Un
      autre communisme? Compromis historique, eurocommunisme, union de la
      gauche* (Paris: Hachette, 1977); Eric Hobsbawm and Giorgio
      Napolitano, *The Italian Road to Socialism* (London: Journeyman,

1977); Editorial Cambio 16, *El Partido Comunista español, italiano y francés cara al poder* (Madrid: Editorial Cambio 16, 1977); Bernardo Valli (ed.), *Los Eurocomunistas* (Barcelona: Dopesa, 1977); Norberto Bobbio *et al.*, *Gramsci y el 'eurocomunismo'* (Barcelona: Editorial Materiales, 1978). A good guide to the early literature is Sarah Bernstein and Stewart Lawrence, 'Eurocommunism as Current Events and Contemporary History: A Critical Bibliography', *Radical History Review*, 23 (1980); more recently, see O. A. Narkiewicz, *Eurocommunism, 1968–1986: A Select Bibliography* (London: Mansell Publishing, 1987).

2. The PCP emerged as the best-organised political force after the April 1974 'revolution of the carnations' and, in alliance with the Armed Forces Movement (MFA), dominated Portuguese political life in the aftermath of the Caetano dictatorship. A combination of over-ambition, tactical errors and internal divisions soon undermined the PCP's hold on power. In France, the PCF participated in government between 1981 and 1984 in alliance with the socialists, but very much as a minor partner.

3. See Fernando Claudín, 'The Democratic Road to Socialism', in his *Eurocommunism and Socialism* (London: NLB, 1978) pp. 65–6. Claudín, a key member of the PCE hierarchy until his expulsion in 1964 for 'fractional activity', offers one of the most cogent analyses of the theoretical shortcomings of eurocommunism from a non-aligned Marxist perspective.

4. See Stephen White, *Gorbachev and After* (Cambridge: Cambridge University Press, 1992).

5. Zbigniew Brzezinski, *The Grand Failure* (London: Macdonald, 1989). The book, the manuscript of which was completed in August 1988, carried the sub-title 'The Birth and Death of Communism in the Twentieth Century'. A more influential, and controversial, study prompted by the collapse of communism was Francis Fukuyama, *The End of History and the Last Man* (London: Hamish Hamilton, 1992).

1 Voluntary Euthanasia: From the Italian Communist Party to the Democratic Party of the Left

Philip Daniels and Martin J. Bull

INTRODUCTION

The collapse of the communist regimes of the Soviet Union and Eastern Europe has had a profound impact on the Italian Communist Party (PCI). Although the PCI had progressively distanced itself from the Soviet model in the post-war years, and from the mid-1960s had been a consistent critic of the 'real socialism' of the Eastern bloc regimes, the party could not remain immune from the 'crisis of communism' which swept Eastern Europe in late 1989. The decision of the PCI at its Nineteenth Congress in March 1990 to dissolve itself and form a new party of the left was precipitated by the revolutionary changes occurring in Eastern Europe. The PCI's process of fundamental reform had commenced, however, with the accession of Achille Occhetto to the leadership of the party in June 1988, more than a year before the collapse of the Berlin Wall. Occhetto inherited a party with severe electoral and political difficulties. He responded to the PCI's crisis with the 'new course' strategy designed to create 'a party of government' through change and adaptation of the PCI's ideology, programme and organisation. The party had taken only the first steps in this process of renewal when the upheavals in

1

Eastern Europe in late 1989 radically altered the contours and pace of change. Occhetto seized the opportunity to embark upon a bold but risky political project that sought to accelerate and deepen the process of party reform and adaptation. The process culminated in the decision of the Twentieth Congress (1991) to dissolve the PCI and launch the Democratic Party of the Left (*Partito democratico della sinistra*, PDS).

This chapter analyses the transformation of the PCI into the PDS, focusing on the significant role played by the party leader, Occhetto, and the deep internal divisions which his actions caused. It also analyses the final birth of the PDS (after two years of inner turmoil) and evaluates the electoral and political propsects of the new party on the basis of its first two years in existence. A prerequisite to understanding the nature and course of the PCI's transformation is the crisis the party underwent throughout the 1980s, and this is where the first section begins.

THE 1980S: A DECADE OF CRISIS

The 1980s were difficult years for the PCI. The successes of the early 1970s were rapidly reversed as the party became caught up in a web of electoral, organisational and political decline. In electoral terms, the party experienced a gradual but virtually uninterrupted decline of its vote from the mid-1970s onwards. As Table 1.1 shows, the PCI lost over 2.3 million votes in national elections over the period 1976 to 1989. Of particular concern to the PCI was the loss of support among young voters, and the electoral retreat in the party's traditional heartlands of the 'Red Belt' of central Italy and in the industrial working-class communities of the large northern cities (Milan, Turin and Genoa). The sources of this electoral decline were manifold and varied. The decline was in part attributable to the party's failure to adapt effectively to processes of socio-economic change which had resulted in a smaller and more heterogeneous

Table 1.1   The PCI–PDS's electoral performance since 1976

Election	% vote	Votes
1976 Chamber of Deputies	34.37	12,622,728
1979 Chamber of Deputies	30.38	11,139,231
1979 European Parliament	29.55	10,322,539
1980 Regional Elections	29.92	10,601,080
1983 Chamber of Deputies	29.89	11,032,318
1984 European Parliament	33.30	11,624,183
1985 Regional Elections	28.66	10,713,950
1987 Chamber of Deputies	26.61	10,284,975
1989 European Parliament	27.60	9,552,518
1992 Chamber of Deputies (PDS)	16.1	6,300,000
1992 Chamber of Deputies (*Rifondazione comunista*)	5.6	2,200,000

Sources: Unpublished PCI–PDS documentation.

working class. Despite the party's efforts to broaden its appeal, the losses among the traditional working-class bedrock of support were not offset by compensatory gains among emerging social groups. In addition, the PCI's policy failures, the crisis of communist ideology and the party's marginal role in national political life from the late 1970s onwards contributed to electoral decline.

The electoral malaise was matched by a weakening in the PCI's organisational machine. Although the PCI retained a vast organisational network and commanded considerable resources, from 1977 onwards party membership declined every year without exception. As Table 1.2 shows, membership dropped by almost 400,000 during the period 1977 to 1989. The most worrying aspect of this decline was the steep fall in membership among 18 to 24-year-olds: they fell from 11 per cent of membership in 1975 to just over 2 per

Table 1.2   Membership of the PCI–PDS since 1976

Year	Membership	New recruits	Net losses
1976	1,814,317	175,948	–
1977	1,814,154	130,166	163
1978	1,790,450	103,310	23,704
1979	1,759,295	95,619	31,155
1980	1,751,323	91,149	7,972
1981	1,714,052	82,317	37,271
1982	1,673,751	67,905	40,301
1983	1,635,264	63,719	38,487
1984	1,619,940	65,157	15,324
1985	1,595,668	61,939	24,272
1986	1,551,576	51,442	44,092
1987	1,508,140	49,501	43,436
1988	1,462,281	42,574	45,859
1989	1,421,230	47,722	41,051
1990	1,319,905	57,828	101,325
1991 (PDS)	989,665	52,280	330,240

Sources: Adapted from *Organizzazione, Dati, Statistiche*, prepared by the Statistics section of the PCI for the seventeenth congress (1986) and eighteenth congress (1989) of the party. Data for 1989 and 1990 from *L'Unità*, 13 January 1991 (p. 13). Data for 1991 from *L'Unità*, 28 March 1992.

cent in 1988 (Table 1.3). In the same year (1988) little more than 7 per cent of all members were under 30 years old, while almost 34 per cent of membership was over 60 years old (compared with 18 per cent in 1975). The PCI's problem of generational turnover in membership was partly attributable to the 'ageing' of the population and lower levels of interest in traditional forms of political participation among young cohorts. In addition, it reflected the PCI's specific difficulties in securing a strong electoral and organisational presence among young voters, a problem

Table 1.3   Age profile of PCI membership, 1985 and 1988

Age	% of membership 1985	% of membership 1988
18–24	2.93	2.14
25–29	6.52	5.02
30–39	21.38	19.15
40–49	19.25	20.85
50–59	19.43	18.89
60–69	15.82	18.94
70–79	9.96	9.75
80+	4.71	5.26

Sources: Adapted from *Organizzazione, Dati, Statistiche*, prepared by the Statistics section of the PCI for the Seventeenth congress (1986) and Eighteenth congress (1989) of the party.

clearly evident in the weakening of its own youth movement. The problems of a declining and ageing membership were compounded by a significant reduction in the levels of party activism and participation at section level. These developments were alarming for a party which attached such importance to a mass, active membership and the erosion of the party's organisational strength stirred a wide debate within the PCI.[1]

The PCI's electoral and organisational weakening were symptomatic of the party's political difficulties in the 1980s. Indeed, some party figures warned of the dangers of a so-called French syndrome in which party decline and an internal crisis of confidence would gather an irreversible, self-reinforcing momentum. The lack of a credible alliance strategy and political isolation at the national level were at the heart of the PCI's political impasse. The party's 'democratic alternative' strategy, formulated in 1980, failed to attract support from other parties and the PCI, lacking political allies, seemed destined to remain excluded from national government. Electoral and political competition with the Socialist Party (PSI), led by Bettino Craxi, thwarted attempts by the PCI to regain the national political influence it had enjoyed briefly in the mid-1970s. Craxi's explicit strategy sought to isolate the PCI, to make it appear a redundant force and erode its electorate in order that the Socialists would be able to usurp the Communists' position as the leading force of the Italian Left. At local level too, much of the power the PCI had gained in the mid-1970s was lost as a result of electoral decline and desertion by erstwhile coalition partners. This political decline at national and local level was compounded by a weakening of the trade union movement which had been a traditional source of communist strength and influence.[2]

OCCHETTO'S LEADERSHIP AND THE 'NEW COURSE'

When Achille Occhetto succeeded Alessandro Natta as general secretary of the PCI in the summer of 1988 he thus inherited a party bereft of allies at the national level and declining both electorally and organisationally. Under the leadership of Natta, fundamental disagreements between the right and left alignments within the PCI had effectively paralysed the party. The left wing of the party, grouped around Pietro Ingrao, attributed the PCI's decline to the party's dilution of its radical programme of reform, its failure to defend working-class interests and its lack of contact with the new social movements. According to this perspective, the PCI's recovery depended on a reaffirmation of the party's radical identity and closer links with the social movements. The moderate right wing of the party (the *riformisti* or *miglioristi*), led by Giorgio Napolitano, contended that the PCI's anti-capitalist rhetoric was at the root of the party's crisis. In order to become a party of government, the PCI should move in the direction of European social democracy and formulate a clear programme limited to 'improving' capitalist society. The centre of the party, located around the leadership, had mediated between these two currents, while leaning clearly towards the right. Any genuine reform of the PCI, therefore, had to contend with profound internal divisions over the very identity of the party.

From the outset of his leadership, Occhetto made clear his intention to depart from the cautious renewal which had characterised Natta's direction of the party during the period from 1984 to 1988. Occhetto's readiness to reform was soon evident as he embarked upon a policy of ideological, organisational and political renewal. This *nuovo corso* (new course) sought to reverse the PCI's decline, to give it a new identity and create a force capable of securing a role in government.[3] The period from late 1988 to the spring of 1989 saw an intense debate within the PCI as it prepared for its Eighteenth Congress in March 1989, called to ratify Occhetto's proposed changes. In spite of some predictable internal opposition, principally from the Ingrao left and the traditional pro-Soviet grouping led by Armando Cossutta, the new direction indicated by Occhetto was approved by the Central Committee and embodied in the political document and in the proposals for party reform prepared for the congress. In the pre-congressional voting in party sections and federation assemblies the Central Committee's documents received overwhelming support: approximately 95 per cent of the members' votes were in favour and less than 4 per cent backed Cossutta's alternative proposals.

The Eighteenth Congress, Occhetto's first as general secretary, indicated the first concrete changes of the 'new course' strategy.[4] In his keynote address, Occhetto clarified the party's 'democratic alternative' strategy and rejected any possibility of a return to the 'historic compromise' strategy with the Christian Democrat Party (DC) – 'a phase of our political history which is over'. The 'democratic alternative' strategy, Occhetto argued, would end the DC's centrality in the political system and usher in a new system of governmental alliances based on programmatic agreements among the parties and forces interested in political, economic and social reform. He also indicated some changes in the broad outlines of the PCI's ideology and pro- gramme, distancing the party still further from communist orthodoxy and moving closer to mainstream European social democracy, and reaffirming the PCI's commitment to the construction of 'a united and democratic Europe', arguing that the European Community was the appropriate arena in which to tackle transnational problems. He rejected both 'capitalist individualism' and 'bureaucratic collectivism' as models of development. However, he acknowledged the market as 'a yardstick for the efficiency of the entire economic system, as well as its irreplaceable source of propulsion' and argued that the socialist move- ment could find a new identity through a focus on the need for democratic control and regulation of the market system.

The congress delegates also approved significant changes to the PCI's organisational and decision-making structures. The PCI had already shifted some distance from the tradi- tional criteria of democratic centralism, evolving an increas- ingly open, pluralistic, participatory mode of internal party life in which centralist norms increasingly gave way to de- mocratic practices. The new party statute adopted at the Eighteenth Congress effectively removed democratic cen- tralism as the organisational norm for regulating internal party life. Although the ban on organised factions remained in place, the new statute granted members the right to use party instruments and premises for 'the free circulation of ideas'. In practice, for a number of years the PCI had toler- ated a significant level of internal party pluralism that per- mitted informal, non-organised 'opinion currents'. These informal tendencies reflected significant internal policy differences and they were readily identifiable since their proponents openly expounded their positions in public. Debates within the leadership were well publicised in the party press, and Central Committee and Executive Com- mittee meetings received full press coverage. There had been some pressure during the 1980s for the recognition and institutionalisation of currents in order that competing policy positions and political lines would become more transparent. However, a move in this direction was resisted at the Eighteenth Congress on the grounds that organised currents would 'crystallise positions', hinder internal party debate and risk paralysis of the party. Nevertheless, the congress delegates approved a series of changes designed to enhance internal party democracy and to make the PCI's decision-making procedures more transparent. Most notably, the delegates decided (with the leadership openly divided on the issue) that elections to all executive posts in the party should be by secret ballot (431 were in favour, 158 against the change, while 37 abstained). Proponents of this change argued that it would give greater authority and legitimacy to those elected and permit a freer evaluation of their performance in office. Lastly, the new party statute adopted at the congress guaranteed women at least 30 per cent representation in all leadership organs.

THE PCI'S 'NEW BEGINNING'

The first nationwide test of the electorate's response to the PCI's 'new course' was provided by the European Parliament elections in June 1989.[5] The PCI's vote held up better than anticipated. Although the party lost over 700,000 votes compared with the 1987 general election, as a result of the lower turnout its percentage share of the vote rose from 26.6 per cent to 27.6 per cent. The PCI was also comforted by the Socialist Party's modest 0.5 per cent gain, a result that enabled the communists to widen their electoral lead over their rivals on the left.

For Occhetto, the Euro-election results represented a popular endorsement of the PCI's 'new course' and enhanced his authority within the party. Nevertheless, profound internal differences remained over the nature and scope of his reform programme. Occhetto and his supporters viewed the changes made at the Eighteenth Congress as only the first stage in the renewal of the PCI, a process that would be completed by eventually tackling the question of the party's ideological heritage and its relationship to the search for a new identity. The first tentative move in this direction, however, demonstrated that key elements in the PCI opposed fundamental changes to the party's identity. On the twenty-fifth anniversary of the death of the former leader and founder of the post-war PCI, Palmiro Togliatti, the party daily, *L'Unità*, published an article by a leading party intellectual, Biagio De Giovanni, proposing that the former party leader should be liquidated from the party's heritage on the grounds that anybody in the PCI associated with Stalin was incompatible with the party's new identity.[6] The article, and a simultaneous proposal to remove Togliatti's name from the front page of the party weekly *Rinascita*, provoked fierce opposition from influential figures such as Ingrao, Natta and Pajetta, and sparked an intense debate which dominated party activity during the summer of 1989. Faced with such opposition, Occhetto was forced to backtrack somewhat. In an article in *L'Unità*, he argued that *discontinuità* (the chief characteristic of the 'new course') did not necessarily mean a rejection of the past; rather, the party had to break with the practice of 'change in continuity', which had implied that renewal could only take place within the framework of the party's heritage.[7]

If internal opposition made Occhetto cautious in moving too quickly, it did so at a time when the communist world was embarking upon rapid and unprecedented change. Consequently, by the late autumn of 1989, Occhetto's strategy of gradual reform of the PCI looked sluggish when set against the rapid transformations occurring in the Eastern bloc regimes. When Eastern bloc communist parties, beginning with the Hungarian, renounced their communist identities, the PCI was placed under intense pressure to follow suit. From a position of receiving support and encouragement for its programme of renewal, the PCI now found itself derided for its apparent conservatism and caution compared with the East European parties. In response to the dramatic changes occurring in the communist regimes, on 12 November 1989 Occhetto proposed the dissolution of the PCI and the foundation of a new, non-communist party of the left. The proposal deepened the PCI's internal crisis and brought unprecedented levels of division inside the party. The opposition to Occhetto deeply resented what they saw as the rapid pursuit of the East European communist parties into oblivion. They argued that Occhetto's proposal to dissolve the PCI was precipitate, for the Italian party had established its full independence from the CPSU and could in no sense be tainted with the charge of ideological complicity with the Eastern bloc regimes. In Occhetto's view, however, the PCI could not remain immune to the crisis of international communism and therefore fundamental reform of the party was imperative.[8]

With some justification, Occhetto insisted that the collapse of the communist regimes had merely hastened, not motivated, the fundamental reform of the PCI. He had, after all, embarked upon his 'new course' from the beginning of his tenure as party secretary a year before, and it had been slowed down primarily by the strength of competing alignments within the leadership and the wider party. The rapid changes in Eastern Europe thus provided Occhetto with the opportunity to propose a fundamental *svolta* (turning-point) in the PCI's development and break the stultifying inertia of internal compromise.

Occhetto's proposals were quickly endorsed by the party secretariat and the *direzione* (the Executive Committee) but they encountered strong opposition at the meeting of the Central Committee on 20 November 1989. Some of Occhetto's fiercest critics attacked the way in which he had made the proposals in public (at a meeting with veteran partisans in Bolognina) without first consulting the party. By raising the issue of a change to the PCI's name in the public arena, Occhetto created a momentum and expectations which the opposition within the party could not arrest. In addition to the expected opposition from the pro-Soviet *cossuttiani* and the Ingrao Left, the 'no front' also contained leading *berlingueriani* like Natta, Pajetta and Tortorella who had until then backed Occhetto's 'new course' for the party. In their view, the changes proposed by Occhetto were rash and amounted to an unnecessary renunciation of the party's history and ideals. In addition, they attacked the vagueness of Occhetto's proposals with regard to the groups and forces that he expected to attract to the new political formation. The opposition of these leading party notables could not, however, prevent Occhetto from winning the backing of the Central Committee: 219 members voted in favour of Occhetto's proposals, 73 voted against and 34 abstained. The divisions within the Central Committee did not simply coincide with the traditional internal alignments of 'left', 'centre' and 'right'. The opposition of some of the older *berlingueriani* and the strong backing for Occhetto from the *quarantenni* (the 40-year-olds), including some from the Ingrao Left, illustrate that generational differences to some extent traversed the traditional internal alignments.

It was far from certain, however, that Occhetto would gain the support of the wider party in the section and federation congresses in the run-up to the special Nineteenth Congress. In particular, the popularity of Ingrao among the party's base posed a significant threat. For the first time in its history, the PCI made provision for competing motions to be presented and debated at the special congress. In addition, the competing currents were guaranteed representation among congress delegates in proportion to the support they received in pre-congressional voting. In the event, three competing motions were presented: Occhetto's own, proposing the dissolution of the PCI and the foundation of a new political formation of the left; and two opposition motions, one from elements of the *berlingueriani* and the *ingraiani* sponsored by Tortorella, Natta and Ingrao, and one from Cossutta.[9] The party's right, the *riformisti* or *miglioristi* grouped around Giorgio Napolitano, did not present a motion. Although they had significant differences with the *occhettiani*, particularly over the question of relations with the PSI, they none the less supported the party secretary's attempts to modernise the PCI and to work for greater unity of the Italian Left. In addition, the right risked exposing their own weakness and undermining their influence in the party if they presented a motion which received little backing in the pre-congress voting.

Occhetto's keynote address to the Nineteenth Congress reiterated many of the themes contained in his speech to the Eighteenth Congress.[10] He made it clear that his proposal to refound the party had won majority backing among the party membership and that he had no intention of retreating or compromising with the 'no front'. At the same time, he reassured his opponents in the party that their traditions would still have a place in the new political formation. His aim was to construct a new reformist party, embracing progressive movements and groups, which would be eligible to join the Socialist International. Occhetto adopted a conciliatory tone towards the PSI, welcoming Craxi's pre-congress message conveying the Socialist Party's readiness to work for a recomposition of the Italian Left. However, Occhetto stressed that his proposal differed from Craxi's long-standing ambition to achieve 'socialist unity' under the direction of the PSI. Following four days of heated debate, with unprecendented criticisms of the party secretary, Occhetto won the backing for his proposals from the mandated delegates: 726 voted in favour of Occhetto's motion, 322 supported the Tortorella–Natta–Ingrao motion proposing reform without the abandonment of the party's name and symbols, and 37 delegates voted for Cossutta's motion.

As a result of the vote, the PCI entered a 'constituent phase' open to all progressive forces, in which the 'fundamental programme' and organisational structure of the new political formation would be agreed. Occhetto appealed to the 'no front' to accept the sovereign decision of the congress and avoid damaging obstructionism during the constituent phase. He hoped that his opponents, representing around one third of the party, would participate in the building of the new formation. In an attempt to counter the threat of a schism during the constituent phase, each of the three alignments was given proportionate representation in the organs set up to mould the new party. In addition, the delegates agreed that each of the three alignments should be represented on the new Central Committee in proportion to their strength at the congress. The Central Committee was enlarged from 300 to 353 members, made up of 236 *occhettiani*, 105 supporters of the Tortorella–Natta–Ingrao position and 12 *cossuttiani*. Occhetto was re-elected Party Secretary in a vote that reflected the strength of the various currents: in a secret ballot, 213 members voted for Occhetto, 23 voted against and 71 abstained (principally the Tortorella-Natta-Ingrao group), while 5 returned blank ballots. In an effort to placate the 'no front' minority and hold the party together during the constituent phase, Aldo Tortorella, a leading opponent of Occhetto's proposal, was elected to the post of President of the Central Committee (280 votes in favour, 14 against and 15 abstentions). Although the results of the congress confirmed the majority behind Occhetto, they also revealed a consistent third of the party which opposed the dissolution of the PCI and which was resolved to overturn the majority during the constituent phase.

THE TWILIGHT OF THE OLD PCI: THE CONSTITUENT PHASE

According to the decision of the Nineteenth Congress, the new non-communist party would be shaped during the constituent phase and ratified at the PCI's twentieth, and final, congress. Strictly speaking then, the PCI, as an autonomous organisation with control over its own destiny, no longer existed. The party had a temporary and pre-determined life which would end with the Twentieth Congress. The dubbing of the PCI as *la cosa* ('the thing') confirmed the party's transient existence. Occhetto regarded this transitional status as essential if the moulding of the new party were to attract the participation of a large number of non-party members.[11]

The constituent phase did not proceed smoothly, however. A combination of poor election results and a dispute over the authority of the Twentieth Congress ensured that an intense debate continued inside the party. The party's disappointing performance in the local elections of May 1990 was seized upon by the 'no front' as a confirmation of their view that the decision of the Nineteenth Congress was ill-judged and that the struggle against the dissolution of the PCI should continue. The divisions were exacerbated by internal disagreements over the party's stance on the Gulf crisis and the rekindling of a debate over the democratic credentials of ex-leader Togliatti, issues which went to the heart of the debate about the party's future identity. Indeed, the Gulf crisis saw the PCI divided in Parliament for the first time in its sixty-year history, with Ingrao leading other rebels in a public display of defiance of the party line. The constituent phase, rather than concentrating on the nature of the new party, became quickly paralysed by a discussion over whether the decision of the Nineteenth Congress precluded the possibility of party members voting for a 'refounded' PCI at the Twentieth Congress.

As a result of fierce and unresolved disagreement with Occhetto over this issue the two minority opposition alignments (the Tortorella–Natta–Ingrao motion and the Cossutta motion), adopted a unified position around an alternative project which sought the 'refounding' (*rifondazione*) of the PCI. During the summer of 1990 the two opposition alignments withdrew from the working group set up to elaborate the form and identity of the new party. Their unified platform, the *rifondazione comunista* ('communist refoundation'), accepted that renewal of the PCI was desirable but rejected the idea that the changes should entail the abandonment of the party's 'distinctiveness' (*diversità*) as a communist party. In October 1990, therefore, they proposed that the Twentieth Congress should vote to retain the existing party name and symbol with the addition of the words *Democrazia* and *Socialismo* above the red flag. Moreover, they argued that, even if their platform were to be defeated, the Twentieth Congress would mark the beginning of the 'refounding' of Italian communism rather than its end. The *rifondazione comunista* group was divided, however, over the question of adhesion to the new party.

The *cossuttiani* regarded a split as an 'objective necessity' if the word communism disappeared from the party's name. The *ingraiani*, while not ruling out the possibility of a split, continued to stress that their prime objective was to hold the party together. They hoped that this stance would encourage Occhetto to be more accommodating towards the minority alignments. As a result of pressure from Ingrao, the *rifondazione comunista* group reached a common position which committed it to changing the new party from within. This unity was extremely fragile, however, and it was doubtful that it would survive the Twentieth Congress intact.

The unity of the opposition was also undermined by developments in the majority camp in the run-up to the congress. The majority forged between the *occhettiani* and *riformisti* at the Nineteenth Congress began to fragment as the constituent phase progressed.[12] Occhetto attempted, without much success, to keep open a dialogue with the minority in order to reach a compromise and preserve party unity. However, this mediation between the left and right alignments satisfied neither wing of the party. While the *cossuttiani* and *ingraiani* accused the leadership of trying to preclude options apparently left open by the Nineteenth Congress, the *riformisti* grouped around Napolitano placed pressure on Occhetto to respect the wishes of the congress majority and, without hesitation, implement its decisions. The internal divisions were compounded when Occhetto announced his proposals for the name and symbol of the new party. The *rifondazione comunista* group was angered that any reference to socialism had been abandoned and that the hammer and sickle had been reduced in size and placed at the bottom of the new party symbol, an oak tree. Napolitano, on the other hand, expressed reservations about the lack of any direct reference to the Western social democratic tradition in the proposed new name for the party.

More importantly, Occhetto's proposal opened up a significant division on the left flank of the majority. The so-called *sinistra di si*, those on the left of the party who had supported Occhetto's proposals, became increasingly disturbed that the alliance of the *ingraiani* with the more extreme *cossuttiani* threatened to undermine the influence of the radical element within the new party. The *sinistra di sì* feared that the *rifondazione comunista* group would be isolated from the mainstream of the new party or would refuse to participate in its formation. This would allow the centre-right *occhettiani* and *riformisti* to have the major influence in shaping the new party at its crucial early stages. Consequently, in October, a leading member of the *sinistra di sì*, Antonio Bassolino, declared that the majority of the Nineteenth Congress effectively no longer existed. He resigned from the leadership, announcing his intention to present an independent motion to the Twentieth Congress. The motion would accept Occhetto's proposals for the new party's name and symbol but would offer a more radical conception of the new party's identity. This bridging manoeuvre failed to attract large numbers from either the majority or minority alignments, but it none the less meant that the PCI arrived at its final congress with three separate motions regarding the nature and identity of the new party: for a 'Democratic Party of the Left' (*partito democratico della sinistra* – Occhetto), for a 'communist refoundation' (*rifondazione comunista* – Tortorella), and for a 'modern reforming and antagonistic party' (*moderno partito antagonista e riformatore* — Bassolino). In addition, the party was confronted with two proposals for the name and symbol of the new formation: Occhetto's motion proposing the 'Democratic Party of the Left' and the proposal from the *rifondazione comunista* group to retain the name 'Italian Communist Party'.

THE BIRTH OF THE PDS: THE TWENTIETH CONGRESS

The congress, held in Rimini from 31 January to 3 February 1991, had two principal tasks to perform: first, to decide the new party's name and symbol and, secondly, to adopt one of the alternative motions regarding the nature and political identity of the party.[13] It was clear from pre-congressional voting at section and federation level that the majority of congress delegates would back Occhetto's position on both issues (see Tables 1.4 and 1.5).

With the launch of the Democratic Party of the Left (PDS) assured, the major issues at stake at the congress were the form and identity of the new party and whether Occhetto could convince the opposition minority to participate in the new formation. The questions of party identity and the possibility of a schism were immediately embroiled with the issue of the Gulf War. Occhetto's opening address contributed in large part to this with his call for an immediate ceasefire and withdrawal of Italian forces. Occhetto's stance was essentially a tactic to placate the *ingraiani* and thus stave off the threat of secession by up to one third of the party. However, this attempt to mediate between the PCI's left and right merely exacerbated the turbulence

Table 1.4   Party name and symbol

Section congresses	10,548
Members voting	383,749
% of membership voting	29.2%
Democratic Party of the Left	
Voters	268,504
%	71.4%
Italian Communist Party	
Voters	107,533
%	28.6%
Abstentions	7,712

Source: Twentieth National Congress of the PCI.

Table 1.5   The three motions

Voters participating	385,462
% of membership	29.3%
Occhetto	256,804
%	67.39%
Communist Refoundation	102,690
%	26.95%
Bassolini	21,106
%	5.54%
Abstentions	4,302

Source: Twentieth National Congress of the PCI.

within the party. Its immediate effect was to antagonise the *riformisti*, aligned with Napolitano, who saw the policy as damaging and unrealistic and feared that it represented an attempt by Occhetto to shift the axis of the party majority from the centre-right to the centre-left. For the minority alignments, Occhetto's position on the Gulf War was seen as a chance to forge links with the anti-war movement and give the nascent PDS a more radical stamp.

Although the stance on the Gulf War provoked internal turmoil and invited ridicule from most of the other major parties, Occhetto was able to use the issue to strengthen his hold on the party in two ways. First, Occhetto's call for a ceasefire helped to persuade virtually all the *rifondazione co-munista* group to adhere to the PDS. Secondly, the dispute between the *riformisti* right and the *ingraiani* left enabled the *occhettiani* centre to widen its base and consolidate control of the party. This was achieved by allowing the congress to vote on three alternative motions relating to the Gulf War, with Occhetto's being finally accepted. Occhetto was able to attract support from across the party and, by distancing his position somewhat from that of the *riformisti*, both assuage the left and gain greater room for manoeuvre.

The organisational principles to be enshrined in the new party's statute had been a source of deep disagreement during the constituent phase and continued to present major problems at the congress. The minority alignments, fearing permanent exclusion from the new party's decision-making organs, had argued for a federal structure permitting organised groups, guaranteeing proportionate representation on party bodies and requiring qualified majorities for all key decisions. The majority, supported by the *esterni* (delegates from outside the party), rejected a federative solution on the grounds that it would sanction parties within the party and effectively paralyse the decision-making capacity of the PDS. The preliminary draft of the statute prepared for the congress reflected the majority's support for a unitary party structure with some provision made for organised internal currents. The precise balance, however, between unitary principles and autonomy for organised currents proved difficult to achieve and provoked continued disputes among the various alignments. The resulting statute, approved clause by clause at the congress, is inevitably a flawed compromise between the need to achieve party governability and the recognition of internal differences. A new organ, the National Council, replaces the Central Committee, and is structured to represent the 'political sensibilities' within the PDS. In addition, both sexes are guaranteed a minimum 40 per cent representation on the National Council. The minority succeeded in amending a clause which would have required all political initiatives to be agreed by the leadership. The new clause simply requires that the leadership is notified of any political initiatives emanating from the currents. The proposals to replace the section with a new local structure, the *unioni comunali* (communal unions), were resisted by the minority and for the time being existing sections and the new communal unions will exist side by side. Financial resources remain under central party control although currents will be guaranteed funds for their activities. Finally, the new

statute retains individual adhesion as the basis of membership and makes no provision for group affiliation to the
PDS as proposed by the minority alignments.

The main business of the congress, the launch of the
PDS, was achieved with 807 votes in favour, 75 against and
49 abstentions. The numbers reflected Occhetto's success
in carrying the principal elements of the old PCI into the
new formation. Significant opponents of the *svolta* ('the
turning-point') such as Angius, Bassolino and Chiarante
voted for the new party. Ingrao voted against the formation
of the PDS, although he agreed to join it and promised to
endeavour to construct a communist left within the new
party. Over 300 delegates were absent from the vote, including the *cossuttiani* who had decided to break away and form
a new communist party, the *Rifondazione Comunista*.

HEALTHY ACORN OR WITHERED OAK? THE PDS'S FIRST TWO YEARS

The PDS has had a series of problems since its formation in
February 1991. From the outset, the internal conflicts
sparked by the PCI's dissolution have made party unity
tenuous. Although the Twentieth Congress succeeded in
averting a major split (only the small group of hard-line *cossuttiani* seceded), the struggle over the identity of the PDS
continued as the *ingraiani* made clear their intention to establish a communist wing in the nascent party (calling
themselves 'democratic communists'). With the exception
of the *cossuttiani*, all the currents present in the PCI were
transplanted into the PDS along with the new group of
esterni (a motley collection of non-PCI elements of the left).
Fundamental differences remained over the political and
ideological identity of the PDS and its alliance strategy.
These divisions in the new party did not simply coincide
with those alignments in favour and those against the dissolution of the PCI. For the *riformisti* on the party's right, the
ultimate goal for the PDS was the reunification of the

Italian Left. However, the *ingraiani* and other elements of the party's left feared that this would entail a rightward drift and eventual absorption by the PSI, which they regarded as an irremediable conservative force under Craxi's leadership. In order to avert this, the *ingraiani* favoured closer links with social movements which would give a radical identity to the PDS. For the *riformisti*, courting the radical social movements (so-called *movimentismo*) risked perpetuating the 'culture of opposition' and making the PDS unattractive as a pole around which to build an alternative governing coalition.[14]

The problems of a divided party are likely to be exacerbated by the new organisational principles which permit the coexistence of institutionalised currents. For example, representation on the rather bloated National Council reproduced faithfully the strengths of each of the alignments according to the congressional results: the 'centre' (Occhetto, 53 per cent), the 'reformists' (Napolitano, 15 per cent), the 'left' (Tortorella, 27 per cent) and the Bassolino faction (5 per cent). This system will not attenuate the factional rivalry and problems of party management which a number of socialist and social democratic parties in Europe have encountered since the mid-1970s.

Ultimately, the success of the PDS will be judged on its capacity to attract a level of electoral support comparable to that achieved by the PCI and on its ability to 'unblock' the Italian political system through the promotion of an alternative governing alliance which excludes the Christian Democrats. The electoral performance of the PDS is clearly of critical importance to the party's future: it was the key issue which had convinced Occhetto that fundamental reform of the party was necessary. From the outset he sought to create a new type of party formation which would attract support not only from the traditional parties of the left but also from the so-called hidden left (*sinistra sommersa*) and the new social movements. Occhetto hoped that the constituent phase would generate interest among these potential supporters and involve them in the formation of the new party. The policy met with some success as a number of leading left-wing intellectuals and newly formed left-wing clubs participated in the preparatory work of the constituent phase and were represented by 315 delegates (*gli esterni*) at the Twentieth Congress. Many were disillusioned, however, with the results of the congress and complained that their contribution was marginal as a result of the struggle between the competing internal alignments of the old PCI. Their main criticism, however, was that the new statute effectively institutionalises currents and therefore undermines the role of individual party members. As many of these 'outside' delegates readily admitted, the adhesion of these small left-wing clubs and groups to the PDS is likely to be of only marginal electoral significance. There is also little evidence to suggest that the PDS can attract significant support from the new social movements, which tend to reject traditional party forms of political participation.

Occhetto's hope, reaffirmed at the Twentieth Congress, was that the PDS would broaden the electoral constituency of the old PCI by attracting disillusioned Socialist voters, 'progressive catholics', the 'hidden left' and first-time voters. This ambitious electoral strategy is likely, however, to encounter a number of severe difficulties. First, it is not clear what sort of programmatic appeal can be devised to attract and hold together such a disparate constituency. Many of the target groups focus on new issue concerns (ecological problems, for example) which may conflict with the traditional value priorities of the party's industrial working-class constituency, and this constituency now has the alternative of voting for *Rifondazione Comunista*.[15] Secondly, there is the risk that the rapid dissolution of the PCI, a move opposed by around a third of the party, could result in a significant exodus of party members and a demobilisation of significant numbers of party activists. As Table 1.2 shows, the old PCI lost more than 100,000 members in 1990 and the decline in membership has continued in the new party; official PDS figures give party membership as 989,665 in 1991, of which 52,280 were new members. The PDS organisation has been further weakened by the party's severe financial difficulties and the cuts made necessary by the secession of *Rifondazione Comunista*. This weakening of party organisation, traditionally so vital in mobilising the communist vote, may undermine the electoral performance of the PDS. Thirdly, the attempt to give the PDS a broad appeal might so dilute its identity that erstwhile communist voters will desert the party. Finally, the inclusion of 'democratic communists' in the PDS who are committed to forging a radical identity for the new party could frighten off potential new voters: not surprisingly, in the immediate aftermath of the Twentieth Congress, the party's electoral rivals depicted the PDS as nothing more than the PCI with a new name.

The PDS faced its first major electoral test in the parliamentary elections of April 1992. The results were a major setback for the new party: the PDS won only 16.1 per cent of the vote compared with the 26.6 per cent won by the PCI in 1987. This haemorrhage in support, enormous by Italian standards, was in large part attributable to the unexpectedly strong electoral performance of Communist Refoundation which won 5.6 per cent of the vote and 35 seats in the Chamber of Deputies. In addition, exit polls indicated that levels of abstentions were quite high among former PCI voters and that some votes had been lost to new political formations such as the Greens, the Network and the Northern Leagues. The PDS predictably performed best in areas of traditional PCI electoral strength: the new formation emerged as the leading party in the 'Red Belt' of central Italy but, with the strong showing of Communist Refoundation in these regions, the PDS vote declined by approximately 10 percentage points compared with that of the PCI in 1987.

The PDS leadership gave an upbeat interpretation of the party's performance, claiming that the result represented a promising start for a 'new' party and focusing on the fact that it had matched the PCI's position as Italy's second largest national party. In addition, the party alleged that a large number of would-be PDS voters had unintentionally voted for Communist Refoundation as a result of confusion over the party emblems printed on the ballot papers. The left of the PDS gave a more critical assessment of the party's performance in the election and attacked the leadership for its failure to take advantage of the electoral backlash against the governing coalition.

The fragmentation of the ex-PCI vote produced a significant rebalancing on the left of the party spectrum. The electoral lead of the PDS over the PSI was reduced to 2.5 per cent, compared with the 12.3 per cent lead which the PCI held over the PSI in the 1987 parliamentary elections. The PSI emerged as the leading party of the left in 44 of the 94 provinces, compared with its lead in only 9 in the 1987 elections. The rebalancing on the left was due entirely to the shrinkage and splintering of the ex-PCI electorate.[16]

Nevertheless, despite the loss of about 10 per cent of the old PCI's vote, the very launch of the PDS has posed a fundamental challenge to the PSI, particularly when viewed in the context of the impact of the revolutions in Eastern Europe on Italian national politics generally.[17] The domestic politics of post-war Italy were, for fifty years, shaped significantly by divisions originating in the cold war period. The parties of the centre-right, and most recently the Socialists, claimed consistently that the PCI's alleged ambivalence over Italy's membership of the Western camp and its alleged ideological incompatibility with a capitalist democratic system excluded it as a legitimate party of government. This *conventio ad excludendum* persisted despite the PCI's acceptance of Italy's NATO membership, its strong commitment to the European Community, its longstanding independence from the Soviet Union and its consistent critique of the failings of Eastern bloc regimes.[18] However, the rapid changes occurring in the Eastern bloc and the shifting pattern of East–West relations has made that remnant of the cold war, the *conventio ad excludendum*, increasingly untenable. In this sense, the collapse of the communist regimes of the Eastern bloc and the dropping of the communist label from the name of the new party have removed a stigma that had consistently thwarted the PCI's efforts to achieve domestic legitimacy as a party of government.

In addition, the PSI's disappointing performance in the 1992 national election and the subsequent vortex into which the Socialists and the Christian Democrats entered, as a result of their deep implication in the corruption scandals and misuse of public resources, have reinforced the PDS's image as the principal party of the left. Although the PDS has not remained untainted by the scandals under investigation by Italian magistrates since the early summer of 1992, the party has so far avoided the political price being paid by the established governing parties. They have undergone the resignation of both leaders (Craxi and Forlani) and are desperately attempting to recycle themselves as 'new' parties, ironically mimicking the PCI's transformation which they had not long ago derided.

That the 'Communist question' is a thing of the past has been confirmed at both the national and European levels. At the national level the PDS was invited to participate in Azeglio Ciampi's government in April 1993. The appointment of Ciampi (ex-Governor of the Bank of Italy) as the first 'non-party' Prime Minister in the post-war period symbolised the total discrediting of the Italian system of party government. The PDS accepted posts in the new government but within hours pulled out as a consequence of a vote in Parliament which upheld the Socialist leader Craxi's parliamentary immunity from prosecution by the magistrates for alleged corruption. Although there was no direct linkage between these two issues, the PDS (and it was not alone in this) interpreted the latter as confirmation that the old politics still prevailed and called for immediate elections.[19] At the European level, meanwhile, the PDS, in abandoning its links with the communist world, has been accepted by the international non-communist left. This process, in fact, was begun by the PCI in June 1989 when the party left the communist grouping in the European Parliament and formed a new group, the United European Left, with the Danish *Bonde* and one Greek SAP deputy. In 1993 the PDS completed this development by joining the Socialist Federation and Socialist International.

In short, despite the continued presence of 'democratic communists' inside the party and the persistence of ideas about the party's 'distinctiveness' amongst many members, there can be little doubt that the transformation enacted by the PCI, in conjunction with the changes in Italian politics which that transformation partly caused, has legitimised the PDS in the eyes of others and made it an acceptable candidate for government.

CONCLUSION: THE PDS'S LONG-TERM PROSPECTS

It is still too early to predict the long-term prospects of the PDS. As argued above, the first two years have been difficult ones for the new party: the persistence of internal divisions over the identity and political strategy of the PDS, the unexpected force of the electoral challenge from *Rifondazione Comunista* and the poor showing by the PDS in the 1992 national election have confirmed the difficulties the party faces in halting, let alone reversing, the electoral decline which the PCI suffered from the late 1970s onwards. Any assessment of the party's prospects is complicated by the dramatic changes which have transformed the character of Italian politics since early 1992. As already noted, the birth of the PDS itself has contributed in large measure to the redrawing of the contours of the post-war Italian political system. With the collapse of the Eastern bloc regimes and the transformation of the PCI, communism as an external and internal threat has evaporated, and the cement of anti-communism which underpinned Italian post-war coalition formation has crumbled.

The Italian political system is in a state of flux characterised by high levels of electoral volatility, the growth of a 'politics of discontent' and significant reforms to the institutional basis of the system. The 'unblocking' of the political system promises the prospect of competing coalitions of parties alternating in government. Although Occhetto's reforms of the PCI were designed to transform it into an acceptable party of government and thereby 'unblock' the system, he could not have anticipated the rapid demise of the DC-dominated regime. The new, fluid political situation in Italy offers the PDS a potentially favourable context in which to establish itself. For the first time in the post-war period there is the real prospect of alternation in government, with the PDS at the core of a progressive/reformist political alignment. The collapse of the Socialist Party's vote since early 1992 gives the PDS a greater chance of leading a potential progressive alliance. The new electoral system, which markedly reduces the level of proportionality, will underpin the PDS's dominance in the Red Belt of Central Italy and, to the extent that the new procedures facilitate alternation in government, is likely to give the party a key role in coalition formation – the primary objective of Occhetto's reforms.

NOTES

1.   Contributions to this debate include M. D'Alema, 'Per essere un moderno partito riformatore', interview in *Rinascita*, 3 May 1986, no. 17, pp. 4–5; M. D'Alema, 'Idee e regole per un partito che si riforma', *Rinascita*, 14 May 1988, no. 17, pp. 28–30; E. Ferraris, 'La riforma delle strutture del partito e del loro modo di lavorare', in *Il rinnovamento del Pci e della sua organizzazione dopo il 17 Congresso* (Rome: C. Salemi, 1987), pp. 32–82; and V. Chiti, 'La riforma del partito per gli anni novanta', *Critica Marxista*, anno 27, nos 1–2, pp. 177–97.
2.   For a general overview of the PCI's decline, see S. Hellman, 'Italian Communism in Crisis', in R. Miliband, L. Panitch and J. Saville (eds), *Socialist Register 1988* (London: Merlin Press, 1988), pp. 244–88; P. Ignazi, *Dal PCI al PDS* (Bologna: Il Mulino, 1992); M. Lorusso, *Occhetto: Il Comunismo Italiano da Togliatti al PDS* (Florence: Ponte alle Grazie, 1992).
3.   For a detailed analysis of the initial phases of the 'new course', see G. Grant Amyot, 'The PCI and Occhetto's New Course: The Italian Road to Reform', in R. Y. Nanetti and R. Catanzaro (eds), *Italian Politics: A Review*, vol. 4 (London: Pinter, 1990), pp. 146–61. Also see M. Prospero, *Il Nuovo Inizio: dal PCI di Berlinguer al Partito Democratico della Sinistra* (Chieti: Métis Editrice, 1990).

4. A full account of the Eighteenth Congress is contained in M. J. Bull and P. Daniels, 'The "New Beginning": The Italian Communist Party under the Leadership of Achille Occhetto', *Journal of Communist Studies*, 6/1 (1990), pp. 22–43. Occhetto's speech is reproduced in *The Italian Communists: Foreign Bulletin of the PCI* (Rome), no. 1 (1989), pp. 15–89.

5. For a detailed account of the Euro-elections, see P. Daniels, 'The Italian Communist Party and the European Parliament Elections of June 1989', *Journal of Communist Studies*, 5/4 (1989), pp. 194–199.

6. Biagio De Giovanni, 'C'erano una volta Togliatti e il comunismo reale', *L'Unità*, 6 August 1989.

7. Achille Occhetto, 'Il nuovo corso e discontinuità, non è demolizione del passato', *L'Unità*, 14 September 1989.

8. Occhetto's key speeches during this period are reproduced in M. De Angelis (ed.), *Achille Occhetto: Un indimenticabile '89* (Milan: Feltrinelli, 1990). Important interventions in the debate are contained in G. Moltedo and N. Rangeri (eds), *PCI: La Grande Svolta* (Rome: Edizioni Associate, 1989). On reactions in the party, see C. Valentini, *Il nome e la cosa: Viaggio nel Pci che cambia* (Milan: Feltrinelli, 1990).

9. The texts of the motions are reproduced in *The Italian Communists: Foreign Bulletin of the PCI* (Rome), no. 1 (1990).

10. Occhetto's speech is reproduced in *The Italian Communists: Foreign Bulletin of the PCI* (Rome), no. 1 (1990), pp. 100–59.

11. Primarily through the national programmatic conference (Rome, 22–24 October 1990) held during the constituent phase. A selection of contributions to this conference can be found in *Critica Marxista*, anno 28, nos. 5–6 (1990).

12. On the political position of the *riformisti*, see G. Napolitano, *Al Di Là del Guado: La scelta riformista* (Rome: Lucarini, 1990) and G. Polillo and P. Valenza (eds), *Noi Riformisti: per una Cultura di Governo della Sinistra* (Napoli: Cuen, 1990).

13. On the congress, see S. Hellman, 'La difficile nascita del Pds', in S. Hellman and G. Pasquino (eds), *Politica in Italia: Edizione 92* (Bologna: Il Mulino, 1992), pp. 111–35.

14. On divisions in the PDS, see G. Pasquino, 'Un problema della sinistra: organizzazione e leadership nel Pds', in G. Pasquino, *La Nuova Politica* (Bari: Laterza, 1992), pp. 37–60.

15. Significantly, *Rifondazione Comunista* has overtaken the PDS in some northern cities: for example, in the June 1993 municipal elections, in Turin it polled 14.6 per cent of the vote compared with 9.5 per cent for the PDS and in Milan its vote was 11.8 per cent compared to 9.4 per cent for the PDS. The PDS's long-term programme provides an insight into the attempt to broaden its target groups. See the party's publication, *L'Italia verso il 2000: Analisi e proposte per un programma di legislatura* (Rome: Editori Riuniti, 1992).

16. Indeed, the Socialist Party's vote fell by 0.7 per cent (from 14.3 per cent in 1987 to 13.6 per cent in 1992), demonstrating the party's failure to benefit from the haemorrhage in the ex-PCI vote and the decline in support for the Christian Democrats.

17. The changes in Italian politics in the 1990s are too vast to detail here. For an overview, see Martin Bull and James Newell, 'Italian Politics and the 1992 Elections: From "Stable Instability" to Instability and Change', *Parliamentary Affairs*, **46**/2, (1993).

18. Predictably, the PDS swiftly condemned the coup attempt by hard-liners in the Soviet Union in August 1991.

19. The whole issue of participation in the Ciampi government, however, provoked deep division in the PDS. The moderate wing of the party attacked Occhetto's decision to withdraw his ministers and abstain in the vote of confidence on the new government; the left of the party criticised the leadership for its lack of opposition to the new government.

2 The French Communist Party and the End of Communism

Peter Morris

In the midst of the political turbulence that gripped and then engulfed the socialist regimes of Eastern Europe in Autumn 1989, *Le Monde* published a cartoon in which the general secretary of the French Communist Party (PCF), Georges Marchais, is seen declaring proudly to the leader of its parliamentary group, André Lajoinie, 'We're on our way to becoming the most powerful communist party in Europe.'[1]

The cartoon has a double significance. The leadership of the PCF, and Marchais in particular, have long been an easy target for satirists of all sorts and the fact that they should be is an implicit acknowledgement of the central role that the party has played within the French political system for much of the last fifty years. It is indeed part of the self-defining legitimacy of French communism that its leader should attract such opprobrium from his opponents, since this shows the intensity of the hatred that pursues the PCF and is thus a tribute paid by bourgeois vice to revolutionary integrity.

Yet the cartoon was also a sharp comment on two widely perceived characteristics of contemporary French communism. The first is the doctrinal and organisational sclerosis that has left the party wedded to a discredited orthodoxy that no one else now accepts and that has vanished from the areas of Europe which it once dominated. The second is the marginalisation of the PCF within the French political system. To the outside observer, it can appear that French politics has become not so much anti-communist (for it was always that) as a-communist; and the latter condition is highly damaging to a party whose influence within the system always depended on the ubiquity of its *presence* in French society. Thus Marchais and the leadership are condemned not simply for having identified French communism with the state socialism of Eastern Europe but for having brought upon their own party the same disaster that occurred beyond the Berlin Wall. One could go further and argue that the party was only saved from the fate that overtook the Eastern European parties whose achievements it had so tenaciously defended by the fact that it has become so peripheral to the realities of the exercise of power in present-day France.

One consequence of such an analysis would be that the French communists' response to the collapse of the international communist order can be reduced to three propositions: (i) that they did not like it; (ii) that it had no effect whatsoever on their own strategic choices and analyses; and (iii) that it was simply another nail in the coffin of their ambitions to be a major political force within France. Each of these three propositions is, as we shall see, plausible. But they do not, separately or together, provide a complete analysis of the challenges that the events of 1989–91 posed to the PCF and of the responses that it made to them. The purpose of this chapter is thus, in the first place, to describe how the party did deal with the crisis of East European socialism and then to analyse what its response reveals about the intellectual and political universe inhabited by present-day French communism. The impact, if any, of the events on its future prospects will also be considered.

BACKGROUND

The PCF response to the 1989 revolutions was conditioned by its existing attitudes towards the states of Eastern Europe, attitudes that were nothing if not straightforward. The PCF has always distinguished itself by the intensity of its commitment to what it long referred to as proletarian internationalism and now calls international solidarity. From the time when Stalin defined an internationalist as 'someone who is ready to defend the USSR without reserve, without hesitation and without condition', the PCF believed that the Socialist Commonwealth established in and around the Soviet Union represented a qualitatively superior model of civilisation to anything available in the capitalist West. In his book *A quoi sert le PCF?* (the best analysis of French communism before its fall), Georges Lavau pondered what he saw as the incomprehensible absolutism of the party's support for the socialist world that came into being between 1917 and 1945 and found an answer in the theory of the two antagonistic camps into which the world is divided.[2] From this vision of a world divided into the forces of good and evil the PCF has never deviated; it explains events as separate in time as the strategic retreat into revolutionary defeatism after the Nazi–Soviet Pact of 1939 and the opposition to the Gulf War in 1991.

There were, of course, periods of tension between the PCF and the Communist Party of the Soviet Union (CPSU) in the years that followed the death of Stalin. In 1956 the French party refused to admit the existence of Khrushchev's secret speech denouncing Stalin's crimes against the Soviet party and shortly afterwards supported the attempts of the conservative faction in the Kremlin to engineer a change in the Soviet leadership. After the death in 1964 of the PCF general secretary Maurice Thorez, who had held the position since 1930, the party showed a growing willingness to condemn political repression in the Soviet Union and even, during the 1968 invasion of Czechoslovakia, to criticise an action undertaken by the USSR in the name of proletarian internationalism. In the early stages of the party leadership of Georges Marchais, who became secretary general in 1972, following Waldeck Rochet, who had held the position since 1964, the PCF embarked with gusto on the politics of eurocommunism. It emphasised both the autonomous nature of its model of socialism and its right to determine its domestic strategic choices. Thus, in the run up to the 1974 presidential elections it disregarded Soviet unease at its core political strategy of winning power through a governmental alliance with the Socialist Party and complained bitterly – and publicly – at the support given by the Soviet ambassador to François Mitterrand's rival, Valéry Giscard d'Estaing. Party spokesmen were prepared to denounce both human rights abuses in the USSR and the barrack-room uniformity that Moscow, supported by its East European allies, sought to impose on the international communist movement. In 1978 the party publishing house brought out *L'URSS et nous*, a study of the USSR written by five prominent communist intellectuals.[3] Their analysis was insufficiently revisionist for non-communists; but it was extremely unwelcome to Moscow, which responded with a long denunciation of the book in *Kommunist*, the theoretical journal of the central committee of the CPSU.

The PCF's global vision, however, was unchanged. It remained that of an aggressive imperialism constantly straining, like some blood-stained Sisyphus, to prevent its inevitable demise at the hands of a socialism whose superiority was every day demonstrated in the societies of Eastern Europe. In 1979, when the party had not yet retreated into defiant isolationism that resurfaced with its approval of the Soviet invasion of Afghanistan and led, *inter alia*, to the virtual suppression of *L'URSS et nous*, the PCF Congress declared that the record of existing socialist societies was overall a proud one. Though the term used – *bilan globalement positif* – has since come to haunt the party, it unquestionably defined what French communists felt. Throughout the 1980s the instinctive response was to support East European leaderships when, as in Poland, they came under pressure. Delegations of the Polish Workers' Party received a rapturous welcome at party congresses and the Solidarity movement (whose banning by General Wojciech Jaruzelski the party refused to condemn) was abused with equal vigour. In 1985 amendments from a departmental federation criticising the Romanian regime were rejected by the party and at the 1987 Congress the PCF's foreign policy minister, Maxime Gremetz, referred to his 'fruitful relations' with his Romanian counterpart. At the same congress a delegate criticised the party for having been inadequately supportive of its East European comrades during its eurocommunist period.[4] As if to reassure him and those who felt like him, Marchais had already stated in his opening address that 'existing socialism ... has already shown its ability to resolve the problems of famine, poverty, unemployment, infant mortality, social security, illiteracy, education, sport and culture'.[5]

Thus the core belief in the moral, but also practical, superiority of existing socialist regimes remained intact. It is this that explains why the party leadership was initially underwhelmed by the blaze of publicity that surrounded the Russian party's adoption of *perestroika* in the mid-1980s. Just as the party had found it difficult to come to terms with the radicalism of Khrushchev, so now it barely concealed its suspicion of the dynamism of Mikhail Gorbachev. Outside commentators claimed that Marchais was about as keen on *perestroika*, let alone *glasnost*, as was the East German leader Erich Honecker. For a long time, the official line was that since the PCF had renounced in the name of its strategic independence any idea of a universal model of socialism it had no need to copy innovations that came from outside its own experience. At the 1988 Conference of the Portuguese Communist Party – whose leader, Alvaro Cunhal, was a long term-enemy of anything that smacked of 'wet' communism and had memorably declared during the eurocommunist period of the 1970s that 'there will be no parliaments in a socialist Portugal' – Marchais declared that 'what is happening in the Soviet Union in no sense constitutes a model for other communist parties; it is specific to the USSR'.[6] A year earlier a delegate from the communist heartland of Seine Saint Denis told the PCF Congress that if it wanted a good example of what was meant by *perestroika* it need look no further than the action that the then party leader Thorez took in 1930 to expel the Barbe Celor group.[7] Even in 1989, when, as will be seen, the leadership had come to view the

Soviet experiment with greater official enthusiasm, it still in-sisted, using Gorbachev himself as authority, that 'the idea that perestroika should apply everywhere is un-marxist and simply stupid'.[8]

From its beginnings, however, *perestroika* nevertheless pre-sented the PCF with a more difficult problem than that it had to face after Khrushchev's secret speech. It showed the extent to which the party leadership was no longer able to monopolise the definition of what constitutes French com-munism. The myth of the Communist monolith in France has always had to incorporate the existence of dissidents and out groups – Jacques Doriot in the 1930s; André Marty/Charles Tillon in the 1950s; Laurent Casanova/Marcel Servin in the 1960s; Jean Elleinstein/Henri Fiszbin in the 1970s. Yet throughout its history the leadership had always managed to isolate its opponents and to destroy their identity as communists. The significance of *perestroika* was that it revealed the extent to which the leadership had lost this power. Successive waves of dissidents – the so-called *ren-ovateurs, reconstructeurs, refondateurs* – could now use *pere-stroika* to challenge with impunity, if not with success, the orthodoxies of the leadership group in their headquarters (one is tempted to say bunker) in the Place du Colonel Fabien.

The reason for this is that *perestroika* hit the PCF at a time when its domestic position was weaker than at any time since 1941. The story is too familiar to need more than a brief recapitulation. In the 1981 presidential and legislative elections, the struggle for control of the French left between the PCF and Mitterrand's revived Socialist Party (PS) ended in the decisive victory of the latter. Marchais won only 15 per cent of the vote in the first round of the presidential elections and the entry of four Communist ministers into the Socialist government of Pierre Mauroy was a testament to the historical myth of left unity rather than the necessary recognition of communist power.

During the 1980s the process of marginalisation con-tinued and accelerated. As Table 2.1 shows, the PCF's share of the vote in national elections slumped from 15.1 per cent

Table 2.1   Communist share of the votes in French elections since 1958 (mainland only)

	Votes	Percentage
Legislative Elections 1958	3,870,184	18.9
Legislative Elections 1962	4,003,553	21.84
Legislative Elections 1967	5,029,208	22.46
Legislative Elections 1968	4,435,357	20.03
Presidential Election 1969	4,808,285	21.27
Legislative Elections 1973	5,084,824	21.40
Legislative Elections 1978	5,793,139	20.61
Presidential Election 1981	4,415,028	15.48
Legislative Elections 1986	2,663,734	9.69
Presidential Election 1988	2,005,995	6.76
Legislative Elections 1988	2,765,761	11.32
Legislative Elections 1993	2,268,931	9.14

Source: A. Cole (ed.), *French Political Parties in Transition (1990);* Le Monde, *Dossiers et Documents: 21 mars–28 mars 1993 Élections Législatives.*

in the 1981 presidential contest to 9.7 per cent in the 1986 parliamentary elections to 6.7 per cent in the presidential election of 1988. Between 1978 and 1988 the number of Communist voters fell from 5.8 million to 2.8 million; in large parts of France the party has ceased to exist as a credible political force. It is indicative of the party's decayed image that in 1988 it managed to poll only 9 per cent of the 18 to 25 age group. French political sociologists are fond of drawing a distinction between the world of politics and government and the institutions of what they call civil society. Here too, the influence of the PCF has manifestly declined. It no longer enjoys prestige amongst France's powerful (or at least vocal) intellectual class and though it continues to control the leadership of the *Confédération Générale du Travail* (CGT, General Workers' Union) the number of workers who remain within what used to be the country's largest union movement has fallen, according to some sources, to 500,000.[9]

The result of accelerating electoral decline, exclusion from central government after 1984 and the national unpopularity of Marchais was that dissident groups within the party started to challenge the leadership. The initial opposition group came out into the open after the party's disastrous performance in the 1984 European elections and subsequent withdrawal from the new Laurent Fabius government. The *renovateurs*, as they were known, were headed by Pierre Juquin, former party spokesman and a member of the political bureau, and Marcel Rigout, a minister in the Mauroy governments of 1981–4. In 1988 Juquin stood for president and managed to poll nearly a third of the vote of the party's official candidate, André Lajoinie. In the municipal elections of 1989 the party was unable to prevent the re-election of dissident communists as mayors in important urban centres like Orly and Le Mans.

Juquin's decision to stand for the presidency inevitably led to his – and his supporters' – expulsion from the party. Yet the departure of the Juquinistes has not led to an end to internal dissidence. The *reconstructeurs*, and more recently, the *renovateurs* headed by another former communist minister, Charles Fiterman (see below), have continued to express open disagreement with the leadership. One reason for the impunity with which they are able to do this is that many of them hold elected office as deputy or mayor and are thus evidence of the party's continuing electoral strength. To lose their nominal affiliation would be yet further evidence of the decline in the presence of French communism.

Decline at home has been mirrored by isolation abroad, and in particular by the growing deterioration of the party's relations with its former partners in the eurocommunist movement. After the 1989 European elections, the Italian Communist Party (PCI) withdrew its 22 euro-deputies from the Communist Group in the Strasbourg Parliament, leaving the seven PCF euro-deputies in a rump group of fourteen, the so-called *coalition des gauches*. Subsequently the PCI asked its supporters among the Italian immigrant community in France to withdraw from the PCF, to which they had traditionally adhered, and to create a separate organisation. A more practical problem for the party has been the drying up, even before the end of Soviet communism, of financial support from the CPSU.

THE PCF AND THE EVENTS OF 1989

(i) The Crisis of Autumn 1989

The socialist internationalism to which the PCF is so committed was demonstrated once again in 1989 at its central annual ritual, the *Fête de L'Humanité*, held every September in a Paris suburb. The Bulgarian, Czech and East German parties all had large stands (the Italian one was tiny, and closed for most of the time), and in his keynote speech Marchais lauded the achievements of the German Democratic Republic, then about to celebrate its fortieth anniversary: 'We have never despaired of the socialist societies or of their capacity to find within themselves the strength that will enable them to overcome the barriers to a full realisation of their potential'.[10] A month later Lajoinie and the veteran communist leader Gaston Plissonier, went to East Berlin to represent the PCF at the fortieth anniversary of the GDR.

By October 1989 the communist world of Eastern Europe was entering its death throes, a phenomenon that even the PCF could not ignore. In studying the reaction of the party to the overthrow of the regimes in East Germany, Czechoslovakia, Bulgaria and Romania, it is useful to draw a distinction between the crisis response as the events unfolded in the autumn of 1989 and the more considered analysis that emerged once the leadership had had time to digest the overthrow of the *partis frères*.

For much of autumn 1989, the term used by the party leadership to describe the tumultuous events in East Germany was *'bouillonnement'*, which can best be translated as 'effervescence'. This 'effervescence' was explained in two ways. In September and October, *L'Humanité* denounced the West German authorities for fomenting trouble in order to get their hands on a highly qualified, and cheap, labour force and proclaimed that in terms of economic growth, full employment and comprehensive social security the GDR was indeed a model.[11] The emigration movement thus became no more than the 'wholly legitimate desire to travel'. Georges Marchais told the October meeting of the Central Committee that many young East Germans were telling him that 'we're doing very nicely in East Germany but we want more liberty, we want to be able to travel wherever we like'.[12]

The shared characteristic of these two explanations is, of course, that they absolve the socialist nature of the regime from any responsibility for what was going on. At the October meeting of the Central Committee this line was still being held and the party press did its best to avoid any commentary on the growing turmoil by its traditional tactic of blanket coverage of domestic social unrest and dire warnings about the threat to national sovereignty posed by the EC summit at Rome. Subsequently, as regime disintegration throughout Eastern Europe became unstoppable, the PCF simply tried to show that every concession made by the collapsing parties was evidence of their democratic good faith and strategic grasp of the situation. The day after the Berlin Wall came down, Marchais sent a telegram to Egon Krenz congratulating him on his 'decision' and declaring that moments like these which we share with our German comrades are not simply days of joy, but days of confidence and optimism.[13]

Only in Maxime Gremetz's speech to the Central Committee meeting in December was the term *bouillonnement* replaced by *bouleversement* (upheaval) and the famous phrase *bilan globalement positif* declared to be an incomplete definition of the PCF's analysis of the East European regimes. Almost immediately afterwards the party had to face the torrent of abuse that rained down on it once the Nicolae Ceaucescu tyranny in Romania disintegrated. The non-communist press seized upon the fact that Marchais had holidayed in Romania as recently as 1984 and that in November 1989 the party, unlike its Italian counterpart, sent a delegation to the Romanian Party Congress.

(ii) PCF Analysis of the Crisis

In one sense the PCF could draw sustenance from the violent denunciations of its alleged relationship with the Ceaucescu dictatorship. For it was able to point out, quite correctly, not only that political leaders of many other parties had long cultivated good relations with the Bucarest regime, but also that Marchais had declared on French television early in 1989 that what was going on in Romania had nothing to do with socialism. The PCF delegation to the 1989 Romanian Party Congress strongly, and publicly, criticised abuses of human rights in Romania and spoke of a fundamental disagreement between the two parties over the definition of socialism. Its democratic credentials thus reasserted – at least to its own satisfaction – the party could then move on to a three-pronged analysis of what had happened throughout Eastern Europe and its own relationship to the discredited parties.

The first point made was that French Communists could not be blamed for failing to appreciate what was going to happen since nobody else had either. The dramatic events of autumn 1989 were, as Gremetz told the December 1989 meeting of the Central Committee, largely *imprévisible* (unforeseeable). In his 1990 book, *Démocratie*, Marchais justified the party's failure to foresee the collapse by appealing to two very different authorities – Vaclav Havel, who declared a fortnight before the Prague demonstrations that nothing would happen in Czechoslovakia, and the Romanian prime minister, who said that he had not realised how extensive was the apparatus of repression constructed by Ceaucescu.[14] As the immediacy of the events receded, the party went

further and started to imply that the Western, and thus capitalist, media had deliberately sought to engage in disinfor-
mation about the extent of the upheavals that provoked
regime overthrow. In the September 1990 issue of the
Cahiers du Communisme, for example, Jacques Fath dwelt on
the claims, which subsequently proved to be false, of mass
executions in the Romanian city of Timisoara and of the
beating to death by the Czech security forces of the young
dissident Martin Smid.[15]

The PCF did not, however, try to pretend that what happened was simply the result of capitalist manipulation. A
second and more important theme is that of solidarity betrayed. The leadership repeatedly claimed that it had con-
tinually told the East European leaderships that all was not
well with their society and that major reform was necessary.
A familiar tactic of French Communist dialectic – that of
showing that the only bad communist is a dead communist
– was brought into use to condemn the dismal heritage of
Brezhnevism in Eastern Europe (and, as we shall see, the
Soviet Union). The fact that Marchais had poor personal relations with Brezhnev and that in 1977 the CPSU had toyed
with the idea of engineering a putsch against the French
party leadership facilitated the idea that the East European
parties were run by narrow-minded reactionaries, corrupted
politically, if not personally, by power and guilty of pervert-
ing the principles of communist party life. The Czech and
East German leaders came in for particular criticism on this
account. At the 1990 PCF Congress, held at Saint Ouen,
Marchais stated that

> imprisoned in their out of date attitudes, the leaders of
> these countries saw only danger in the new challenges of
> modernisation – and hence of democratisation – which
> actually represented a great opportunity for socialism. ...
> We do not regret these regimes but we do regret that
> their leaders' policy was so unpopular that their popula-
> tions rose up against it.[16]

Writing in *Cahiers du Communisme* in October 1990, Yves Moreau argued that it was the absence of political liberty that brought the East German regime down – its people enjoyed social rights but their political rights were not fully recognised.[17] The significance of the observation lies, of course, in its continuing refusal to denounce the achievements of the East European states, a point to which we shall return. It also introduces the third element in the PCF analysis of the events of 1989 – the extremely difficult circumstances in which socialism had been established there. This is a theme to which French communists return time and again. In the case of the Soviet Union, Marchais sees the roots of Stalinism as lying in *'la longue tradition de la Russie'* but also in the aggressiveness and violence of a capitalist West that constantly sought to overthrow the new socialist order. Elsewhere, the term repeatedly used to describe the state of Eastern Europe before the communist takeover is *'arriération'* – 'backwardness'. Barracks socialism is attributed to the fact that, with the exception of Czechoslovakia, East European societies were characterised not only by great poverty but also by a total absence of a democratic political culture. Thus Jacques Fath argues that the political traditions of a France that had experienced its industrial and political revolutions two centuries ago were bound to be different 'and in many ways superior' to those of countries that had 'only recently escaped from feudalism and poverty'.[18]

(iii) Lessons of the Crisis

The 'developmental' argument is important because it provides the link between the recognition of the failure of the deposed regimes in Eastern Europe and the PCF's continued insistence on the absolute superiority of its concept of socialism. For what emerges most clearly from the party's analysis of the 1989 events is that French communism has nothing to learn from the collapse of the communist states.

Nowhere in the party literature is there any sign of a crisis of confidence on the part of its 'official mind'; what emerges instead is the reiteration of a number of explanations of why what had happened elsewhere could not ever happen in a scientifically socialist France and why, in consequence, socialism retains all its authority. This, of course, raises the two questions of what constitutes the 'official mind' of present day French communism and whether that mind is responsible, as most outsiders would claim, for the dire condition in which the party now finds itself. But before considering these two points, we need to describe how the PCF rationalises its unshakeable belief in the future of socialism at both national and international level.

Once the errors of the East European regimes had been explained away, it became possible for the PCF to go onto the offensive in its defence of the achievements of socialism. The counterpart to the 'backwardness' thesis is a recognition of the achievements of the socialist regimes in developing the societies they controlled. In *Démocratie* Marchais admitted that the phrase *'bilan globalement positif'* presented difficulties in the light of what had happened and he said on television that he would not now use it.[19] More generally, however, the emphasis is firmly on East European socialism's success in putting an end to illiteracy and hunger and in helping to preserve world peace after the defeat of Nazism and in the face of imperialist aggression. (One party official has even said that the chronic level of absenteeism in Soviet factories was evidence of how free a society the USSR was.)

The PCF has also continued to hold on to the principles of communist internationalism and to laud the heroic struggles of the remaining socialist states. This has been very notable in the case of Cuba. In 1990 Fidel Castro's regime took on the mythical status of heroic adversary of imperialist aggression – communist David to Uncle Sam's Goliath – that North Vietnam had enjoyed in the 1960s. The party press published in book form *'Conversations au clair de lune'*, a lengthy interview by Jean Edern Hallier with Castro, and at the 1990 Congress an emotional appeal was made to send a boat full of supplies to Cuba (*'un bateau pour Cuba'*) to break the United States embargo (the boat duly sailed from Le Havre and reached Havana four weeks later). The party has continued its traditional programme of exchanges of messages and personnel with progressive forces everywhere. The aged Gaston Plissonnier paid two visits to Vietnam in 1989 and the following year flew to South Yemen for the anniversary celebrations of its communist regime.

Among the remaining socialist states was, of course, the Soviet Union itself. From autumn 1989 there was a change of tone in the PCF attitude to *perestroika* and to its symbol, Mikhail Gorbachev. Marchais visited Moscow in September 1989 and declared on his return that the PCF was fully behind the reform movement. By 1990 he was implicitly referring to himself as the best Gorbachevian around (it is impossible not to remember the late 1940s party description of Thorez as the best Stalinist in France) and thereafter the PCF never gave up on its defence of *perestroika*.

Yet what matters is the way in which the reform movement was presented. *Perestroika* was always portrayed as a democratic revolution within the Revolution, the continuation rather than an abandonment of the heritage of 1917. It was a testament to the vitality of the Communist Party of the Soviet Union rather than a sign of its decay. The CPSU thus became the initiator of the reform programme – a writer in *Cahiers du Communisme* even claimed in March 1992 that the true founder of *perestroika* was Yuri Andropov – and is praised for abandoning the attempt to control popular forces and for concentrating instead on its authentic role as a movement of the political *avant garde*. The emphasis on the role of the party is essential because it legitimises the central element of communism as a political doctrine.

The PCF did not try to conceal the growing difficulties faced by Gorbachev from 1990 onwards and Marchais, in *Démocratie*, spoke complacently of the hesitations, contradictions, errors that had occurred.[20] But it did not, at least openly, side with the conservative factions in the CPSU. It reserved its hostility for the 'economic radicals who preach

a market liberalism that Giscard d'Estaing would recognise'
and – above all – for Boris Yeltsin, categorised as early as
1990 as a populist poujadist.[21] Open criticism of Gorbachev
himself only surfaced at the time of the Gulf War when he
was condemned for abandoning the historoic mission of the
Soviet Union as defender of 'the camp of progress' against
United States imperialism.

By now the picture is becoming clear. The lesson of
Eastern Europe is that the regimes failed not because they
were socialist but because they were insufficiently socialist.
The PCF refuses to see any relevance to its own situation
in what had happened, a refusal justified by reference to
its own programmatic legitimacy and by its analysis of the
global situation. So far as their own position is concerned,
orthodox French communists argue that by the 1970s they
had accepted that socialism was inherently linked with
democracy. Constant reference is now made to the adoption in the 1970s of a *'socialisme aux couleurs de la France'*
and to the political liberalisation enshrined in the 1976
Party Congress (when eurocommunist enthusiasm was
at its height), by the abandonment of the dictatorship of
the proletariat and the adoption of a *socialisme autogestionnaire. L'URSS et nous*, which had been hidden almost as
soon as it was published, returned to prominence in party
propaganda.

Thus the PCF claims that its programmatic vision would
have been capable of managing the transformation of
Eastern Europe from capitalism to socialism. For the central
point about its response to 1989 is the determination to
hold on to that vision. The party is, and remains, glad to be
red. Communism, the social vision inaugurated by the
social science of Marx and Lenin, retains all its potency as
explanation and as praxis. At one level this simply means
that socialist Bulgaria was better than capitalist Turkey.
More basically it means that the core tenets of Marxism –
the iniquities of capitalism, the necessity of revolution, the
decisive role of the party – continue to structure the
content of the party's mind set. In his 11 November 1989
broadcast, Marchais asserted that while socialism faced

problems of development, capitalism was – and must inevitably remain – in a state of systemic crisis. Nothing that
has happened since, in Eastern or Western Europe, has led
the French communists to depart from that view.

IMPACT OF THE EVENTS

(i) Policy

Thus the dissolution of the East European regimes did
nothing to lessen the certainty of the PCF belief that *le capi-
talisme ne se corrige pas, il se combat*. The immediate consequence of this was that the party could face its future – but
also its past – with confidence. It is significant that, early on
in *Démocratie*, Marchais pays a warm tribute to the party's
most famous – or notorious – leader, Maurice Thorez, and
subsequently offers as partial excuse for the party's failure
in 1956 to come to terms with the secret speech of
Khrushchev the fact that 1956 was a year in which the international class struggle was particularly acute owing to the
Soviet intervention in Hungary and the Anglo-French aggression at Suez. (The resonance of the terms used – inter-
vention/aggression – is unmistakable.)

More importantly, the PCF has denied the need for any
change to its programme or structure, both of which are
characterised by the rejection of social democracy. Since
leaving governmental office – power would be too strong a
word – in 1984 the PCF has condemned the prudent,
market-friendly policies of the Socialist governments and
has championed all protest movements by low-paid groups
and other victims of French modernisation. Efforts made by
the Michel Rocard government (1988–91) to reorganise the
financing of the social security system were denounced, and
even led to the PCF parliamentary group joining with the
Right in voting a censure motion. The PCF now advocates
the end of the directly-elected presidency in France and a
return to a fully parliamentarian regime.

Refusal of programmatic social democracy goes hand-in-hand with an equally insistent rejection of social-democratic political structures. The incapacity of these structures to achieve real change is a permanent theme in PCF discourse. At one level this enables the party to dwell on the series of corruption scandals that have affected the French Socialist Party in recent years as evidence of its subservience to financial interests; its publishing house has produced *La Rosenklature*, an exposé of the Socialist Party's domination of the apparatus of French public life. Not until June 1993 did Marchais propose the abandonment of the Leninist principle of democratic centralism as the defining characteristic of a revolutionary party. In February 1990 the role of the latter had been spelled out in *Cahiers du Communisme*. If free discussion was to be encouraged (and how could it not be in a party pledged to *socialisme autogestionnaire?*) the imperatives of party discipline and respect for majority decisions, and the illegality of appealing outside the party against those decisions, retain their importance.[22]

There is nothing surprising in this. As Marchais told the 1990 Congress, 'Our party was born out of social democracy, from which it has liberated itself for ever.' Thus the choice made at the 1920 Tours Congress to abandon the Second International is still valid; *autogestion* is the present-day equivalent of the revolutionary syndicalism that characterised French labour politics at the turn of the century; the workers' cause must remain unpolluted by the vice of *'parlementarisme petit bourgeois'*.[23] The party has no intention of returning to the political and programmatic alliance – *union de la gauche* – that it constructed with the Socialist Party in the 1970s and that it regards as a betrayal of its ideals (and the cause of its electoral problems).

One consequence of the PCF's position is its hostility to the europeanism that is at the centre of France's foreign and economic policy. For the official mind of French communism, the integrationism of the European Community is a betrayal of economic and political sovereignty to the interests of international capital; using language that comes straight from the traditional nationalism of the party lexicon, *Cahiers du Communisme* has described the Jacques Delors/François Mitterrand plans as threatening Europe with 'the uncontrolled spread of the power of the banks (including American and Japanese bankers) and the growth of a television *sans frontières* dedicated to the diffusion of American mass (i.e. non) culture'.[24] In 1992, as France entered on the process of ratifying the Maastricht Treaty, the party proclaimed its *'non' radical* to further economic and political integration and campaigned for a 'no' vote in the September referendum (the parallel with Jean Marie Le Pen's *Front National* – France's other 'anti-system' party – is obvious).

(ii) Party

We have seen that the events of 1989 occurred at a time when the leadership of the PCF had already lost its ability to consign its internal critics to silence or to the political wilderness. If some opponents of the leadership, like Juquin, had quit, others had not. Thus the group of *refondateurs* around the ex-ministers Charles Fiterman, Jack Ralite and Anicet le Pors moved into action. In an October 1989 letter to the Central Committee (which *L'Humanité* did not publish in full), Fiterman spoke of the need to 'refound a modern communist identity' and went into the sensitive area of the significance of democratic centralism. When the Berlin Wall came down, hitherto loyal members of the leadership group, like Guy Hermier, Philippe Herzog and the CGT leader, Henri Krasucki, all criticised the globally positive assessment of the socialist regimes.

Subsequently, dissidence has been a permanent feature of PCF politics, with the Fiterman/Herzog group using party institutions like the regular meetings of the Central Committee. In April 1992, for example, Fiterman gave a press conference during the Central Committee meeting to publicise his opposition to ratification of the Maastricht Treaty. The dissidents also prepared joint actions with ex-members of the party like Marcel Rigout.

It would be wrong to assert that the intra-party authority of the PCF leadership has been unaffected by the collapse of the East European regimes. The decision of the CPSU in February 1990 to consider dropping democratic centralism posed what was potentially the greatest difficulty for the simple reason that democratic centralism is the central tenet of the party's value system. Yet what is chiefly impressive about the intra-party response to the 1989 crisis is the ability of the leadership group around Marchais to withstand what might seem to have been a basic challenge to their legitimacy. Why this should be is something to which we will return in the conclusion. For the moment it is enough to point out that the critics have not attempted to launch a frontal assault on the leadership – and that the leadership has not sought to liquidate the most prominent dissidents like Fiterman (who remains a member of the Political Bureau). Instead, the PCF headquarters tries, wherever possible, to exclude dissidents from positions of responsibility within the local party machinery and the official press continues its traditional propaganda tactic of denouncing them as ignorant of, if not actually hostile to, the concerns of the French working class.

The ability of the leadership to keep control of the party was demonstrated by the Soviet coup of August 1991 and the end of the USSR. Once again the PCF leadership was the target of those inside, as well as outside, the party, who accused it of failing to denounce the overthrow of Gorbachev with sufficient energy. (It is worth noting that President Mitterrand was similarly criticised.) Certainly *L'Humanité's* reports of the events limited its criticisms, like the Political Bureau statement of 19 August, to a condemnation of the *'conditions d'éviction'* of Gorbachev. Fiterman and Herzog distanced themselves from the language of the declaration. The party also attempted, unsuccessfully, to withdraw from circulation its weekly supplement, printed before the failure of the coup, which dealt with the state of Soviet society under the blunt title *L'Echec* (the failure). Once again the leadership used the events both during and after the coup to prove the correctness of its analysis/vision. The last months of the USSR had given the apparatus ample opportunity to underline the failures of *perestroika*. Gorbachev's inability to reassert his authority after the coup; the growing power of Yeltsin; and the measures taken against the CPSU and its allied organisations, allowed the party to articulate once again its favourite themes of the iniquity of attacks on that democracy which the PCF has always defended as an integral part of its socialism.

CONCLUSION: THE FUTURE OF FRENCH COMMUNISM

'Future' can seem an improbable term when talking about the PCF. For the prospects of the party appear as bleak as ever. In the regional (and departmental) elections of March 1992 the PCF wholly failed to profit, as it had hoped, from the collapse of the political authority of the governing Socialist Party, which received fewer votes than at any time since 1971. The fact that it polled 8 per cent of the total (some 800,000 votes more than in the European elections of 1989) was claimed to be 'encouraging'. But given the much higher turnout of March 1992, this was in no sense the beginnings of a recovery and its share of the vote in the departmental council elections which took place on the same day was 6.94 per cent. In a traditional area of strength, the Limousin, the official party list was crushed by the dissidents around Marcel Rigout, and in the Ile de France communist councillors refused to accept leadership directions over the choice of the new regional executives.

The PCF's 1992 tactics were repeated in the 1993 legislative elections and involved trying to annex every sectoral grievance – for example, the dockers' resistance to government efforts to change their employment statute – in an attempt to develop the party's trade union profile. They brought few results. It is true that the election of twenty-four Communist deputies meant that the PCF was able to preserve a parliamentary group and that it won back eight seats lost to the Socialist Party in the 1980s. Yet the party won only 9.18 per cent of the first-round vote. Electoral stagnation goes hand-in-hand with organisational decline. The party press was in crisis and the losses of *L'Humanité* rose from 17 million francs in 1989 to 30 million in 1991.[25] The result of this was that a quarter of the newspaper's staff were sacked. Party membership (Table 2.2) is under 200,000 and the collapse of the Soviet Union has deprived it of the financial support which it had received throughout its history.

Writing in the 1970s, Ronald Tiersky explained the durable power of the PCF within the French political system in terms of its ability to combine the roles of trade union (tribune) pressure group; party of government; symbol of a revolutionary alternative to the shortcomings of bourgeois democracy; and provider of a counter community for the victims of capitalist society.[26] The position now looks very different. For all that the CGT remains influential in one or two industrial sectors (the docks, the Paris underground) and that communist municipalities remain strong in the most deprived areas (Seine Saint Denis, Val de Marne) of the Ile de France, the tribune function of the party that Georges Lavau identified has largely gone. The revolutionary mystique no longer

Table 2.2   Estimates of Communist Party membership

1960	300,000
1966	341,000
1970	380,000
1974	450,000
1978	520,000
1984	380,000
1986	320,000
1990	200,000

Source: C. Ysmal, *Les Partis Politiques sous la Ve République* (1989); 1990 figure, *L'État de la France, 1992.*

mobilises and the PCF has ceased to be a potential partner in government.

It is thus easy to conclude that there is no future for the PCF any more than there is for the parties in the East with which it identified for so long. Nevertheless our analysis cannot end there. A full assessment of the PCF needs to take account of two further, and related, points that modify – even if they do not transform – the dominant impression of accelerating collapse.

The first is that electoral communism has not disappeared. The statistics show that some two million French electors remain prepared, even in elections where the PCF has no hope of winning, to vote for it and that municipal communism is still a reality. French communism continues to have its *notables* and its voters who continue to see the party as a vehicle for their everyday – if not its ideological – aspirations.

The second point concerns the continuing existence within France of a communist community. A fascinating poll of 1000 delegates to the 1990 Party Congress shows that only 59 per cent had been prepared to vote for Mitterrand in round two of the 1988 presidential election, compared with 89 per cent of round one communist voters.[27] The poll also shows that 96 per cent of the delegates continue to believe in the revolutionary mission of the PCF and 95 per cent in the reality of the class struggle. Only 18 per cent of party militants continue to have faith in the reality of proletarian internationalism; but 60 per cent remain loyal to the principles of democratic centralism. The activities of the *refondateurs* attract considerable media attention (as intra-party dissent has always done) and highlight the decline in the legitimacy of the party's formal authority structures. Yet the existing leadership group remains in place and it is not evident that it is about to be displaced.

Such survey findings help to understand the persistence, if not the vitality, of the organisational culture of French communism at a time when so many of its ideological and structural resources have disappeared. It is not enough to explain this solely in terms of the power of a self-perpetuating oligarchy which dominates its decision-taking bodies – the fact, for example, that the majority of the members of its 'parliament' (the Central Committee) are salaried officials. Nor is it enough simply to underline the long-standing nature of party activists' commitment to communism: 66 per cent of the delegates to the 1990 Congress dated their identification with the communist movement from before 1964 and only 3 per cent since 1986. French communism is undoubtedly experiencing an existential crisis. Yet it continues to provide a haven – the counter community of which Tiersky speaks – for an alienated section of the French people, a haven that depends upon its image as the purveyor of a revolutionary alternative to the dominant power structure in France.

Understanding the PCF requires, in other words, an appreciation of the politics of belief. The analogy of the French Communist Party and a church is not a new one; it was in the late 1940s that Raymond Aron and others developed the notion of communism as a secular religion. The last ten years have proved in France, as elsewhere, that the religion has lost its promised land and much of its congregation. That the institutional communism of the PCF has survived better than its counterparts in Eastern Europe may simply reflect the fact that it is not important enough to warrant destruction. But to PCF believers present difficulties are ultimately less important than the survival of the communist Word. It is this that enables its leadership – its priesthood – to survive.

NOTES

I am grateful to Martin Bull and Dennis Kavanagh for their helpful comments on earlier drafts of this chapter.

1.   *Le Monde*, 12/13 November 1989.
2.   Georges Lavau, *A Quoi sert le PCF?* (Paris, 1981), pp. 362ff.
3.   A. Adler, F. Cohen, M. Décaillot, C. Frioux,and L. Robel, *L'URSS et nous* (Paris, 1978).

4.   George Marchais's report to the 1987 PCF Congress, p. 176.
5.   Ibid., p. 23.
6.   *Le Monde,* 13 October 1989; *Le Point,* 16 October 1989.
7.   1987 PCF Congress report, p. 176.
8.   G. Marchais, *Démocratie* (1991), p. 109.
9.   *Le Monde,* 14 December 1989.
10. *Le Monde,* 30 December 1989.
11. *L'Humanité,* 13 September 1989, 10 October 1989.
12. *Le Monde,* 13 October 1989.
13. *Le Monde,* 12/13 October 1989.
14. Marchais, *Démocratie,* p. 89.
15. *Cahiers du Communisme,* September 1990, p. 80.
16. George Marchais speech quoted in *Le Monde,* 19 September 1990.
17. *Cahiers du Communisme,* October 1990, p. 88.
18. *Cahiers du Communisme,* February 1990, p. 85.
19. Marchais, *Démocratie,* p. 122.
20. Ibid., p. 115.
21. *Cahiers du Communisme,* June 1990, p. 80.
22. *Cahiers du Communisme,* February 1990, pp. 86ff.
23. *Cahiers du Communisme,* March 1990, p. 23.
24. *Cahiers du Communisme,* November 1989, p. 62.
25. *Libération,* 23 December 1991.
26. R. Tiersky, *French Communism 1920–76* (Columbia University Press, 1974).
27. *Le Monde,* 3 January 1991.

3 The Spanish Left: Towards a 'Common Home'?

Paul Heywood

The collapse of communism in Eastern Europe and the subsequent disintegration of the Soviet Union have presented fundamental challenges to the communist parties of Western Europe. It is no exaggeration to talk in terms of potentially terminal crisis: both the role and the relevance of communism in the late twentieth century have been called sharply into question since the dramatic events of 1989–91. The very survival of communism as a meaningful political force on the world stage is open to question. In Spain, the *Partido Comunista de España* (PCE) had already undergone a near fatal crisis in the late 1970s and early 1980s – an experience which not only predates the general crisis of European communism by a decade, but has also conditioned the Spanish response to it. Thus, it is possible to speak of two crises in the recent history of Spanish communism.

Two points in the Spanish case require emphasis. First, the gradual re-emergence of the PCE as a significant player on the domestic political stage since its electoral nadir of 1982 has been intimately associated with the launch of a wide-ranging alliance of left-oriented groups. Known as *Izquierda Unida* (IU, United Left), this formation originated in 1986 as an anti-NATO platform and its formal establishment in early 1987 prefigured similar developments which have taken place in other European countries. Secondly, the PCE – uniquely among West European communist parties – has operated since 1982 in the context of uninterrupted opposition to a governing socialist party, the *Partido Socialista Obrero Español* (PSOE). Relations between the PCE and PSOE have always been particularly bitter, the legacy in part of mutual recrimination over the defeat of the Second Republic during the Spanish Civil War. The PCE, both in its own right and under the auspices of the IU (in which it is the dominant force), has been vehement in its attacks on the supposed abandonment of any socialist principles by the PSOE since assuming power. Thus it was with no small degree of *Schadenfreude* that leaders of the PSOE seized upon the collapse of communism to argue that their party should assume the role of 'common home of the left', inviting PCE militants to join them. The official response, in spite of a series of electoral setbacks for *Izquierda Unida* since 1989, was one of withering disdain.

None the less, noteworthy developments have taken place within both the IU/PCE and the PSOE. The rejection of all *rapprochement* with the PSOE by the IU/PCE leadership never won universal support from the membership, and several figures of political weight have journeyed across the historic divide. Moreover, the PSOE has since the mid-1980s been engaged in a major project of ideological reformulation, reflected in initiatives such as the *Manifiesto del Programa 2000*, which sought to establish the party as the dominant force of the social-democratic left not just on the Spanish stage, but also in the forthcoming context of a politically united Europe.[1] This chapter analyses the background to these developments, their impact, and some future implications for the politics of the left in Spain.

THE FIRST CRISIS OF CONTEMPORARY SPANISH COMMUNISM

It was widely anticipated by political activists and pundits alike that the PCE would assume the dominant role on the Spanish left after the death of General Franco in November 1975.[2] After all, the PCE had been the main bulwark of opposition to the dictator throughout his rule – a point repeatedly emphasised by both the Franco regime and the communist leadership. The Socialist Party, meanwhile, appeared riven by internal crises. The leadership-in-exile, based since 1947 in Toulouse, had seemed caught in a time-warp, endlessly replaying the details of the splits which had undermined the Republican cause in the Civil War. The PCE disparagingly dismissed the Socialists for having been *'de vacaciones'* during Franco's rule. As if to lend support to the Communists' wounding charge, by the early 1970s Socialist militants from the Spanish interior had begun to challenge the Toulouse-based leadership over its failure to appreciate the reality of socio-economic and political change both in Spain and elsewhere. The years 1972–4 were marked by a bitter power struggle which eventually brought Felipe González and Alfonso Guerra to prominence at the head of a numerically small and faction-ridden party.[3]

It was natural to assume that, in any post-Franco democratic settlement, the PCE would play a role analogous to that of the *Partito Comunista Italiano* (PCI) in Italy. Moreover, the PCE leadership deliberately stressed its links to an emerging West European communist order which claimed ever greater distance from the overarching influence of the CPSU in Moscow. Santiago Carrillo, secretary-general of the PCE since 1960, became the leading exponent of 'eurocommunism' along with Enrico Berlinguer. In the brief political life of eurocommunism – first launched officially in 1975 with a joint statement in Rome by the PCI, PCE and PCF and reinforced by the Madrid 'eurocommunist summit' of March 1977 – the Spanish party was the most committed and dynamic exponent of the new trend. A few weeks later, Carrillo published *'Eurocomunismo' y Estado*, widely seen as a blueprint for the future of West European communism.[4] In June 1977, as the first democratic elections in Spain for over forty years drew near, confidence in the PCE was riding high: the party looked first to establish itself as the cornerstone of the new democracy and then lead a steady advance towards socialism.

The dream was cruelly shattered. The PCE fared badly in the elections compared with its Socialist rivals, winning just under 10 per cent against the latter's near 30 per cent and, as the PSOE marched inexorably towards a crushing victory in the 1982 general elections, the Communist Party virtually disintegrated (see Table 3.1). Acrimonious internecine struggles within the leadership, a collapse in membership, and the loss of prestige amongst the intellectual elite which had been drawn to the PCE by its opposition to Franco, all combined to leave the party on the verge of extinction. In the 1982 election, its support fell to under 4 per cent.

Four principal and related reasons can be adduced for the PCE's precipitate eclipse. The first two relate less to the PCE itself than to the context within which the transition to democracy occurred in Spain. In terms of image, the PCE leadership, associated principally with Carrillo and the legendary *'Pasionaria'* (Dolores Ibárruri), looked out of touch compared with the youthful and dynamic Felipe González, leader of the PSOE, and Adolfo Suárez, principal architect of the political transition. Inevitably, Carrillo and Ibárruri evoked memories of the past, most particularly of the Civil War, in which they had both played significant roles. In a period where consensus and moderation were the watchwords of democratic progress, the PCE leadership provided an uncomfortable reminder of bitter division, and was therefore unlikely to perform well in any electoral contest.[5] The party's freedom of manoeuvre was also severely circumscribed by the need to avoid antagonising the so-called *poderes fácticos*, especially the military. The PCE's legalisation in April 1977 was made possible only by Carrillo's promise of compromise: the PCE dropped its call for a provisional government and constituent assembly, pledged respect for the monarchy and the red-and-gold flag and accepted the continuity of judicial and administrative institutions – indeed, allowed the terms of the transition to be dictated by former Franco regime apparatchiks such as Suárez. Although it is arguable that the PCE had little option over any of these issues, it is equally the case that many communist militants felt betrayed.

The third and fourth reasons relate more to developments within the PCE. At a general level, eurocommunism – on

Table 3.1 *Parliamentary representation, 1977–93: General Elections*

Party	1977			1979			1982			1986			1989			1993		
	%V	S	%S	%V	S	%S	%V	S	%S	%V	S	%S	%V	S	%S	%V	S	%S
PSOE	**29**	**118**	**34**	**31**	**121**	**35**	**48**	**202**	**58**	**43**	**184**	**53**	**40**	**175**	**50**	**39**	**159**	**45**
PP	8	16	5	6	9	3	26	106	30	26	105	30	26	107	31	35	141	40
CDS	–	–	–	–	–	–	3	2	1	9	19	5	8	14	4	–	–	–
UCD	35	165	47	36	168	48	7	12	3	–	–	–	–	–	–	–	–	–
PCE/IU	**9**	**20**	**6**	**11**	**23**	**7**	**4**	**4**	**1**	**5**	**7**	**2**	**9**	**17**	**5**	**10**	**18**	**5**
CiU	3	11	3	3	8	2	4	12	3	5	18	5	5	18	5	5	17	5
PNV	2	8	2	2	7	2	2	8	2	2	6	2	1	5	1	1	5	1
Others	14	12	3	11	14	3	6	4	2	10	11	3	11	14	4	6	10	3

(Rounded percentages; %V = percentage of votes cast, S = seats won, %S = percentage of seats; 1989 parliamentary election results include March 1990 re-staging of election in Melilla.)

Key: PSOE – Socialist Party; PP – Popular Party (variously known prior to 1989 as AP/CD/CP); CDS – Social and Democratic Centre; UCD – Union of the Democratic Centre; PCE/IU – Communist Party/United Left; CiU–Convergence and Unity, a right-leaning Catalan nationalist party; PNV – Basque National Party; Others – mainly Basque regionalist and separatist groups, as well as regional parties from Andalusia, Aragón, Valencia, the Canary Islands, Navarra and Galicia.

Sources: Luis Moreno, 'Las fuerzas políticas españolas', in Salvador Giner (ed.), *España: Sociedad y Política* (Madrid, 1990), pp. 297–8; *El País*, 7 June 1993; author's calculations.

which the PCE set such store – was never a precisely elaborated strategic or tactical approach. Instead, the term is more usefully seen as a rubric which covered the response of leading figures in the Spanish, Italian and, for a short while, French parties to the perceived political bankruptcy of Marxist–Leninist revolution in advanced capitalist societies. The response was centred around three key themes: the identity between socialism and democracy, independence from Moscow, and the belief that the transition to socialism could be achieved peacefully.[6] The theoretical inconsistencies of eurocommunism, especially in regard to its analysis of the role of the state, together with its specific embrace of pluralism, ensured that it would never win unquestioning support from those militants for whom communism derived its identity by reference to 'the struggle' and to Moscow. The concessions to parliamentary democracy led many to question the communist identity of those parties which espoused ideologically dubious eurocommunism.

However, there were other militants within the PCE for whom eurocommunism promised an exciting avenue for progress. Many had been involved in the opposition to Franco within Spain, and believed the new developments would lead to their winning a deserved voice in the party once the leadership returned from exile in Paris. They were to be disappointed, for Carrillo was never prepared to relax the rules of democratic centralism. The mismatch between the eurocommunist rhetoric of openness and democracy and the reality of rigid control as exercised by the PCE leadership provides the final reason for the party's collapse. In the immediate aftermath of the return to democracy in Spain, latent tensions within the PCE were held in check as the party played its full part in supporting consensual change. However, Carrillo's readiness to collaborate with Suárez's Union of the Democratic Centre (UCD) government proved a bitter pill to swallow for militants who had struggled so long against Franco. In particular, the October 1977 *Pacto de la Moncloa*, an all-party austerity package which sought to impose a moratorium on economic debate and allow attention to be devoted instead to political issues, appeared to punish the working class for Spain's economic difficulties. Following this shock, Carrillo's unilateral declaration later in the year that the PCE would drop 'Leninism' from its party statutes opened the floodgates of internal dissent.

At the PCE's IX Congress in April 1978 relations *within* the leadership began to break down. In the central debate on Leninism, Carrillo's wishes prevailed after he presented the issue in terms of a debate on his record. Although – in spite of the growing misgivings of a number of leaders – the PCE remained officially committed to a policy of moderation and pluralism, this stood in marked contrast to the heavy-handed manner in which it was imposed on the membership. Herein lay the crux of the PCE's crisis: for Carrillo, democratic centralism was a defining characteristic of communism – a lesson he had internalised while in the Soviet Union at the time of the Spanish Civil War. Party discipline and loyalty were not negotiable, no matter what the rhetoric of eurocommunism might suggest. To concede on this point would be to risk the very identity of the party.

Unsurprisingly, in the context of unrestricted political activity under the new Spanish democracy, a growing number of PCE members began to question their loyalty to the party. A major haemorrhaging of support became clear as early as 1978: membership fell from 201,757 in 1977 to 171,332 a year later – a drop of nearly 18 per cent (see Table 3.2). Disagreements within the PCE were exacerbated still further by the Soviet invasion of Afghanistan in 1980. Those militants still loyal to Moscow supported the action as a blow against imperialism. Referred to as 'Afghans', these pro-Soviets had become increasingly unhappy at what they saw as the PCE leadership's sell-out to bourgeois interests in Spain. Others, though, felt that the PCE's commitment to eurocommunism should entail not just an express condemnation of the Soviet invasion, but also greater internal democracy. These *'renovadores'* were to become increasingly disenchanted at the continued imposition of democratic centralism within the PCE. Disputes within the party at the start of the 1980s at times reached almost labyrinthine

Table 3.2   Membership of the PCE, 1977–91

1977	201,757
IX Congress (April 1978)	240,000
July 1981	132,069
XI Congress (December 1983)	84,652
December 1987	62,342
October 1991	55,000

Reliable figures are virtually impossible to ascertain. The figures given above are those claimed by the PCE, although they have been disputed by some observers. Botella, for instance, believes that the figure for 1978 should be reduced to around 175,000.

In terms of the profile of PCE membership, figures are again difficult to obtain. A report on the delegates who attended the PCE's IX Congress, published in *Nuestra Bandera*, 93 (1978), indicated: (i) that there was a clear imbalance between men (87 per cent) and women (13 per cent); (ii) that 45 per cent of delegates had joined the party between 1971 and 1978, compared with 32 per cent between 1961 and 1970, 14 per cent between 1940 and 1960, and 9 per cent before 1939; (iii) that occupational categories were industrial workers (39 per cent), non-manual workers (15 per cent), professionals (32 per cent), small businessmen and self-employed (3 per cent), agrarian workers (3 per cent), students (4 per cent) and 'others' (4 per cent).

Sources: Juan Botella, 'Spanish Communism in Crisis: The Communist Party of Spain', in Michael Waller and Meindert Fennema (eds), *Communist Parties in Western Europe: Decline or Adaptation?* (Oxford: Blackwell, 1988), p. 70; José Amodia, 'Requiem for the Spanish Communist Party', in David S. Bell (ed.), *Western European Communists and the Collapse of Communism* (Oxford: Berg, 1993), pp. 103, 108, 119.

complexity: there were disagreements between the PCE leadership and that of the *Comisiones Obreras* (CC OO, Workers' Commissions), between the PCE and its Catalan counterpart, the *Partido Socialista Unificado de Cataluña*

(PSUC), and – within both the PCE and the PSUC – between 'Afghans', *'renovadores'* and the *'oficialistas'* who supported the leadership. However, it was the divisions between the Madrid-based PCE leadership and regional federations which were truly to shatter the communist movement.

Relations between the PCE and the Catalan PSUC had been on a downward spiral since the start of the transition. Carrillo's insistence in the wake of the 1979 general elections – in which the PCE vote had remained more or less static at just over 10 per cent – that the PSUC should maintain the same ideology, policies and organisational methods as the PCE, inevitably led to confrontation. In an anti-Madrid move, the V Congress of the PSUC voted in January 1981 to reject eurocommunism. This exacerbated internal divisions in the PSUC whilst the PCE's insistence that it reinstate eurocommunism as a minimum condition of participation in its X Congress in July 1981 split the Catalan party irrevocably. By the time of the congress, divisions within the PCE had reached a point of no return.[7]

At the X Congress, Carrillo refused any semblance of compromise, pointing to the attempted coup on 23 February 1981 by Lieutenant-Colonel Antonio Tejero as justifying collaboration with Suárez. In a four-hour-long report by the secretary-general, the PCE's actions since the death of Franco were virulently defended, freedom to express dissident opinion was denied and democratic centralism was specifically reaffirmed. However, further division was foreshadowed by Roberto Lertxundi, leader of the Basque communists, who argued that Carrillo's approach foreclosed any possibility of genuine eurocommunism. Although the PCE leadership was comfortably re-elected, its victory would prove to be pyrrhic.

After the X Congress, Carrillo embarked on a 'clean-up' campaign. The *renovadores* were given minimal representation on the executive committee and the vast majority of key posts went to *oficialistas*. In response, Lertxundi declared that the only hope of progress for the Basque Communist Party (EPK) would be to ally with the left nationalist Basque grouping, *Euskadiko Ezkerra* (EE). An attempt by the PCE leadership to prevent the merger simply exacerbated the crisis. Lertxundi held a conference in Madrid which won open support from several leading *renovadores*. Carrillo then demanded that those members of the PCE's central committee who had signed a motion supporting the EPK should be expelled unless they presented a 'satisfactory self-criticism'. Refusal to conform led to the expulsion of several leading figures, including Manuel Azcárate, Pilar Brabo, Julio Segura and Jaime Sartorius.[8]

From this point onward, the PCE embarked on a highly public process of hara-kiri. By the start of 1982, membership of the party had fallen to less than half its 1977 level. The expulsions continued unabated and became the subject of almost prurient press attention. In March 1982, a disastrous showing in the Andalusian regional elections saw the PCE achieve just 8.5 per cent of the vote, winning 8 seats out of 109 in what was traditionally one of its strongholds. Since the municipal elections of 1979 the PCE had lost 150,000 votes, more than half its support, in the region – a result made the more painful by the dramatic success of the PSOE, which gained over 500,000 votes compared with 1979, won an absolute majority in every province, and took 66 seats. The PCE leadership refused to discuss the Andalusian fiasco, leading to calls for the resignation of the secretary-general. Hopelessly divided, the party was in no shape for the general elections of October 1982. His credibility as a eurocommunist in tatters, Carrillo resorted in the election campaign to bitter attacks on the PSOE. In the event, the PSOE achieved an historic victory, taking over 10 million votes to secure an absolute majority for the first time in Spanish parliamentary history. The PCE, meanwhile, saw its level of support fall by over 1 million votes from 1,911,217 (10.6 per cent) in 1979 to 865,267 (3.9 per cent) in 1982, leaving it with just four deputies compared with 22 in the outgoing parliament. The subsequent resignation of Santiago Carrillo caused little surprise and even less mourning.

IZQUIERDA UNIDA AND THE (STILL) REBIRTH OF SPANISH COMMUNISM

The scale of the PCE's defeat was such that the party might easily have been relegated to the fringes of mainstream political life. That it was able to stage a revival, albeit a slow and painful one, paradoxically owes much to the PSOE. The route to recovery emerged over the issue of NATO membership. A central plank of the PSOE's election manifesto had been the promise of a referendum on NATO membership, with the clear implication that the government would support withdrawal.[9] In the event, it soon became apparent that the PSOE government had revised its position on NATO. Given the massive unpopularity of NATO membership, the PSOE's *volte-face* opened the way for the emergence of serious political opposition to its left – a point reinforced by the lack of any obvious socialist content to the new government's economic policies as it embarked upon the 'reconversion' of Spain's industrial base. Ultimately, the NATO issue served as the cornerstone of a new political initiative in Spain, *Izquierda Unida* (IU), which loosely united the PCE with a series of other left-oriented groups in a wide-ranging anti-PSOE and anti-NATO coalition.

In the short term, though, the PCE's first priority was to restore some semblance of unity and direction after the bloodletting of the previous three years. Carrillo was replaced as secretary-general by Gerardo Iglesias, an Asturian mineworker widely seen as his *protégé*. However, as the example of King Juan Carlos had already shown, those groomed for succession have a habit of confounding their predecessor's hopes. Rather than act as Carrillo's proxy, Iglesias embarked upon a revision of the PCE's internal functioning and political strategy. The result was a further period of open division within the party. In the years 1983–5, the PCE was riven by the most divisive internal confrontation in its modern history. Carrillo, feeling betrayed by Iglesias's embrace of the *renovadores'* vision of eurocommunism, incessantly attacked his successor in public meetings.

These attacks, though often pitched in personal terms, reflected far more complex divisions within the party. Socio-economic and political developments in Spain since the mid-1960s had altered the nature and meaning of militancy within the PCE: the traditional blue-collar working class had shrunk markedly as a proportion of the workforce as a 'new middle class' of technicians and white-collar workers grew rapidly, associated largely with the world of commerce and the service sector (see Table 3.3). The political conditions of parliamentary democracy effectively converted the party into just one more mass-membership organisation, a circumstance which was always likely to favour those parties, such as the PSOE, which were *perceived* by the public as being more mainstream. With the personal risk which had been attendant upon members of the PCE during the Franco dictatorship gone, discipline was far harder to impose. No longer could the threat of denunciation to the Francoist authorities be held like a sword of Damocles over party members; no longer did expulsion from the party

Table 3.3   Evolution of occupational groups in Spain, 1965–75

	Percentage increase
Professionals	89.7
Administrative, commercial and technical employees	54.6
Entrepreneurs and managers	51.2
Service workers	43.1
Supervisors and skilled workers	37.2
Self-employed	−6.7
Agricultural workers	−30.4
Farmers not employing others	−38.5
Unskilled workers	−49.7

Source: J. F. Tezanos, *Estructura de clases y conflictos de poder en la España postfranquista* (Madrid, 1978), pp. 194, 196.

carry the threat of cutting off their very livelihood. This fact alone helps to explain the divisions between *renovadores, oficialistas* and 'Afghans', between different generations (exile and internal), between centre and periphery. Whereas previously party discipline was central to the PCE's very survival, now dissident voices increasingly made themselves heard.

Ironically, in March 1985 Iglesias turned the tables on Carrillo by instructing him to respect the PCE's official line or face expulsion. Refusal to comply led to his demotion the following month to the rank of ordinary base militant: 'the purger, purged', as *Cambio 16* described this turn of events.[10] Six months later Carrillo left the PCE to set up an alternative party, the *PCE Marxista Revolucionario* (PCE-mr), later the *Partido de Trabajadores Españoles* (PTE). In the meantime, Ignacio Gallego – a veteran member of the executive committee and a leading 'Afghan' – had in early 1984 founded the *Partido Comunista de los Pueblos de España* (PCPE), loyal to the Soviet Union.[11] Thus, with three parties claiming to represent its true heritage, Spanish communism in late 1985 presented a panorama of hopeless division and confusion. Unsurprisingly, the 'official' PCE, headed by Iglesias, performed disastrously in the Galician regional elections of December that year, winning just 1.1 per cent (less than 14,000) of the votes cast.

However, Iglesias had already begun to stress the need to develop an alliance of leftist forces which recognised the emergence of new social movements in Spain.[12] The NATO referendum, delayed by the PSOE government until March 1986, provided the catalyst for translating the plan into reality. A PCE National Conference in early 1986 agreed on a three-point plan which called for a policy of electoral alliances with other non-socialist forces of the left, the rejection of any coalition with supporters of Carrillo, and opposition to NATO membership as the central plank of party policy. Following the PSOE's narrow victory in the March referendum, an *ad hoc* electoral platform known as *Izquierda Unida* was established in order to offer 'a credible leftist alternative' (Iglesias) which would appeal both to traditional communists and to green, feminist and peace groups in the general elections of June 1986.

In the event, the *Izquierda Unida* coalition performed only marginally better than the PCE had done in 1982, but all the same the trend was encouraging: the party's level of support rose to 4.6 per cent, and it secured 7 seats. More important than the results was the fact that the coalition offered a new direction and established the PCE at its centre. Its creation – a response to the potentially fatal crisis of the PCE – prefigured in some senses developments which would take place in other countries in the wake of the events of 1989. However, Gerardo Iglesias proved unable to unify a party which still bore the scars of deep division. Although a worthy and committed leader, he lacked the charisma to challenge González. Now that *Izquierda Unida* had joined battle on the field of electoral politics, voter response became as central as dues-paying membership. Herein lay a conundrum for IU: many of those in the 'new social movements' from whom the coalition sought support were likely to be precisely those who set least store by participation in the formal mechanisms of what they saw as bourgeois parliamentary democracy. A further marginal increase in support for the IU in the June 1987 European elections proved insufficient to placate party militants and, at the PCE's party congress in February 1988, Iglesias was replaced as secretary-general by a somewhat reluctant Julio Anguita, head of the party list at the 1986 general elections in Andalusia, the PCE's most successful region.

Both charismatic and enigmatic, Anguita provided both the PCE and the IU with the leadership they sought. A native of Córdoba (Andalusia), where he had been mayor, the new PCE secretary-general cut an impressive figure, lambasting the PSOE over the allegations of political corruption which had been gaining ground since González first assumed power in 1982. With a heavily didactic tone, he repeatedly emphasised the need for the left to behave ethically, an ironic echo of one of the *leitmotifs* of the PSOE's founding father, Pablo Iglesias. In a further parallel, Anguita's almost homiletic orations disguised the lack of any obviously identifiable Marxist content to his thought. Under his leadership, it could be argued that the PCE made good its effective conversion from a Marxist to a catch-all political party. Given the nature of the IU coalition, ideological rigour was always likely to be at a premium; instead, IU represented a focal point for various progressive positions of distinct provenance. In addition to the PCE, the other main forces in IU initially comprised the Pasoc (a small socialist group which claimed continuity from that sector of the PSOE which had been defeated in 1972–4), Ignacio Gallego's PCPE, the tiny federalist Progressive Federation set up in 1984 by the former Communist, Ramón Tamames, a few maverick groups (the *Partido Carlista*, the *Partido Humanista* and *Izquierda Republicana*) and various independents such as Cristina Almeida.[13] Together they claimed a combined membership of around 100,000, of which the PCE accounted for roughly two-thirds (62,342 members in 1987).

With Anguita at the helm, IU made steady headway in public opinion polls. The PSOE came under increasing pressure in 1988 as growing discontent with the government's economic policies culminated in a general strike of 14 December, which won massive public support. Although Spain had enjoyed spectacular economic growth since entry to the EC in January 1986, there was widespread feeling that the benefits of this success had become excessively concentrated in the hands of a small minority whilst the government became ever more arrogant in power. Chastened by the scale of the strike, the government attempted to adopt a more conciliatory tone, but relations between the PSOE and the General Workers' Union (*Unión General de Trabajadores* – UGT) broke down completely as it became clear that González was not prepared to countenance any fundamental shift in policy. As the PSOE appeared to abandon the interests of a reduced 'traditional' urban, working-class constituency in favour of business and financial groups, IU was able to mount effective attacks on the government in the name not just of the so-called 'new social movements', but also of the economically marginalised. IU's progress was reflected by its performance in the two major electoral contests of 1989: the European elections of 11 June and the general elections of 29 October. In both cases, IU emerged as the only force which could point unequivocally to tangible advances.

IU AND THE EVENTS OF 1989–91: THE SECOND CRISIS OF SPANISH COMMUNISM

Ironically, just as communism in Spain seemed to be emerging from a protracted period of crisis, so communism in Eastern Europe entered its death throes. The impact of this on both the PCE and the IU has been profound. Initially, Anguita's response to the unfolding drama in the 'real socialist' states was relaxed, even upbeat. In October 1989, just prior to the general elections, he remarked that seven years earlier he had predicted the collapse of communism in Eastern Europe. That the collapse had finally happened, he argued, carried no special implications for IU which was embarked upon a four-year plan for continued growth and progress.[14] However, for all Anguita's sanguineness, by the end of 1989 unmistakable lines of division which had marked the first crisis of Spanish communism were beginning to reappear. Once again, the PCE was faced with three critical issues: the role and relevance of a communist party in what looked increasingly to be a definitively post-communist age, relations between the party leadership in Madrid and regional centres, and disputes over the party's structure and direction. However, in the post-1989 crisis these concerns were overlain by the wider issue of how the PCE related to IU: would it remain the dominant party within the coalition, should it dissolve itself as a political party and become one component faction of IU, should IU itself be relaunched as a political party?

The single most important issue concerned the very future of the PCE. For several figures in IU, the PCE had become something of an irrelevance. Some, such as the writer Juan Marsé, openly questioned what it meant to be a communist in the 1990s. Others – including Enrique Curiel, a former leading *renovador* in the PCE – argued that the only way forward lay in collaboration with the Socialists as part of the 'common home of the left' proposed by the PSOE. He found support from the veteran communist, Santiago Carrillo, who argued that, as the barriers which had separated communists and socialists since the Bolshevik Revolution were now crumbling, all leftist forces should join a new socialist formation, forcing the PSOE in a progressive direction. Carrillo maintained that there was no political space for an alternative government to the left of the PSOE; the new formation, unlike IU, should not be opposed to the ruling party.[15]

To the surprise of many, Anguita responded to such calls by insisting with ever greater vehemence on the need to maintain the PCE intact. Despite being hailed as a Spanish precursor to Achille Occhetto, Anguita set his face against emulating the Italian communists and relaunching the PCE under a different identity. In early 1990, the PCE secretary-general said he was prepared to countenance any necessary reform of ideas which derived from the Bolshevik Revolution, but the party would remain communist. He did not make clear, however, what he understood a communist party to be in the 1990s. Given the loss of linkage to the CPSU, the abandonment of cadre membership, and full acceptance of parliamentary democracy and the constitutional monarchy, it would appear that some vague obeisance to Marx and democratic centralism remained the only defining characteristics left to Anguita. Beyond that, the PCE seemed barely distinguishable from any other leftist catch-all political party.

None the less, in an interview with the leading daily, *El País*, in late November 1990, Anguita declared that all discussion of the PCE's future had been 'settled' [*zanjado*] until after the May local and regional elections. The PCE leader reiterated that he anticipated its continuation as a communist party, and argued that 'you have to be Marxist' to understand its role in IU:

You have to know what it means to be a marxist force. The PCE, in this phase, has no other programmatic policy than that which has been approved by *Izquierda Unida*. In the PCE's congress theoretical, but not programmatic, documents will be approved. That is, the party renounces the elaboration of a programme because that task corresponds to *Izquierda Unida*. The PCE reserves for itself theoretical formulations, the capacity to analyse from a marxist standpoint. For example, Salvador Jové holds the economy portfolio in the PCE, as well as in *Izquierda Unida*. In IU he develops programmes, and in the PCE he analyses. That is, he deals with political theory, elaboration, reflection, while *Izquierda Unida* is concerned with concrete programmes for society. Is that so difficult to understand?[16]

Clearly, the PCE secretary-general had no intention of renouncing either the party's communist or Marxist heritage.[17] Anguita had earlier expressly rejected the suggestion that he might solicit the PCE's entry to the Socialist International, and set the limit of accommodation with other political forces at the level of 'contacts'. The relationship between PCE and IU was described as one of 'complete symbiosis', as they were seen as two organisations with coinciding policies. The one concession Anguita was prepared to make was that, as IU continued to grow, the PCE's role within it would change from the leading one to being just 'fundamental'. None the less, Anguita insisted that IU could not turn into a political party since this would be to betray its very identity. Because IU already existed, there was no need to follow the example of the Italian communists.[18]

For all Anguita's certainty, others in IU and the PCE were not persuaded. Although, officially, any links with the PSOE had to be on the basis of the latter moving towards IU, rather than vice-versa, since early 1990 various contacts became established between communists and socialists. In the European parliament, IU euro-deputies joined with their Italian [ex-]communist colleagues in a group called 'For a United Left in Europe', acting in concert with the socialist group. Fernando Pérez Royo, who headed the IU list in the 1989 European elections, became a strong supporter of greater unity between communists and socialists and, much to Anguita's annoyance, backed the policies of PSOE prime minister, Felipe González. Furthermore, Alonso Puerta, the Pasoc euro-deputy, became a leading supporter of his party's application for observer status in the Socialist International prior to full membership. Indeed, Puerta apparently sent Anguita a portrait of Pablo Iglesias, founder of both the PSOE and UGT, in order that it should act as a stimulus to dialogue with the socialists.[19] At union level, talks commenced in 1990 between the UGT and the CC OO over the possibility of eventual merger. Antonio Gutiérrez, the CC OO leader, strongly supported Occhetto's initiative and argued that the PCE should move faster and further in the direction of reform, although he rejected the PSOE's notion of a 'common home of the left'.[20]

Most significant, though, was the growing number of contacts established with other leftist forces at regional level. In Madrid, the PSOE regional president, Joaquín Leguina and IU's regional leader, Isabel Villalonga, reached agreement on substantive administrative and policy matters. In Andalusia, local leaders of the Pasoc threatened to leave IU altogether following disagreements on coalition strategy, while further tension emerged with the national leadership in Catalonia and the Basque Country. Regional autonomy, with all seventeen Spanish regions granted their own parliamentary legislatures since the return of democracy, highlighted an acute ambiguity within centre–periphery relations. On the one hand, both the PCE and IU stood as national movements with a central leadership based in Madrid; on the other, a key policy objective has been to support moves towards full federalism, which would logically undermine the organisational unity of both movements. Indeed, Catalonia already presented a special case: the PSUC, formed in 1936 as the Catalan branch of the PCE, is unique in being the only sub-national communist party ever allowed full independent membership of the Third International. Its autonomy has developed to the extent that there is now effectively no formal link between the PSUC and the PCE. By the same token, *Iniciativa per Catalunya*, the Catalan equivalent to *Izquierda Unida*, is autonomous, although formal coordination with IU is maintained via a liaison committee. Tensions between central initiatives and regional demands for accommodation with more narrowly nationalist groups represent a critical challenge for IU and have given rise to damaging divisions within the movement.

Rafael Ribó, leader of both the PSUC and *Iniciativa per Catalunya*, has gone furthest in the direction of establishing ties with non-communist groups, offering vital support to the governing Socialists in various important Catalan municipalities. This went against the express wishes of Anguita, whose particular aim was to undermine the charismatic PSOE mayor of Barcelona, Pascual Maragall. Ribó, a close personal friend of Achille Occhetto, also proposed the establishment of *comités de enlace* (liaison committees) with left nationalist parties, such as *Euskadiko Ezkerra* in the Basque Country, the Valencian *Unitat del Poble Valenciá*, *Esquerda Galega* in Galicia, and the *Partit Socialista de Mallorca*. His long-term aim was that IU should be simply one member of a state-wide political force.

The differences between Ribó and Anguita were aired publicly prior to the Basque regional elections in October 1990, when the Catalan leader criticised Anguita's decision to present a separate slate instead of forming an electoral pact with *Euskadiko Ezkerra*. At root, Anguita and Ribó held diametrically opposed views on the future direction of the Spanish left, with the latter favouring a development very much in line with that sponsored by Achille Occhetto, while the former took up a position more analogous to that of the orthodox Pietro Ingrao. Although the two leaders shared the same view of IU as a movement composed of various forces rather than a single force representing the sum of its various parts, they differed fundamentally on its relations with left nationalist groups. Equally, they disagreed on the optimal form of state, with *Iniciativa per Catalunya*

proposing a confederal state against IU's more convent-
ional federalism.[21]

The disputes between Ribó and Anguita found their
reflection in various other Spanish regions. Within IU, Ribó
won support from the Andalusian euro-deputy Pérez Royo,
the president of the Valencian branch, Albert Taverner,
various independents in Seville and the Galician branch of
the CC OO. IU's secretary-general in Galicia, Anxel
Guerreiro, agreed that a move towards convergence with
nationalist parties was 'unstoppable', but insisted that IU
would retain its dominant position. However, some CC OO
leaders in Vigo favoured establishing a 'special relationship'
with *Esquerda Galega*, whose leader, Camilo Nogueira, held
talks in early 1990 with Ribó. The Catalan leader also
invited the Andalusian branch of IU to attend meetings of
Iniciativa per Catalunya in an autonomous capacity, but
Anguita's dominance in his own territory prevailed and the
invitation was rejected. In Valencia, tensions emerged
between the PCE secretary-general, Pedro Zamora, and
various IU municipal representatives: a significant number
of IU councillors in the Valencian *Ayuntamiento* favoured a
pact with *Unitat del Poble Valenciá*. Conflicts also came to the
fore in the Balearic Islands: while nationalist socialist parties
in Mallorca and Menorca were happy to establish accords
with *Iniciativa per Catalunya*, the former expressly rejected
any agreement with *Izquierda Unida*.

The importance of the divisions between Catalonia and
Madrid is emphasised by the fact that the former region
represents a major centre of strength for IU, providing
nearly 20 per cent of its seats in the Spanish Congress.
Equally, such divisions have posed major questions as to
the precise nature of the relationship between *Izquierda
Unida*'s leadership in Madrid and its regional branches.
Unsurprisingly, such open divisions cost IU electoral
support. Elections in Andalusia in June 1990 and the
Basque Country in October saw IU perform disastrously. In
Andalusia, IU support fell by 40 per cent, a desperately
disappointing result given the context of a massive, nation-
wide campaign against the PSOE related to the corruption

scandal surrounding the then deputy prime minister, Alfonso Guerra. The PSOE, instead of suffering widely expected damage, saw its vote and absolute majority increase – despite a protracted internal struggle.[22] IU, on the other hand, performed particularly poorly, nowhere more so than in Anguita's home province of Córdoba. Widespread accusations that the PSOE 'bought' Andalusian votes through extensive subsidies failed to mask the fact that – in the wake of the collapse of communism in Eastern Europe – IU signally failed to capture the public imagination. Anguita's insistence on the continued independent existence of the PCE within IU was widely interpreted as a major factor in the defeat, especially since the party which made most gains, the *Partido Andalucista*, had ditched its formerly Marxist identity and socialist name in favour of a more narrowly nationalist stance. Such an interpretation appeared confirmed by the May 1991 municipal elections, in which IU did badly in Seville in spite of an overall rise in support throughout Spain.

Unlike Andalusia, the Basque Country, with its complex web of nationalist forces, always offered little prospect of success for IU; none the less, just over 14,000 votes (1.4 per cent) resulted in no seats and gave rise to further debates over the coalition's purpose and direction. These received a full airing at IU's 2nd Federal Assembly, held in Madrid from 23 to 25 November, 1990. Discussion centred on the fact that IU had been plagued by internal dissent for over a year, presenting a public image of interminable debates over its structure and political orientation rather than confronting major social issues. In his opening speech, Anguita called for an end to debates which could be 'understood only by affiliates'. None the less, organisational issues, particularly the composition of IU's presidency, dominated much of the assembly. The leadership's proposal that a closed list be voted on survived a challenge from the Andalusian delegate, Luis Carlos Rejón, and the new presidency thus continued to reflect the PCE's prominence with seven members, compared with five from Pasoc, five independents and two from *Izquierda Republicana*.[23]

In fact, the assembly resulted in a clear overall victory for Anguita's line: closer links and electoral agreements with the PSOE were firmly rejected, and IU's full autonomy, with the PCE's continued dominance within it, was confirmed. Indeed, Manuel Parejo, a delegate from Extremadura, described the PSOE's 'common home of the left', as an attempt to build a 'common whorehouse of the left,' whilst Francisco Herrera from Madrid spoke of the 'common grave of the left'.[24] Anguita insisted, in line with his statements since 1989, that any move towards the PSOE could come about only on the basis of an agreement over policies – a decidedly remote prospect. However, in an attempt to calm fears among IU's constituent groups that the PCE would seek continued domination, the general coordinator described the coalition as a 'plural house with no predisposition to absorption'.

After the 2nd Federal Assembly, arguments between the PCE and the so-called *'sector crítico'*, comprising Pasoc, the independents and a minority group in the PCE, continued unabated. They were further fuelled in part by the dramatic events of August 1991 in Moscow, which presaged the eclipse of Mikhail Gorbachev and the disintegration of the CPSU's political hegemony. Some leading PCE militants, such as Antonio Gutiérrez and Nicolás Sartorius, immediately called for the party to be dissolved and replaced by a reconstituted IU in order to avoid the increasingly negative associations of the term 'communism'. Anguita, however, refused to countenance any such move, arguing instead that it was more important than ever that the PCE should survive. In early September, the PCE's political commission rejected dissolution by 18 votes to 4, with one abstention, a decision ratified at the party's XIII Congress in December 1991. Meanwhile, in a tactical move, Anguita resigned as general coordinator of IU in late November 1991, confident that he would subsequently be reinstated with increased authority, a development which duly took place in early 1992.[25]

Anguita's response to the August crisis in the Soviet Union was one of studied indifference, based on his continued belief that developments in communism's heartland were of no relevance to the PCE.[26] Relations between the PCE and the CPSU had indeed been strained since the late 1960s, but Anguita's insouciance underplayed the true significance of the events in Moscow. One outcome was that the *sector crítico* within IU derived renewed impetus, reflected in the formal establishment of a critical current known as *Nueva Izquierda* (New Left). Headed by Sartorius, *Nueva Izquierda* repeatedly challenged Anguita's vision both of IU's future direction, and of the PCE's role within it. Debates between the two factions were sometimes arcane. Whereas Anguita continued to insist on defining IU as 'a political and social movement which is registered as a fully sovereign political organisation', his opponents sought to define IU as 'a juridically and politically fully sovereign organisation, which underpins its political action as a unitary political and social movement'. That such fine distinctions confused the electorate was demonstrated in a Sigma Dos survey conducted in April 1992: although 53.7 per cent of IU supporters believed that the coalition should become a political party, 72.6 per cent said they agreed with Anguita against the *sector crítico*.[27]

Further disputes arose over Spain's ratification of the Maastricht Treaty. Anguita's demand for a referendum on the issue ran counter to the views of *Nueva Izquierda*, which supported the government's argument that Spain had no real choice but to ratify. Indeed, the issue of collaboration with the Socialists – supported by leading figures in IU such as Pablo Castellano – re-emerged as a source of tension in early 1993. Nevertheless, by the time general elections were called for June 1993, confidence had been restored within both IU and the PCE. The ruling PSOE was in some disarray, mired in corruption scandals and widely blamed for economic recession, whilst opinion polls in late 1992 and early 1993 had pointed to a sharp rise in support for the communist-dominated coalition.

In the event, high hopes were to be dashed yet again. The election campaign was marked by two crises which severely disrupted IU's plans. First, three IU deputies and leading members of *Nueva Izquierda* – Sartorius, Castellano and

Cristina Almeida – withdrew from the coalition's electoral list for Madrid in protest at being given low positions on the list (designed to ensure that they were not re-elected, apparently as punishment for their support of the Maastricht Treaty). The move cost IU support in the Spanish capital, where all three enjoyed a strong personal following. Secondly, just weeks before the vote, Anguita suffered a mild heart attack which forced his retirement from the remainder of the campaign.

On 6 June, IU's overall vote rose by more than 370,000 to just over 2.2 million (9.56 per cent), but its total of 18 deputies was just one more than in the outgoing parliament. The result was a severe blow to IU leaders, who had hoped to capitalise on the PSOE's apparent unpopularity. Ultimately, however, Felipe González played highly effectively on fears of a right-wing victory and was able to retain sufficient support to scrape back into power, albeit with a minority government. For the PCE, the results confirmed that talk of its demise had been much exaggerated, even if they did little to clarify its longer-term prospects.

CONCLUSION: TOWARDS A COMMON HOME OF THE LEFT?

The IU leadership's official line of rejecting any proposal to join a 'common home of the left' under the aegis of the PSOE obeyed a clear political logic, especially since the effective collapse of the *Centro Democrático y Social* (CDS) in the wake of the May 1991 regional elections left the IU as the undisputed third force at national level – a position which was confirmed in the 1993 general elections. Moreover, Anguita had repeatedly insisted on attacking the PSOE so vehemently for abandoning socialist principles that any move towards integration would have carried a considerable cost in terms of his political credibility.

None the less, the IU leadership's determination to stake its claim as the only genuinely leftist force in Spain has not won unanimous support amongst its members. For some, the PSOE – for all its faults – represents the only logical destination for all those of leftist political inclinations. There is a long history of former communists ending up in the PSOE, sometimes via circuitous routes. The list includes figures such as Ramón Tamames, Enrique Múgica and Jordi Solé-Tura, the last two of whom have achieved ministerial status. Indeed, two of the most well-known victims of Santiago Carrillo's machinations as PCE secretary-general, Jorge Semprún and the late Fernando Claudín – both expelled from the party in 1965 – became closely linked to the PSOE after Spain's transition to democracy. Claudín became director of the PSOE's research centre, the *Fundación Pablo Iglesias*, while Semprún was appointed minister of culture in 1985, a post he held until he was replaced by Solé-Tura in March 1991.[28] Other leading ex-communists who have joined the PSOE in recent years include Enrique Curiel, Eugenio Triana, the late Pilar Brabo, Jordi Borja and José María Mohedano.

Curiel, once vice secretary-general of the PCE and seen as a likely successor to Santiago Carrillo, became increasingly disillusioned with IU after the events of 1989. Accusing IU of being more concerned to act as an anti-socialist coalition than an alternative leftist project, Curiel set up the *Fundación Europa* with the aim of bringing back into active political life those leftist intellectuals who had abandoned the PCE during the Carrillo purges of the late 1970s and early 1980s. In late 1990, Curiel and a claimed 200 followers in the *Fundación Europa* joined the PSOE, something of a coup for the Socialists – even though IU argued, with apparent justification, that the figure of 200 was a wild exaggeration. Others who have joined the PSOE as part of its project to establish the 'common home of the left' include José Sanroma, former secretary-general of the extreme left Revolutionary Workers' Organisation. The most spectacular boost to the PSOE's project, however, has come via the *en masse* entry to its ranks of Santiago Carrillo's *Partido de Trabajadores Españoles* (PTE). While Carrillo took the opportunity to bow out of active politics, he had been a leading proponent of the left's 'common home' being built around the PSOE. In what may seem an appropriately ironic epitaph for his long and controversial career, Carrillo sponsored his followers' return to the party he had first joined in 1928, predicting that within a few years the PSOE would be the only serious party on the left. The veteran leader argued that the complexity of the modern workplace meant that any party which seeks only to represent workers' interests would face major problems. *Izquierda Unida* was thus dismissed as being nothing more than a midsummer night's dream.[29]

Although the leaderships of both the PSOE and *Izquierda Unida* maintained a mutual lack of official communication, significant realignments were taking place on the Spanish left even before the collapse of communism in Eastern Europe. Clearly, though, the PSOE sought to capitalise on the political discomfiture of the PCE/IU to ensure its hegemony on the Spanish left until into the twenty-first century. Whatever its chances of success (and its own travails in the early 1990s suggested that earlier optimism had been somewhat misplaced), the events in Eastern Europe and the former Soviet Union, as well as emerging trends in Spain, do pose a number of issues which will have a significant bearing on the left's future.

Ideological redefinition raises fundamental questions as to the current status of leftist ideology in the 1990s. In Spain, as elsewhere, the fifteen to twenty years since the mid-1970s have seen what seems to be a gradual draining of clearly identifiable ideological content in the programmatic positions of the left. Both the PSOE and the PCE/IU have moved a long way from their Marxist roots, to arrive at a position where their aims now seem to have more in common with a Fabian-style ethical politics based on moral imperatives than with any teleological vision. The Marxist historian Victor Kiernan once wrote:

> Not many years ago, Marxist and 'bourgeois' history-writing could look as different as chalk and cheese; today they often differ much less obviously.... Marxism may

have grown more reasonable, but less readily recognis-
able.... It is, in short, no longer easy to say who is entitled
to call himself – if he chooses – a Marxist.

Similar sentiments would now seem to apply to leftist political parties. The distinctions which used to mark out
Marxist parties from social-democratic ones have all but disappeared. Indeed, the loss of clear identities may go further
than this, as the example of the PSOE in power suggests.
This is not to argue in favour of a Daniel Bell-revisited 'end
of ideology' thesis, still less to lend support to Francis
Fukuyama's view of the 'end of history'. Rather, it is to
suggest that the left is currently going through a period in
which ideological redefinition is an inescapable, but far
from complete, response to profound socio-economic and
political changes in the modern world. Capitalism has consistently demonstrated an ability to adapt in the face of
seemingly imminent crisis; that same challenge now faces
socialism, however defined.

In the short-term, at least, one socialist response – that
adopted by the PSOE – has been to don a decidedly capital-
ist-looking cloak. In the early 1990s, Felipe González even
began to criticise the very rhetoric of those in his party who
baulked at his market-oriented policies: his attack on the
PSOE's 'tribal language' and the 'pathetic schizophrenia'
which marked the party's public pronouncements on business interests, when everything possible was done to attract
investment, prefigured the split between the prime minister and his long-time deputy, Alfonso Guerra.[30] Guerra
always claimed to represent the true left in Spain, yet he
was the leading force behind the elaboration of the party's
decidedly moderate document, *Programa 2000*.

The issue of a united Europe also poses problems for the
left. Both the PCE/IU and especially the PSOE are committed to a fully integrated Europe (although Anguita argues
that it should be developed on a different basis from that
enshrined in the Maastricht Treaty). However, while
Programa 2000 is confident that the PSOE can play a leading
role in the advance towards a democratic socialist Europe,

the document says nothing about how this can be reconciled with the market-oriented free-trade measures which underlie the logic of economic and monetary union (EMU). Equally, no mention is made of how individual socialist governments would respond to the loss of independent control over macro-economic policy formulation should the right become the dominant force in the key decision-making European fora. Of no less importance is the question of how European political union will relate to the issue of regional nationalism. As has been seen, this issue already poses severe difficulties for *Izquierda Unida*: the global vision implied by its broad policy objectives, not to mention the internationalist Marxist heritage of the PCE, sits uneasily with the narrow nationalist demands of some of its regionalist representatives. Marxists and nationalists have never been comfortable bed-fellows. Moreover, the emergence of a 'Europe of the regions' called for by some nationalist leaders is bound to generate tension with the traditionally highly centralised party leaderships of both the PSOE and the PCE.

Against this, it could be argued – following Rafael Ribó – that *Izquierda Unida* potentially represents a new form of political organisation which can cater for diversity within its overall unity of purpose, a sort of dialectical synthesis of its divergent parts. This leaves the central problem of how the PCE is to fit into *Izquierda Unida*. There is a strong argument that IU cannot itself become a political party, for this would be to betray the conception which lies behind it. However, unless the PCE becomes a component member on the same basis as all others, it will continue to exercise the dominant influence which has already given rise to major disputes. Some members of the PCE executive have recognised this fact.[31] On the other hand, should the PCE refuse to renounce its communist identity, as seems likely, it is hard to envisage how IU can survive in its present form.

Meanwhile, the PSOE's proposal for a 'common home of the left' appears equally beset with difficulties. The PSOE is notorious for its resistance to allowing factional groups, and the price of entry to the 'common home' is likely to be the loss of any independent identity. Certainly, those who in recent years have attempted to maintain a critical line within the PSOE, such as Pablo Castellano through *Izquierda Socialista* or Ricardo García Damborenea with *Democracia Socialista*, have found themselves either marginalised or forced out. There is little to suggest that the PSOE is set to alter an organisational pattern which has marked its entire history, and allow free voice to organised currents of opinion (even though a bitter dispute has broken out over the succession to González between supporters of Alfonso Guerra and more market-oriented 'reformists'). In any case, for many on the left no single party could possibly serve as a 'common home'. For this reason, some – such as Gregorio López Raimundo, former president of the PSUC – have proposed that *Izquierda Unida* should be a plural political formation which encompasses political parties, social movements, professional and cultural bodies, as well as individuals, within a democratic and flexible organisational structure. How this might translate into practice is less than clear.

None the less, it is true that the emergence of so-called 'new social movements' has called into question the 'classic' model of political parties as instruments for the mediation of collective interests. Voluntarist movements involving feminists, peace groups, environmentalists, and youth organisations bring together social sectors which do not necessarily identify with established social and political forces. Party membership in Spain is in any case very low; the boost to party politics provided by the post-Franco return to democracy was never translated into mass affiliation. Indeed, perhaps as a result of the legacy of polarisation which marked the Franco regime, political attitudes in Spain since the return of democracy have been decidedly centrist. According to survey data, on a scale of 1 (far left) to 10 (far right), the ideological self-definition of Spaniards between 1977 and 1987 has veered between a maximum rightist position of 5.5 in 1977 to a maximum leftist position of 4.5 in 1980 and 1983. The period average stands at 4.8.[32]

That the PSOE should have enjoyed such remarkable electoral success since 1982 owes much to its colonising the centre ground. This fact alone poses a problem for the left.

On the one hand, any attempt to capture the support of the 'new social movements' requires the kind of flexibility propounded by some within *Izquierda Unida*, but at the same time is likely to consign any organisation which delivers such flexibility to the margins of mainstream politics. On the other hand, the logic of electoral politics dictates that the left in Spain must continue to cultivate the centre ground if it is to retain power. Thus, unless the left is able to effect a fundamental shift in the *practice* of politics towards a more participative model, then – rather than a 'common home of the left' – there may emerge a 'common home of the centre', in which the most notable difference between the mainstream political parties will reside in their policies over social integration or exclusion: the left will seek to ameliorate the social effects of new technological developments (economic and cultural marginalisation); the right will try to contain state intervention and its consequent high taxes by promoting competition and individualism.

NOTES

1. See Paul Heywood, 'Rethinking Socialism in Spain: *Programa 2000* and the Social State', *Coexistence*, **30**/3 (1993).
2. See, for example, Editorial Cambio 16, *El PC Español, Italiano y Francés cara al poder* (Madrid: Editorial Cambio 16, 1977).
3. On the PCE during the Franco regime, see Gregorio Morán, *Miseria y grandeza del Partido Comunista de España* (Barcelona: Planeta, 1985); Angel Ruiz Ayúcar, *El Partido Comunista. 37 años de clandestinidad* (Madrid: ESM, 1976); Guy Hermet, *Los comunistas en España* (Paris: Ruedo Ibérico, 1972), Paul Preston, 'The Dilemma of Credibility: The Spanish Communist Party, the Franco Regime and After', *Government and Opposition*, **11**/1 (1976); and 'The PCE's Long Road to Democracy, 1954–77', in Richard Kindersley (ed.), *In Search of Eurocommunism* (London: Macmillan/St Antony's, 1981). Until recently, there was far less available on the PSOE during the same period, but see Abdón Mateos, *El PSOE contra Franco. Continuidad y renovación del socialismo español, 1953–1974* (Madrid: Editorial Pablo Iglesias, 1993), José Luis Martín Ramos, *Historia del socialismo español, 1939–77* (Barcelona: Conjunta Editorial, 1989; vol. 4 of the five-volume collection introduced by

Manuel Tuñón de Lara); Richard Gillespie, *The Spanish Socialist Party* (Oxford: Clarendon Press, 1989); Paul Preston, 'The Decline and Resurgence of the Spanish Socialist Party during the Franco Regime', *European History Quarterly*, **18** (1988).

4. Eurocommunism generated a veritable explosion of literature in the late 1970s and early 1980s (see Introduction, note 1). On the Spanish case see, in particular, the works of Fernando Claudín, *Eurocommunism and Socialism* (London: New Left Books, 1978) and *Santiago Carrillo: Crónica de un secretario general* (Barcelona: Planeta, 1983). For further references, see Paul Heywood, 'Mirror-images: The PCE and the PSOE in the Transition to Democracy in Spain', *West European Politics*, **10**/2 (1987).

5. See José María Maravall, *La política de la transición* (2nd edn, Madrid: Taurus, 1984), esp. ch. 5; Richard Gunther, Giacomo Sani and Goldie Shabad, *Spain After Franco: The Making of a Competitive Party System* (Berkeley: University of California Press, 1986), esp. chs 5 and 8; Howard E. Penniman and Eusebio Mujal-León (eds), *Spain at the Polls 1977, 1979 and 1982* (Durham, NC, 1985).

6. Carrillo described the main characteristics of eurocommunism as follows: 'The parties included in the "Eurocommunism" trend are agreed on the need to advance to socialism with democracy, a multi-party system, parliaments and representative institutions, sovereignty of the people regularly exercised through universal suffrage, trade unions independent of the State and of the parties, freedom for the opposition, human rights, religious freedom, freedom for cultural, scientific and artistic creation, and the development of the broadest form of popular participation at all levels and in all branches of social activity. Side by side with this, in one form or another, the parties claim their total independence in relation to any possible international leading centre and to the socialist states, without ceasing on that account to be internationalist.' *'Eurocommunism' and the State* (London: Lawrence and Wishart, 1978), p. 110.

7. On PCE–PSUC relations, see Morán, *Miseria y grandeza*, pp. 593–6, 600–6; Pedro Vega and Peru Erroteta, *Los herejes del PCE* (Barcelona: Planeta, 1982), pp. 68–100; Sergio Vilar, *Por qué se ha destruido el PCE* (Barcelona: Planeta, 1986), pp.185ff.; Gregorio López Raimundo and Antonio Gutiérrez Díez, *El PSUC y el eurocomunismo* (Barcelona, 1981).

8. On the breakdown between the PCE and the Basque Communist Party, see Morán, *Miseria y grandeza*, pp. 596–7; Claudín, *Santiago Carrillo*, pp. 355–66; Manuel Azcárate, *Crisis del eurocomunismo* (Barcelona: Argos Vergara, 1982), pp. 252–82.

9. The UCD government took Spain into NATO following the attempted coup of 23 February 1981. The PSOE's promised referendum was a dominant issue in Spanish politics from 1982 to

1986, and the NATO debate generated a substantial literature. A useful guide to some of the key issues is Federico G. Gil and Joseph S. Tulchin (eds), *Spain's Entry into NATO* (Boulder, Col.: Westview Press, 1988). For the PCE's position, see the special issue on 'Spain and NATO', *ENDpapers Twelve* (1986), pp. 34–65.

10.   'El purgador purgado', *Cambio 16*, **699** (22 April 1985), pp. 30–41; *El País*, 21, 28, 30 April 1985.

11.   On Gallego, see Morán, *Miseria y grandeza*, pp. 628–30.

12.   'Iglesias: "Voy a romper la burocracia"', Gerardo Iglesias interviewed by Enrique Barrueco in *Interviú* (April 1985).

13.   Some of these groups, such as the Progressive Federation and the PCPE, later disappeared as they were subsumed into the IU or their leaders moved in new directions; others, such as the Carlists and Humanists, left of their own volition.

14.   Interview with Anguita in *Cambio 16*, **935** (30 October 1989), pp. 30–33.

15.   Santiago Carrillo, 'La izquierda se unirá', *Cambio 16*, **942** (18 December 1989), p. 20.

16.   'Es y será comunista', *El País*, 24 November 1990.

17.   Maurice Duverger, the French political scientist elected to the European Parliament in 1989 as a candidate on the Italian Communist Party's list, has argued that to abandon the communist label indicates a readiness to move beyond the constraints of a Marxist interpretation which originated in an analysis of nineteenth-century social developments. He also argues that the importance of the events of 1989 resides in the opportunity they have provided to establish a link between the two factions of socialism which have been separated since the 1920s. Duverger, 'El vínculo, *El País*, 30 November 1990.

18.   Anguita, 'No encabezaré la entrada en la Internacional Socialista', *Cambio 16*, **956** (19 March 1990), pp. 29–30. See also, 'Los socialistas y comunistas dialogan en la sombra', *Cambio 16*, **959** (9 April 1990), pp. 10–18.

19.   This was especially ironic, given that as leader of the PSOE Pablo Iglesias was notoriously loath to ally with any other political forces: from 1879 until 1909 the party refused all collaboration, remaining in splendid isolation until finally forced into an electoral pact with republicans in order to escape political marginalisation. See Paul Heywood, *Marxism and the Failure of Organised Socialism in Spain, 1879–1936* (Cambridge: Cambridge University Press, 1990).

20.   Gutiérrez, whose relations with Anguita were cool, accused the PCE secretary-general of 'jomeinismo', a reference to his supposedly Ayatollah-like leadership style. Talks on union merger ultimately broke down over bitterly disputed works' council elections in late 1990.

21.   Julio Anguita interviewed in *Cambio 16*, **988** (29 October 1990), pp. 35–6.

22. The sitting president of Andalusia, José Rodríguez de la Borbolla, was replaced as PSOE candidate at Alfonso Guerra's behest by the incumbent minister of labour, Manuel Chaves – in spite of Chaves's public and vocal resistance to the move. That agreement was not reached until a few weeks before the elections apparently had no impact whatsoever on voters.

23. For details, see *El País*, 25 November 1990.

24. *El País*, 25, 26 November 1990.

25. The pretext for Anguita's resignation was an IU vote to allow the coalition's various federations the right to form themselves into political parties, following the unilateral decision by *Esquerra Unida* in Valencia to do so. See Economist Intelligence Unit, *Spain Country Report 1* (1992), p. 10.

26. José Amodia, 'Requiem for the Spanish Communist Party', in David S. Bell (ed.), *Western European Communists and the Collapse of Communism* (Oxford: Berg Press, 1993), p. 116.

27. *El Mundo*, 30 April 1992.

28. Semprún's experiences as minister of culture provided the backdrop to his autobiographical volume, *Federico Sánchez se despide de ustedes* (Barcelona, 1993), a second volume of memoirs to follow up the remarkable *Autobiografía de Federico Sánchez* (Barcelona: Planeta, 1977), which covered his experiences as leader of the communist underground in Spain during the Franco regime.

29. Santiago Carrillo, interviewed in *Cambio 16*, **993** (3 December 1990). See also, *El País*, 23 February 1991.

30. For details, see Economist Intelligence Unit, *Spain Country Report 1* (1991), pp. 7–9.

31. Francisco Palero Gómez, 'La ruptura con la izquierda conservadura', *El País*, 24 November 1990.

32. Luis Moreno, 'Las fuerzas políticas españolas', in Salvador Giner (ed.), *España. Sociedad y Política* (Madrid: Espasa Calpe, 1990), p. 306.

4 The Portuguese Communist Party: *Perestroika* and its Aftermath

Maria Teresa Patrício and Alan David Stoleroff

Until very recently the Portuguese Communist Party (PCP) appeared to be a bastion of communist orthodoxy modelled along Soviet lines. Indeed, as the only Western European communist party that had been a protagonist in a revolutionary struggle for power (1974–75) since the post-war recuperation of liberal democracy, the ideology and behaviour of the PCP still manifested characteristics that could fairly be labelled 'Stalinist'. In the early 1980's the PCP perceived itself as a *revolutionary* party and it conserved its unity through the effective operation of democratic centralism as it had been learned in the struggle against dictatorship. However, with the advent of *glasnost* and *perestroika* in the USSR, cracks became visible in the windows of the 'party with glass walls'.[1] Individual communist dissidents began to challenge the PCP's enduring orthodoxy. With the overthrow of the East European 'socialist' regimes these fissures deepened and organised groups began to advocate the renovation of the party. The Portuguese Communist Party nevertheless disassociated itself from the crisis of communism and reaffirmed its Marxist–Leninist principles. However, after the attempted coup in the Soviet Union whole walls of this glass house shattered with the vibrations of internal protest and subsequent expulsions. Abandonment of the party by prominent members has become a constant sign of crisis. Yet, despite the radical changes that have occurred, the PCP leadership persists in its commitment to orthodox communist values and goals. The question is whether and for how long the PCP will be able to maintain its defence of orthodox communism whilst maintaining its viability within the Portuguese political system?

The PCP's stalwart defence of what it calls the 'communist ideal' has had its costs. Party membership has declined and its electoral results have suffered. With the wave of highly public defections from the party following events in the USSR in summer 1991, it is unimaginable that the PCP can continue to claim the relative stability in membership that it reported in 1988 just before the breakup of the Eastern European regimes (see Table 4.1). In October 1991 its electoral support fell below 10 per cent for the first time since free elections were introduced in Portugal in 1975. In short, the PCP has resisted pressure to change from both outside and inside the party, while experiencing decline by attrition and isolation. A further question therefore is whether recognition of the high costs involved in holding the line will motivate significant changes in the party's positions and practice?

Table 4.1   Party membership and composition*

	1983	*1988*
Total	200,753	199,275
Workers	115,270 (57.4%)	**(57%)
Women	43,451 (21.6%)	**(22.9%)

*   These are the categories used by the PCP. We do not have the means to break them down into sociological categories.
**   Only percentage reported.
Source: Reports on Organisation to Congresses (PCP, 1984, 1989, 1990).

In this chapter we trace the response of the PCP to the crisis of world communism. We identify the leadership's positions towards events and changes as well as the positions of the various reformist tendencies that appeared and had an impact. However, it is our view that an analysis of the PCP's response to the changes in the Soviet Union and Eastern Europe should not be separated from an analysis of its handling of domestic political problems such as Portugal's integration within the European Community (EC), its alliances and conflicts with the Portuguese Socialist Party (PSP) and the splits within the labour movement. The ideological challenges derived from the loss of external references and support converge with those derived from the rapid structural changes in Portuguese society and the political challenges associated with them. This is particularly important since the PCP's traditional bases of support reside in specific regional communities, namely the Alentejo, and working class collectivities – such as certain industrial sectors, like the metal workers – that have been or are being strongly affected by structural changes. The PCP is thereby faced with the challenge of resisting ideological change and maintaining such traditional bases of support in the face of economic and political change.

PORTUGUESE POLITICS AND THE PCP ON THE EVE OF *PERESTROIKA* AND THE CRISIS OF SOCIALISM

At its X Congress in December 1983 the PCP faced the challenge of working out a defensive strategy due to the situation created by what it considered to be the increasingly 'counter-revolutionary' trend in Portuguese politics and the onset of a deep economic crisis. In spite of this situation, the PCP was in good standing. It was united, apparently impervious to eurocommunist inroads, and its electoral support had increased to 18 per cent in the 1983 legislative elections. It paid little attention to the international situation at this Congress, and when it did, it was to highlight the imperialist offensive led by the Reagan administration in the United States of America. In short, communist ortho-doxy was not only secure in Portugal, it seemed to be con-solidated. The increasingly serious crisis of 'really existing socialism' had few repercussions in the Portuguese Communist Party.

Nevertheless, the economic crisis of 1983–5 initiated a process of decline of the PCP that was not immediately visible at its X Congress. Portugal was entering a process of radical structural change, ironically hidden by the depth of industry's crisis. The crisis hit hard both at heavy industry and the more traditional labour-intensive branches. This was not just a conjunctural crisis of capitalism, nor was it the crisis of 'Fordism' of the more advanced countries. It was a crisis symptomatic of the radical change that the Portuguese economy was experiencing in the capitalist world economy. The degree of employment insecurity and general economic instability reached such proportions that it began to weaken, rather than strengthen, the forms of class identification and association that contributed to PCP support. In particular, the crisis ravaged the Setúbal region, a bastion of PCP support. During this period of economic crisis Portugal was governed by a centre-block coalition led by the socialist, Mario Soares, who during the revolutionary period had been the main nemesis of the PCP in its quest for state power. The coalition government celebrated a pact with the International Monetary Fund (IMF) that led to austerity and exacerbated the PCP's 'Third-World' mental-ity. This encouraged the PCP to develop opposition to this government of 'capitalist recuperation' and imperialism as the basis of its politics against the economic crisis. The PCP could not foresee that the transitional nature of the eco-nomic crisis was a symptom of fundamental change that would leave it strategically in a *cul-de-sac.* Indeed, it would shortly have to make a new tactical about-face when, in 1985, the *socialist* Mario Soares ran for president against the genuinely right-wing candidate of the Centre Democrats. The PCP ended up eating its hat and supporting Soares. This about-face would become typical of the PCP's difficulty in getting out of merely defensive, reactive politics in the following years.

The PCP's leadership of the working class was also undergoing increasing practical challenge. The strategy of politicisation of labour union struggle that the PCP promoted within Portugal's largest union confederation, the *Confederação Geral dos Trabalhadores Portugueses* (CGTP), while mobilising workers in the short run, was not a successful economic strategy. It ended up opening opportunities for the reformist unions to reach agreements and obtain contracts that, in salvaging the chances of hard-pressed firms, contributed to saving jobs and thereby added to the weakening of the CGTP's influence. As the economy began to pick up at the end of 1985 the workers and civil servants were avid even lightly to recuperate spending power that had been brutally reduced throughout the austerity policy. This lead the CGTP to emphasise economic struggle in many of the surviving enterprises, which further undermined the PCP's politicisation strategy.

As a result of the turbulence of this period the PCP saw its vote in the 1985 legislative elections diminish from the 1,031,609 votes of 1983 to 893,180 votes; that is, from 18.1 per cent to 15.5 per cent. However, the Socialist Party had been thoroughly identified with the policies of adjustment in the crisis, and suffered a major defeat in the 1985 legislative elections. The PSP received 20.8 per cent of the vote (down from 36.3 per cent in 1983). These elections also saw the rise of an element of disorganisation on the left due to the formation of a new party, the *Partido Renovador Democrático* (PRD), which received about 20 per cent of the vote. The PRD was an ideologically nondescript entity based upon a personalistic identification with ex-President General Ramalho Eanes. Its projection of an ethical, above-the-other-parties image nevertheless earned it votes from supporters of both the PSP and the PCP. Although the left – taken as a whole and including the newly emergent PRD – had in fact obtained a majority in the 1985 legislative elections, it was irrevocably divided and the right-of-centre PSD (*Partido Social Democrata*), under the new leadership of

economics professor, Anibal Cavaco Silva, formed a
minority government with only 30 per cent of the vote. This
minority government and the favourable circumstances of
economic recovery gave the PSD an opportunity to
transform Portuguese politics.[2]

In 1986 Portugal entered the European Community.
European integration accelerated radical economic and
political changes in Portuguese society. Incorporating
Portugal into the logic of the consolidated capitalist
markets of Europe, integration has restricted the political
economic options of whatever government could come to
power in Portugal and thus further diminished the credibility of the PCP's socialist-derived economic programme. The
new economic space reinforced the perception of the enterprise as a unit of consensual economic performance and
modified the behaviour and strategies of labour. This had a
significant effect upon the left, encouraging reformism. It
also created a new political–cultural space with potential to
diffuse class conflicts. The ubiquitous reference of political
and economic actors to 'modernisation' is a manifestation
of this. The involvement of communists in European institutions at all levels could not help but have feed-back effects
upon the practice of communists within the institutions of
the domestic polity. Moreover, on the question of Europe
as a whole, the PCP's position has moved from defensive
anti-EC nationalism to very minimal reconciliation with the
accomplished fact. Indeed, in 1987 the CGTP, with the
obvious go-ahead of the Communist Party, began to participate in the Permanent Council for Social Concertation, a
neo-corporatist state organisation created in 1984 for
macro-level economic and social negotiation. Until then the
PCP had characterised this organ as bordering on neo-
fascism. Changes of this sort were symptomatic of the
'tailism' of the PCP in regard to the nation's evolution.

In 1987, for the first time since the transition to
democracy, legislative elections produced an absolute majority for a single party, the PSD. As a result, Cavaco Silva
was able to form a stable government and put into effect a
programme of economic liberalisation that would have

further consequences for the PCP. (Leading members of
the government party certainly conceived these liberal
reforms explicitly as a means of weakening and marginalis-
ing the PCP in conjunction with their strategy for creating a
bi-polar electoral party system.) The PCP vote declined to
12.2 per cent nationally in 1987 from 15.4 per cent in 1985.
(The PSP's electoral score remained stable at 21.4 per cent
of the vote.) Most significantly, in the 1987 election a decisive trend of communist voters moving to the right took
place. Thus, by 1988, a great deal of pressure upon the PCP
had accumulated since the X Congress, based upon domestic trends alone. It is certain that this situation, as well as
the build up of a crisis of communism, influenced the emergence of critical currents at the time of the XII Congress.

The PCP's XII Congress was held in December 1988, over
a year into the tenure of the PSD majority government. By
the time the Congress took place, many of the government's structural reforms were on their way to being imple-
mented. At the XII Congress, the party adopted a new
programme, made changes to its statutes and elected
a 'renewed' Central Committee (see Table 4.2).[3] The
Congress recognised the party's failure to meet the objectives it had set itself at the X Congress of 1983. It considered
the fundamental victories of the 25 April 1974 to be intact
but the party acknowledged that 12 years of 'counter-
revolution' (as the PCP refers to the consolidation of liberal
democracy) had been effective. The PCP acknowledged
that it was not possible simply to relaunch the revolutionary
struggle that it had thought merely to have been suspended
with the defeat of late November 1976. The party's new objective was summed up as the goal of achieving an 'advanced democracy'. This objective meant a regime of
democratic political liberties and a democratic representative state, based on popular participation, and would
include social policies that guaranteed an improvement in
living conditions as well as a democratic cultural policy
which would promote individual, social and national eman-
cipation. Economic development should be based upon a
mixed economy.[4] Lastly, advanced democracy called for

Table 4.2   Composition of Central Committee *

	X Congress	XII Congress
Full Members	91	96
Workers	47 (51.6%)	49 (51.0%)
Workers + Employees	68 (74.1%)	69 (71.9%)
Women	13 (14.3%)	12 (12.5%)
Substitutes	74	79
Workers	37 (50%)	39 (49.4%)
Workers + Employees	51 (69%)	(69.6%)
Women	9 (12.2%)	16 (20.3%)
Average Age	40.9	42

*These are the categories used by the PCP.

national independence and sovereignty and a policy of peace, friendship and cooperation with all peoples. 'Advanced democracy' was conceived of as the 'road to Socialism' in Portugal.

PERESTROIKA AND THE PCP

Between the PCP's X and XII Congresses, the world had begun to change. At the time of its XII Congress, in December 1988, *glasnost* and *perestroika* were in full swing. The PCP, however, in clear distinction from other West European Communist Parties, would continue to resist and successfully suppress these influences, forcing them to express themselves outside the party.

The PCP's analysis of *perestroika* at its XII Congress, as reflected in the speech of its secretary-general, Alvaro Cunhal, was basically positive. Cunhal even recognised that the road to socialism was not linear and that important errors could be made. It was in this light that he characterised *perestroika* as a 'process of transformation and advance of socialism' and affirmed that:

> Contrary to what is spread in anti-communist propaganda, *perestroika* does not reflect the failure of socialism; rather, it confirms and enriches its essential characteristics and values – the power of the workers with the guarantee of the full power of the Soviets as the basis of the organisation of the State; the stimulus and the promotion of the creative intervention of the popular masses in all spheres of social life; the quickening of socio-economic development, with the collective appropriation of the main means of production as the base and the well-being of the people as the central objective; the role of the Party as the vangard political force, especially of the process of construction of the new society.[5]

On the basis of this official analysis, it can be observed that either the PCP was particularly optimistic about the potential of Mikhail Gorbachev's policies or it was at least publicly supporting the new leadership and the new line of the Soviet Union, while cautiously figuring out what its true position should be.

Nevertheless, the PCP initially was actually much more ambivalent towards *perestroika*. This was revealed through the duplicity in its analysis of the situation. This analysis concentrated on the leading role of the party and thereby avoided taking a position on the content of many of the reforms introduced in the Soviet Union by Gorbachev. As long as *perestroika* was led by the Communist Party of the Soviet Union (CPSU) it was proclaimed to be a revolutionary process for restructuring socialist society in accordance with the 'communist ideal'. However, during the same period the party made explicit statements criticising not only the weakening of Communist Party hegemony, but the increasing introduction of market mechanisms in other socialist countires. By extension of the logic of these criticisms the party thereby implied that it also disapproved of the programme of economic restructuring in the Soviet Union.

Taking the lead from the Soviet examples of 'openness' and 'transparency', critical members of the party, intellectuals in particular, began demanding change. In clear disregard for party tradition their opposition became increasingly visible and audible in the non-communist press and media.

Opposition to the party's analysis was first expressed publicly by parliamentary deputy and Central Committee member, Zita Seabra. In a series of opinion pieces in the daily newspaper, *Diário de Notícias*, she voiced enthusiastic support for *perestroika*. This unequivocal position regarding democratic change in the Soviet Union translated into advocacy of the abandonment of democratic centralism within the PCP itself. Further criticism of the party was soon forthcoming from a group of prominent intellectuals from Coimbra (Vital Moreira, Veiga de Oliveira, Sousa Marques, Vitor Louro, Dulce Martins and Silva Graca), who came to be known as the 'group of six'. They believed the party was in crisis and called for open reflection on the nature of the party and an evaluation of its past and its role in contemporary Portugal. Their remedial prescriptions were vague. However, two themes in their documents made them adversaries of the party machine: their criticism of democratic centralism and their call for a new leadership.

Initially the group of six confined its criticism to the normal party channels. They even approached Cunhal directly but discreetly in late 1987 with a formal statement of their views in hope of his support. Cunhal and the Central Committee delayed in their response to the six, and when they finally replied it was to reject and refute the criticisms.[6] Cunhal denied there was a crisis within the party and accused the six of objectively weakening the party. A plenary meeting of the Central Committee on 24 February 1988 accused the 'group of six' of serving the interests of the counter-revolution, of reducing the efficiency of the party at a difficult political moment, of underestimating the strength of the party and overestimating the difficulties it faced.

The cautious nature of the Portuguese Communist Party led it to delay and postpone its response to the events in Eastern Europe. This delay presented a window of opportunity for critical or reformist members within the party to organise for change. Vital Moreira, a prominent member of the 'six', identified Cunhal as the major obstacle to the renovation of the party and called upon him to step down from his post of secretary-general. According to Vital Moreira the events in the East demonstrated the collapse of Marxism–Leninism (identifying Marxism–Leninism with Stalinism) and the decline of the Soviet model for socialist society. The critics now demanded the end of democratic centralism and proposed a 'democratic reconversion' of the party.

Although the PCP postponed taking a clear public position on *perestroika* and the crisis of the socialist countries, it did not delay in taking a hard and frontal approach with the internal criticism. The 'group of six', according to the PCP leadership, was lamentable and condemnable. The critics showed clear disrespect for collective decisions taken at the XII Congress and indicated a lack of interest in a CDU[7] victory in the local elections to be held in December 1989. This response would be typical of the position of the established party leadership in the ideological struggle provoked by the crisis of socialism.

On the one hand, the leadership's analysis of the crisis attributed the breakdown of the socialist regimes to errors and deviations in the implementation of Marxist–Leninist principles, thereby acknowledging that political problems, and not mere imperialist manipulation, were at issue. But the party also asserted, first, that these errors did not condemn the principles themselves and, secondly, that the PCP was not guilty of equivalent practices. On the other hand, the leadership sought to control debate on these issues, impeding criticism from attaching to communist principles or being expressed outside of party channels. According to the leadership of the PCP, the negative events

in Eastern Europe were being used by anti-communist
forces, and some 'social-democratic' members of the party,
to attack and weaken the PCP. The criticism of Marxist—
Leninist principles and the public call for abandonment of
any element of this organic whole was considered grounds
for disciplinary action.

The treatment of Zita Seabra, who was personally and
politically close to the 'group of six', was intended to serve
as an example of the meaning of communist discipline to
other critics. She was dismissed from the Political Commission and the Central Committee in May 1988. She was
finally expelled from the party in January 1990, following
her publication of an open letter in a daily paper calling
upon the PCP to change its name, drop Marxism–Leninism
and democratic centralism and relinquish its ties to the
internationalist communist movement.[8] Nevertheless, the
activity of the critics found support among reform-minded
party members. Well known party members such as Barros
Moura (Member of the European Parliament), José
Magalhães (deputy in the National Assembly), José Luis
Judas (a leader of the CGTP union confederation), and
José Saramago (a prominent novelist), added their voices in
support of some sort or degree of renovation of the PCP.
These renovators became known as the 'third way'. Some
agreed with the positions of 'the six', while others expressed
different views on the collapse of the Berlin Wall and on the
crisis of communism in the East. In this period the 'group
of six' was the most visible and polemical group owing to its
explicitly eurocommunist message and its recourse to non-
party means of communication. But the activities of the
loosely organised critical 'third way' indicated that militants
were disturbed by the political and ideological paralysis of
the party.

The need to discuss openly the events in Eastern
Europe, as well as other issues of concern to the left, led
the 'group of six', the 'third way' and other non-party independents to create the *Instituto de Estudos Sociais* (INES).
INES was created as a civic association solely intended to
be a forum for discussion and debate. Nevertheless, and

somehow predictably, the PCP viewed this association with great apprehension, distrust and a fair amount of suspicion. In spite of its members having guaranteed that INES had no intention of becoming a party, the PCP continued to see this forum as a risk for party unity. The party identified the real aims of INES as being fractionalist, with the intention of creating a pressure group to influence the internal debate of the party.[9] In spite (or because) of the fears expressed by the PCP, INES quickly and quietly disappeared.

With the approaching local-municipal elections in December 1989, the PCP succeeded, with the critics' tacit agreement, in postponing debate over recent events in Eastern Europe until May 1990. While the PCP's overall electoral results decreased in the local elections of December 1989, it did manage to obtain some important accomplishments. The most significant was the victory in the municipality of Lisbon of a coalition between the PCP and the Socialist Party over a rival coalition of the Social Democratic Party, the Democratic Social Centre and the Popular Monarchist Party. This local coalition was extremely important for the PCP, for it fostered its hopes that a coalition with the Socialist Party could be formed at the national level.

However, the leadership of the PCP was well aware of the growing discontent of its militants. Seventy-six-year-old Alvaro Cunhal had suffered a serious illness during the previous year and concern with the question of his substitution and succession had to be taken seriously. As the rank and file increasingly demanded a discussion of the events of Eastern Europe and the Soviet Union, the party pre-empted the critics' demands for a congress and took the initiative by calling instead for an extraordinary congress. This initiative permitted the established leadership to structure the debate, elaborate the congress agenda and control the election of delegates. The extraordinary congress was to serve as a means to end the internal questioning and reimpose discipline, preferably avoiding a split within the party. The five points which were selected as the Theses for the Congress reflected these objectives:

1. the events in the socialist countries and their repercussions;
2. the restoration of monopoly capitalism in Portugal;
3. the struggle for a democratic alternative;
4. the communist ideal and the nature and identity of the PCP;
5. the immediate tasks to strengthen the party.

Cunhal's pre-congress discourse indicated the party's future line following the congress. He maintained that the PCP never followed the East European model of socialism, and that it had and maintained a distinct practice and style firmly rooted in Portuguese society. The PCP, according to Cunhal, had 'a clear and tranquil conscience, and would continue to present itself with its head high and its feet firmly on the ground'.[10] Among other positive attributes, Cunhal claimed that the PCP had established deep roots in the working class and in the popular masses, had creatively expanded democratic centralism into a more democratic process, had developed a new concept of collective leadership and collective work, had distinguished real authority from formal authority, had fought and prevented the cult of the personality from developing, and had maintained its cadres living a modest and dedicated lifestyle as revolutionaries totally devoted to the cause of the Portuguese people. At the XII Party Congress the PCP had expanded the notion of advanced democracy.

Preparations for the extraordinary congress, however, displayed similar patterns to those of earlier congresses. Key critics were excluded as delegates to the congress and, with the agenda pre-determined by the Political Committee and the Central Committee, there was little the critics could do to alter its content (see Table 4.3). José Luis Judas, leading communist trade unionist in CGTP-Intersindical, having been excluded from the congress, presented an alternative and integral set of theses for the extraordinary congress in a press conference outside the framework of party institutions. Judas defined the failure of 'existing socialism' and the exhaustion of the Soviet model in terms of the lack of

Table 4.3   Age of delegates to X, XII and XIII Congresses

Age	X Congress	XII Congress	XIII Congress
less than 30	23 %	13.6%	12.6%
from 30 to 50	60.4%	66 %	64.9%
over 50	16.6%	19.6%	22.8%

Source: Reports of Credentials Committee to Congresses (PCP, 1984, 1989, 1990).

democracy at all levels, the incapacity of social and economic development within a military framework, the lack of integration of the Soviet Union and Eastern Europe in the world economy, and the centralised and bureaucratic organisation of the economy (see Table 4.4). In an explicit criticism of the PCP, Judas affirmed that it was insufficient for the PCP to claim that it had taken measures to ensure that those same errors and mistakes would not have occurred in Portugal. A believable self-criticism must go further than a belated recognition of errors. Renovation required that the PCP criticise the communist parties which remained in power in Eastern Europe. The self-criticism should contain explicit recognition of the internal hierarchical organisation where the right to information is withheld and compartmentalised. Judas supported the creation of political platforms, the abandonment of democratic centralism, and the substitution of Cunhal. Finally, Judas defended the unity of the communist-led CGTP with the socialist-led *União Geral dos Trabalhadores* (UGT, General Workers' Union), a position shared by many communist trade unionists.

When the XIII (Extraordinary) Congress was finally held in May 1990, the PCP approved a set of theses in marked contrast to those of Judas. The mistakes of the East

*Table 4.4   Social composition of delegates to PCP Congresses**

	X Congress December 1983	XII Congress December 1988	XIII Congress May 1990
Industrial workers	42.7%	41.9% (a)	33.5%
Agricultural workers	6.9%		4.9%
Employees	22.3%	29.3%	29.9%
Fishermen	(b)	1.2%	0.7%
Farmers	2.4%	1.2%	1.6%
Intellectuals	15.2% (c)	16.1% (c)	9.1%
Technicians			9.8%
Small and Medium Entrepreneurs	(b)	2.5%	3.0%
Others	10.5%	7.8%	7.4%
Women	19.3%	18.2%	18 %
Total Number Delegates	2114	2090	2061

*These are the categories used by the PCP.
(a) figure given by reporter for industrial and agricultural workers not disaggregated;
(b) no figure given;
(c) figure given by reporter for intellectuals and technicians not disaggregated.
Source: Reports of Credentials Committee to Congresses (PCP, 1984, 1989, 1990).

European regimes were analysed as the result of five major weaknesses.

1. A highly centralised political power taking arbitrary and repressive decisions, progressively separated from the wishes and control of the masses and workers.

2. Severe limitations on political democracy, and on the rights and liberties of the citizens.
3. An excessively centralised and State-controlled economy with a heavy bureaucratic apparatus taking decisions from afar and without regard for the role of the market, leading to the stagnation of the productive forces.
4. The authoritarian nature of the party, which led to confusing party and State structures and functions.
5. The imposition of Marxism–Leninism as a dogmatic State doctrine.[11]

The PCP's discussion of the errors of the socialist regimes was prefaced with a reminder of the great feats accomplished by socialism in those countries, such as the creation of a strong industrial base and developed agriculture, the elimination of illiteracy, the generalisation of culture and education, the achievement of a high scientific level, the development of public health and social security, and the elimination of unemployment. The crisis of the Soviet Union and Eastern Europe was reputedly caused not because the communist goal or project led to this, but because party and State policies had distanced themselves from the fundamental orientations and practices leading to the construction of a new society. Having easily, even if not so quickly, explained the collapse of socialism, the next difficult question for the leadership of the PCP was to explain to its members why it had not noticed the errors and informed the party. The PCP response was that it had noticed certain situations and procedures that it considered negative, but it had failed to appreciate how severe the situation had become. The PCP had naively accepted the explanations offered by the leadership of those communist parties, failing to give sufficient attention to the negative accounts. The PCP accepted self-criticism for this, but there was no further explanation of what negative situations the PCP knew about, what explanations were naively accepted, and why this information was kept from the rank and file.

In spite of the failure and collapse of socialism in Eastern Europe, the PCP reaffirmed its commitment to the 'communist ideal'. This included full commitment to the guiding principles of Marxism–Leninism and democratic centralism. The PCP's support for *perestroika* remained contradictory. It was seen as a timely attempt to re-establish the real communist ideals which had suffered through the 'mistakes and errors' of the communist leadership. It is notable that the PCP's purported support for Gorbachev's *perestroika*, or his attempt to correct the errors of socialism, failed to take into account the reintroduction of capitalist market mechanisms.

The leadership of the PCP waited until the XIII Congress to demand communist discipline. This implied acceptance of the theses approved by the majority or resignation from the party. The resignations that followed were thus individual acts in protest at the majority outcome of the congress.[12] Innovations originating from the congress included the creation of the new post of Adjunct-Secretary-General, thus easing the question of Cunhal's succession without actually resolving the question of a new leadership as demanded by the critical sector. Carlos Carvalhas, a senior PCP deputy in the European Parliament, was elected to the new position with only one abstention. The congress was meant to end the debate on the renovation of the party, and end the discussion on the collapse of the socialist regimes. It only partially succeeded in these objectives for the discussion would be reopened following the abortive coup of August 1991 in the Soviet Union.

Following the congress, much of the critics' activity subsided. It appeared that the critics and loyal renovators had squandered their chance of entering the 'window of opportunity' provided by the ideological crisis associated with the defeat of the communist regimes. The critics were unable to articulate support for the piecemeal pragmatic adjustments in the programme that had been taking place with a medium-term strategy of alliances with renovators loyal to the party and more moderate elements of the leadership.

FROM *PERESTROIKA* TO COLLAPSE OF THE USSR,
FROM INTERNAL STRUGGLE TO CRISIS IN THE PCP

The period between the XIII (Extraordinary) Congress and
the collapse in the Soviet Union were marked by the continuing advance of the liberalising and modernising trends
in the Portuguese political economy. The economic growth
that coincided with Portugal's entry into the EC continued
and could not favour the PCP. In general it has not contributed to the credibility of the left as a whole. The
progress of the liberalising programme of the Social
Democratic government placed the PCP in a thoroughly defensive position. It had already experienced the reversal of
most of what it considered to be the 'victories' of the revolution of 1974–5, especially following the so-called 'anti-
socialist' Constitutional Revision, the extinction of the
Agrarian Reform and the re-privatisation of many firms of
the nationalised public sector.

This conjuncture has not been favourable to the construction of a frontal popular opposition to the government or to
capital. The unions, in particular, have vacillated in recent
years between negotiation of a social pact with the employers'
associations and the government and resistance to revision
of labour legislation. Workplace conflict, measured in terms
of strike frequency and density of participation, has decreased significantly over the last few years. Thus, with regard
to industrial relations, things have not gone smoothly for the
PCP. Significant conflicts have occurred amongst communist
trade unionists as well as between the PCP apparatus and the
CGTP over issues such as the co-signing of the 'Social and
Economic Agreement' or the general attitude towards the
UGT labour confederation.

Politically, the PCP remains isolated in spite of repeated
attempts to construct coalitions with the Socialist Party.
Although the PSP had been willing to enter local electoral
coalitions with the PCP, such as in Lisbon, it refused to
consider seriously the constant calls of the PCP leadership
for an alliance in national legislative elections.[13] The only
alliance the PCP succeeded in establishing following the

disintegration of its electoral alliance with the MDP/CDE and the internal strife-ridden Green Party, was with the leftist pro-Albanian UDP.

In January 1991 the presidential elections gave the PCP its first opportunity to test its support since the struggle with the critics and dissidents of the party (see Table 4.5). The party presented its own candidate for President, the newly elected Adjunct-Secretary-General, Carlos Carvalhas. Incumbent Mário Soares had the support of the government and the

Table 4.5   National and regional distribution of vote for Communist candidate in first round of presidential elections, January 1991

Districts	Votes	Percentage
Aveiro	17,887	5.53%
Beja	33,796	37.52%
Braga	26,158	7.07%
Bragança	3,869	5.06%
Castelo Branco	10,559	9.21%
Coimbra	19,083	8.84%
Évora	33,313	35.40%
Faro	20,481	12.00%
Guarda	5,809	5.95%
Leiria	14,969	7.18%
Lisboa	174,181	17.01%
Portalegre	17,271	23.03%
Porto	75,492	9.21%
Santarém	34,996	14.96%
Setúbal	113,232	31.77%
Viana do Castelo	18,397	7.55%
Vila Real	5,736	5.11%
Viseu	9,869	5.13%
Açores	3,010	3.21%
Madeira	3,652	3.49%
Country Total	632,625	12.92%

PSP and was re-elected with 70.4 per cent of the vote. Carvalhas obtained 12.9 per cent (the rightist Basílio Horta received 14.1 per cent and the far left/UDP candidate Carlos Marques 2.6 per cent) (see Table 4.6). The PCP leadership evaluated Carvalhas's electoral results positively and considered them a vindication of its positions.[14]

The coup of 19 August in the Soviet Union coincided with the pick-up of the campaign for the legislative elections of October 1991. The coup, and the PCP leadership's reaction to it, would not only have a dramatic impact on the efforts developed by the PCP since the breakdown of socialism to re-establish its credibility with an electorate beyond its core support base; it would also lead to crisis in the core group itself. The degree of the PCP leadership's commitment to orthodoxy would be confirmed both by the content of its reaction as well as by its willingness to absorb very high costs in terms of organisational stability and electoral support, in order to defend its position.

The PCP's approval of the coup in the Soviet Union was immediate. Even before the outcome of the communist coup was known, the Political Commission of the PCP issued a declaration of support. The PCP's hasty statement of support for a military coup unveiled in an instant its pent-up opposition to the reform and restructuring taking place in the Soviet Union during the preceding years. As

Table 4.6   National results of presidential elections, January 1991

	Votes	Percentage
Mário Soares (incumbent)	3,448,216	70.43
Basílio Horta (CDS)	688,866	14.07
Carlos Carvalhas (PCP)	632,625	12.92
Carlos Marques (UDP)	125,999	2.57

Source: Diário de Notícias, 14 January 1991.

with the Soviet invasion of Czechoslovakia in 1968, support
for the military coup placed the PCP within the vanguard of
the most conservative forces associated with the Soviet establishment. The outcome of the coup was therefore very
embarrassing for the leadership of the PCP and brought it
to its most serious crisis ever. In the immediate aftermath of
the coup the PCP was practically put on trial by the media
and other political parties, and Cunhal and other prominent PCP leaders were reduced to resorting to numerous
excuses and pathetic denials to explain away the statement
of support for the coup in the precipitous declaration by
the Political Commission.

As soon as news of the coup and the Political
Commission's reaction were known, the critics identified
with the 'third way' came out of hibernation and resumed
their activity by taking the lead in criticism of the PCP for its
position. Several prominent PCP members not only resigned, but made public denunciations of the party. An
open meeting of the PCP militants protesting the position
of the Political Commission was organised in a Lisbon hotel.
It was presided over by José Luis Judas and Euro-deputy,
Barros Moura, and was attended by over a hundred people.
A document was drafted to the Central Committee condemning the coup and protesting against the support of the
leadership. As a result of the shock of the situation this
internal protest movement turned into a new and broader
campaign to renovate the party. The existing leadership,
once again, was considered a fundamental problem in the
renovation of the party and, once again, the critics
requested that the next congress be brought forward.
Meanwhile individual resignations from the party
continued.[15]

Within a week, however, the PCP leadership appeared to
have recuperated from the drama of the failed coup in the
Soviet Union and from the critics' renewed demands and
went on the counter-attack in its classical style. In the
Central Committee Cunhal reaffirmed and justified the
Political Commission's note of support for the coup,
criticised capitalist restoration in the Soviet Union, and

labelled Boris Yeltsin reactionary, anti-democratic and dictatorial. The coup was explained as an attempt to halt the counter-revolutionary process that had developed during *perestroika*, permitting reactionaries freely to engage in anti-socialist activities. The ambiguity of PCP support for *perestroika* disappeared in a frankly negative evaluation of its results. *Perestroika* ruined the Soviet economy, substituting an excessively centralised economy with an ill-defined and badly-oriented market economy. According to the PCP it was doubtful whether *perestroika* was still effective in the Soviet Union at the time of the coup. The coup, according to the Central Committee, was a desperate attempt to salvage the socialist character of the Soviet Union. It failed because its protagonists erred in their calculations, objectively making their initiative adventurist. In a further attempt to justify the Political Commission's note, the PCP stated that it was not aware of the anti-constitutional character of the coup until 21 August. The PCP further justified the coup by the events that followed in the USSR. Rather than contain the crisis and destabilisation in the Soviet Union, the defeat of the coup facilitated the rapid advance of an anti-socialist, reactionary process.

As to the direct effect of these events upon the internal affairs of the PCP, the Central Committee took a rigidly orthodox line. It rejected the demand to anticipate the date of the next congress, and refused to accept any challenge to the leadership. According to a member of the Central Committee, 'Alvaro Cunhal would not be another victim of the Moscow coup.' There were few surprises in the Central Committee vote: two votes against and four abstentions. The 'hard-liners' in the leadership demanded that the critics be expelled, while others proposed that any expulsions should follow the up-coming legislative elections. The Central Committee delayed the disciplinary response to the critics' 'divisionist' activity. As the critics had decided to suspend their campaign until after the October elections, the PCP was once again able to hold internal differences in abeyance in order not to prejudice a favourable electoral result for the party. Disciplinary action was set for the post-election period. Nevertheless, resignations still continued.

Following the analysis of the recent events in the Soviet Union the PCP concentrated on internal issues, most particularly the up-coming legislative elections. Debate on external issues was postponed and leading members of the party deferred to Cunhal on matters pertaining to the Soviet Union. Although Carvalhas declared during the election campaign that the events in the Soviet Union had a greater impact upon the intellectuals than upon the masses, the fact was that the collapse of communism in the Soviet Union had a profound impact on local coalitions and brought out contradictions within the trade union movement.[16]

The PCP suffered a major defeat in the legislative elections of 6 October 1991 (see Tables 4.7 and 4.8). It lost one third of its electorate and almost half of its seats in Parliament. For the first time since free elections were introduced following the 1974 coup, the PCP election result fell below the 10 per cent threshold to 8.8 per cent. But not even this electoral setback made the PCP more self-critical; rather, defeat was blamed on the recent events in the Soviet Union and the way the media had used that information against the PCP, on the refusal of the PSP to form an alliance with the PCP, and finally on the political advantage the PSD had, as the incumbent government, to win a new parliamentary majority.

The activity of the critics was denigrated. Cunhal referred to them and other recent drop-outs from the PCP as 'dead leaves'. Following the elections the PCP applied disciplinary action against the last remaining outspoken critics within the party. Judas resigned before his expulsion could be made known, but others were expelled. The expulsions naturally led to further internal protest.

The critics had exhausted all means of bringing about change within the party. The alternative for the expelled was either to create a new organisation, to join the ranks of the PSP (even as an independent on the PSP ticket, as the deputy José Magalhães had done a while before) or to fade

Table 4.7   PCP vote distributed by electoral district in order of concentration, based on vote of 1976

	1976 PCP	1979 APU	1980 APU	1983 APU	1985 APU	1987 CDU	1991 CDU
District							
Setúbal	44.3	46.9	44.0	45.8	38.1	32.7	24.9
Beja	44.0	50.7	47.1	49.5	44.8	38.6	30.4
Évora	43.0	48.8	45.7	47.6	41.2	36.1	27.0
Portalegre	22.0	29.3	26.2	28.0	25.1	20.8	15.2
Lisboa	21.8	26.1	23.1	25.2	20.0	16.5	12.2
Santarém	16.1	21.7	19.0	19.9	16.3	12.6	9.8
Faro	14.5	20.2	16.7	18.7	15.2	10.9	7.2
Porto	8.4	14.5	11.9	13.6	12.0	9.4	6.4
Coimbra	7.2	11.2	9.9	10.6	10.1	7.1	5.0
Leiria	7.3	10.8	9.7	9.5	8.1	5.9	4.5
Castelo Branco	6.6	12.4	10.5	11.1	8.9	7.1	4.5
Viana do Castelo	6.6	9.8	10.0	9.8	8.2	6.2	5.0
Braga	4.1	10.0	8.4	8.8	8.5	6.1	4.5
Aveiro	3.8	7.9	6.8	7.0	6.4	4.4	2.8
Vila Real	3.1	6.1	5.1	5.2	5.9	4.1	2.6
Guarda	2.9	5.4	5.0	4.9	5.2	3.3	2.2
Bragança	2.7	5.8	4.8	4.7	5.3	3.3	2.1
Viseu	2.3	5.5	5.0	4.6	5.0	2.9	2.0
Açores	1.5	3.1	3.0	3.1	4.3	2.3	1.3
Madeira	1.5	3.0	2.9	2.8	3.2	1.9	1.0

into inactivity. A concrete proposal for the creation of a new forum for discussion and activity that would appeal to the dispersed left as a whole surfaced during the meetings of the PCP dissidents. Barros Moura and Judas took the lead of the movement of the new left. The 'Left Platform', a loosely organised left-wing movement, was founded in May 1992, aggregating ex-PCP members as well as disenchanted ex-far-leftists.

Table 4.8   National and regional distribution of PCP vote in legislative elections

Year	Country Total	Percentage
1975	711,935	16.60
1976	786,701	14.39
1979	1,129,322	18.30
1980	1,009,505	16.75
1983	1,031,609	18.07
1985	893,180	15.49
1987	685,199	12.20
1991	501,707	8.80

CONCLUSION

An important problem for an organisation undergoing a contraction of its support and resources is the maintenance of the source of its internal cohesion, that is, what can hold it together in times of recession? It must increase or reinforce its identity. But the traditional social sources of its identity are being undermined.[17] Thus, in a first phase we saw the PCP reinforce its emphasis on communist *values* and on the 'communist ideal'. This emphasis on values in the context of contraction stunted the impulse towards change that may have been in progress and was reflected in the change of the PCP's programme at its XII Congress.

Through one tactic or another, the PCP leadership succeeded in suppressing internal dissidence and any effective challenge to its tradition of communist orthodoxy throughout the period of the crisis of socialism. In this way, the leadership has ensured that the party's latent political crisis and its adjustment to a radically changed environment will have to be managed by the inheritors of that tradition.

The disillusionment with the collapse of the Soviet Union and with capitalist restoration in Eastern Europe was exacerbated by the difficulty that the leadership of the PCP encountered in explaining the events to its militants. The leadership never stepped out of the framework of its traditional references to the Soviet establishment in its attempt to analyse the crisis. The PCP lost its major external source of identification, and has tried to substitute and re-make international alliances with China, North Korea and, of course, its long-standing ally, Cuba. It has also attempted to re-establish ties with the European communist parties of Spain, Greece, France, Italy and Cyprus. This has obviously not compensated for the loss of a traditional centre.[18]

In this chapter we have tried to show how factors of political and social change within Portugal have joined with the crisis of socialism internationally to produce a decline in the PCP. At times the leadership was able to isolate the organisation from the effects of events in the break-up of world communism. At such times, however, the long-term development of Portuguese society came to the fore, maintaining the pressure on the party. In the final period the effects of the international situation converged with domestic problems to throw the organisation into real crisis. How will the PCP emerge from this period? Since the October 1991 elections developments have been rather rapid and the public statements of party leaders have been contradictory. It is risky at present for anyone not privy to the intimate considerations of the Political Commission to make strong predictions. At the party's XIV Congress in 1993, Alvaro Cunhal finally retired as secretary-general. Although his influence remains enormous, his replacement may finally signify a political as well as physical change of generation.

NOTES

1.   Alvaro Cunhal, *O Partido com paredes de vidro* (Lisbon: Edicões Avante!, 1985).
2.   Amongst other indicators of the recovery, 1986 showed an increase in the national product, in real internal demand, a decline in unemployment, a positive balance of payments, a decline in inflation and an increase in real wages.

3. PCP, *XII Congresso PCP: Com o PCP por uma Democracia Avancada no Limiar do Seculo XXI* (Lisbon: Edicões Avante!, 1989).
4. 'Such a project requires a mixed economic organisation not dominated by the monopolies, with sectors of diversified property supported by the State and with its own dynamics, namely, an integrated and modernised State Enterprise Sector, playing a determinant role in the development of the productive forces; a private sector constituted by enterprises of varying dimension with significant support to the small and medium enterprises; collective units of production and cooperatives of the Agrarian Reform; production cooperatives, self-managed enterprises and family farms.' Cunhal, in ibid., p. 43.
5. PCP, *XII Congresso* (1988), p. 29.
6. See *Diário de Notícias,* 17 November 1989, and *Expresso,* 17 February 1990.
7. The CDU (*Coligação Democrática*) was a coalition of the PCP, *Os Verdes* (The Greens), and *Intervenção Democrática.*
8. *Diário de Notícias,* 2 January 1990.
9. See '10 notas sobre o INES', *Avante!,* 1 February 1990.
10. Cunhal's speech in Lisbon on the 69th anniversary of the PCP, *Avante!,* 13 March 1990.
11. Theses, PCP, 1990, pp. 9–10.
12. Judas, for example, accepted the outcome of the congress and remained in the PCP, while Vital Moreira and others of the 'group of six' presented their resignations.
13. The PCP continues to define its electoral strategy in terms of the constitution of a 'democratic alternative to the politics of the Government of the right' (chapter 3 of Theses, PCP, 1990).
14. During the campaign the PCP was constantly subjected to charges of being static and rigid in ideology. Carvalhas would produce a typical response, like the following: 'If you mean by renovation of the party a de-characterisation of the PCP, you are mistaken! We continue to be communists, we have a communist ideal, we have an identity and we will maintain it ....' (*Independente,* 22 February 1991), 'Renovation' was identified by the PCP as the conservation of its communist ideal.
15. Viega de Oliveira of the original 'group of six' resigned, declaring that renovation of the PCP was impossible. Osvaldo de Castro, member of the Central Committee between 1976 and 1982 and ex-parliamentarian, also resigned. With Osvaldo de Castro, nine other party members from the working-class town of Marinha Grande resigned. The only viable alternative for Viega de Oliveira and Osvaldo de Castro was to create a new organisation and/or party of the left. Central Committee member Pina Moura also resigned.
16. The CGTP issued a declaration of unequivocal criticism of the coup, against the will of PCP hard-liners.

17   Since the Soviet model of society was shattered the PCP has had to maintain the loyalty of its militants by reaffirming their social and cultural identification as communists within the Portuguese Communist Party. This identification with the PCP has been so binding that many of the critics, such as the 'third way' held on to their membership and their hopes of changing the party from within in spite of constant disappointed expectations. Some clearly indicated that being expelled was preferable to resignation.

18.   In a meeting held in Portugal (May 1922 in Quinta da Atalaia, Seixal), these six communist parties reflected on the new world order and the revived hegemony of the United States of America. Although these parties recognised that they have different opinions on many issues, according to a communist leader, they share the same spirit of solidarity and are trying to work out forms of co-operation between them.

5 The Decline and Fall of the Communist Party of Belgium

Pascal Delwit and Jean-Michel de Waele

INTRODUCTION

With the exception of a short post-war period, after having secured 12.6 per cent of the vote at the 1946 general elections, the *Parti Communiste de Belgique* (PCB) has never occupied a strong position in Belgian politics. Nevertheless, observers acknowledge that the party's real influence, at least until the beginning of the 1980s, exceeded its electoral performances as a result of its involvement in such bodies as the socialist trade union organisation, the *Fédération générale du travail de Belgique* (FGTB). Communist influence was also discernible in certain associative movements such as the Peace Movement (CNAPD).

During the 1980s, however, the PCB suffered a considerable decline in influence. As far as elections are concerned, in the 1985 general elections it lost its entire parliamentary representation. Until then, it still had two deputies and one senator out of a total of 397 parliamentarians in Belgium. In the light of this decline, the events which took place in the communist world in 1989 and 1991 did not so much disrupt as reinforce, or even exacerbate, trends which were already underway in the PCB.

In order to analyse and understand the reaction of the PCB to the events of 1989 and 1991, this chapter will examine:

119

- the structural reorganisations which took place inside the PCB during the 1980s;
- the distributive curve of electoral results since the mid-1970s;
- the evolution of party membership since the mid-1970s;
- the reasons for the PCB's failure to respond to and adapt to social transformations during the 1970s and 1980s;
- the PCB's position in regard to international matters, notably its silence when faced with the events of 1989, the August 1991 coup and the subsequent disappearance of the Soviet Union;
- internal discussions over the future of the PCB.

THE *PARTI COMMUNISTE DE BELGIQUE* BEFORE 1989

The Evolution of the PCB's Internal Structure

An analysis of the internal structural changes undergone by the PCB prior to 1989 is important for two reasons. On the one hand, it serves to demonstrate the difficulties faced by the party in its attempts to adapt to the evolution of Belgian society. On the other hand, the final stage of 'regionalisation' of the party in 1989 – which led to the creation of a French-speaking and a Dutch-speaking (Flemish) party – was the expression of a desperate attempt by the leadership to take advantage of numerous changes and upheavals taking place throughout the world and bring the PCB's policies and organisational structures up to date.

The PCB was in fact the last Belgian political party represented in Parliament to maintain a national structure. The first modification of its organisation and its functioning took place on the occasion of a Special Congress held in December 1982. Powers which had formerly been attributed to national organs – the Party Congress, Central Committee and Political Bureau – were from this point onwards divided between the national level and the regional or community level, in accordance with Article 15 of the new statutes:

The federal organs of the PCB are competent in all matters of regional and community interest so far as their elaboration and execution are concerned.

National organs of the PCB are competent in regard to:

(a) all problems concerning the Belgian road to socialism; ...
(b) all matters which would remain of national interest in a federal state and, more particularly, international policy;
(c) any questions still to evolve which by virtue of the law remain within the remit of the central government and national parliament; ...
(d) management of party finances and patrimony as well as the policy of cadres.[1]

These changes led to the creation of regional and federal structures – a French-speaking Council and Bureau on the one hand, a Dutch-speaking Council and Bureau on the other – running parallel to the existing national structures. The reforms, which were intended to make up for lost time in regard to regionalisation, in fact resulted in the weighing down of the party's functioning and led to complete paralysis. A state of 'permanent Congress' developed, since members of each of the new organs had to meet in order to renew the PCB's political line and its leadership. Moreover, this attempt at organisational renewal was soon overtaken by the political evolution of the country and by conflicts between competing community interests which appeared and began to multiply inside the PCB. Finally, after numerous discussions which left the party effectively paralysed, the decision was taken in 1989 to create two parties.

For some time, owing to its weakness in terms of both membership and electoral results, the Flemish wing of the PCB resembled a *'groupuscule'* rather than a political party. In fact, the Communist Party had never achieved a breakthrough in Flanders, not even when the PCB's power grew in 1936, nor after the Second World War. By the end of 1986, there were hardly more than 1200 members of the

Flemish party, a number which continued to decline; by 1993, it had fallen to well under 1000. For this reason, the analysis which follows concentrates on the situation in Wallonia and Brussels.

The French-speaking part of the PCB comprises the Brussels and Wallonian 'regional' sections.[2] Its leading organs are the French-speaking Congress, Council and Bureau. The French-speaking communists are organised into 13 federations of varying importance which, to a large extent, correspond to the electoral districts of the French-speaking provinces of Belgium. Historically, the most important federations are those of Liège, Charleroi, Brussels, and of the Borinage and the Centre. They cover essentially the great traditional industrial centres where the PCB once achieved its best electoral results.

The PCB's Electoral Performance

The 1970s were years of relative national stability for the Belgian communists. It appears that they benefited only marginally from the general improvement in the electoral performance of major West European communist parties at the start of the decade, all of which achieved some important successes and managed partially to renovate their political programmes. In Wallonia, the elections of 1971, 1974, 1977 and 1978 saw the PCB obtain respectively 5.9, 5.8, 5.3 and 5.8 per cent of the vote. In Brussels, in the same elections, it obtained 2.8, 4, 2.7 and 3 per cent. It was from 1981 onwards that a significant contraction in the party's support began to appear. Subsequently, the drop was not just confirmed, but grew worse and became faster, as evidenced in the municipal elections of 1982, the European elections of 1984 and the general elections of 1985 and 1987. As shown in Table 5.1, within the space of ten years the PCB lost more than two-thirds of its electoral support in a relatively consistent fashion across the French-speaking community.

The different types of elections bear witness to the homogeneity and continuity of the communist decline. The collapse in support was particularly important in the old

Table 5.1   PCB performance in municipal, general and European
elections, 1976–88

Municipal Elections

Region	1976 (%)	1982 (%)	1988 (%)
BRABANT			
Bruxelles	3.53	1.53	0.85
Anderlecht	3.57	1.78	0.66
Boitsfort	4.43	2.01	1.77
HAINAUT			
Charleroi	4.41	3.82	2.44
Courcelles	13.65	11.12	15.16
Mons	14.04	6.56	2.04
Dour	10.43	3.55	–
La Louvière	7.89	7.42	4.27
Tournai	16.29	7.31	6.21
Mouscron	10.29	3.26	–
Rumes	16.37	10.88	6.34
LIÈGE			
Liège	5.78	4.43	3.04
Seraing	12.16	8.39	5.20
Trooz	12.73	11.98	9.95
Herstal	7.71	5.16	2.71
NAMUR			
Namur	1.76	1.33	0.58

General Elections

Districts	1978 (%)	1981 (%)	1985 (%)	1987 (%)
Bruxelles	2.80	1.95	1.00	0.80
Hainaut	8.71	6.30	3.64	2.40
Namur	2.42	2.18	1.14	0.50
Liège	5.65	4.10	2.62	1.80

Table 5.1   continued

European Elections

Districts	1979 %	1984 %
Brabant	2.10	0.85
Hainaut	7.70	4.31
Namur	2.80	1.43
Liège	5.40	3.02
Luxembourg	2.70	1.23
French Community	5.07	2.75

industrial centres (based on metallurgy, iron and steel, mining, textiles) such as Liège and Hainaut. In the province of Hainaut, the PCB lost three-quarters of its electorate within nine years. This fall was even more clearly shown in the results of municipal elections, which revealed the loss of credit of its local militants.

In Mons, one of the main cities in Wallonia, the PCB vote fell from 14.04 per cent to 2.04 per cent between 1976 and 1988. Over the same period in Dour, an old workers' town, the PCB went from recording 10.43 per cent of the vote to being unable even to present a list of candidates. In Mouscron, an industrial centre in western Hainaut, the party similarly went from receiving 10.29 per cent of the vote in 1976 to being unable to present candidates in 1988. However, thanks to some long-established local personalities, the PCB was able to put up some resistance in certain places like Courcelles, Le Roeux and Quaregnon.[3]

The province of Liège registered equally impressive losses. In Seraing and Herstal, two of the main industrial towns where communist presence had a long history, the PCB vote fell from 12.6 per cent to 5.2 per cent and 7.71 per cent to 2.71 per cent respectively between 1976 and 1988. Again, the influence of a few individuals led to better results in some areas, such as Trooz. However, in the province of Namur and the district of Brussels, the results of the 1988 municipal elections fell below the threshold of electoral credibility, even in places like Anderlecht and the city of Brussels, where communists had been elected in 1976.

The Evolution of PCB Membership since 1975

The evolution of the membership of a political party is obviously an important indicator of its state of health, all the more so for a party which bases – or is theoretically supposed to base – its actions on grounds other than electoral performance. Besides, for parties of the left, membership constitutes a basic index in that the relationship between supporters and electors is generally more stable than in other parties.

According to estimations based on our research, the membership of the PCB in 1975 amounted to somewhat less than 6000. Taking 1975 as a base, it can be seen that within a period of thirteen years the PCB lost at least half its membership. With the exception of the turning-point of 1982–3, when the party lost 11 per cent of its members, the overall fall took place in a regular and continuous fashion. Consequently, by 1988 there remained about 2500 members in Wallonia and 500 in Brussels. By 1993, combined membership in Wallonia and Brussels had fallen to under 2000, with a pronounced collapse evident in the Brussels Federation.

An analysis of the age structure of party members is also very revealing. In 1987, the PCB conducted an internal study of the Walloon federations. Breaking down percentages by age-groups of five years revealed various aspects which require emphasis (see Table 5.2). First, the average age of PCB members is notably high. If the middle of each five-year age group is taken as the mean, then the overall average age of PCB members in Wallonia in 1987 was 51. Secondly, if age-groups are distributed by ten-year intervals, rather than

Table 5.2   Age distribution of PCB members in Wallonia, 1987

Age group	Percentage
20 years and less	1.1
21–25 years	3.3
26–30 years	6.0
31–35 years	8.9
36–40 years	12.0
41–45 years	8.7
46–50 years	7.6
51–55 years	8.7
56–60 years	11.1
61–65 years	10.9
66–70 years	6.2
over 71 years	14.8

five, then just 1.1 per cent of members are 20 years of age or less, whilst 9.3 per cent fall into the 21–30 age group, 20.9 per cent into the 31–40 group, 16.38 per cent into the 41–50 group, 19.8 per cent into the 51–60 group, 17.1 per cent into the 61–70 group, 9.8 per cent into the 71–80 group, and finally 5 per cent are in the 81–90 age group. The very low percentage of those under the age of 30 (10.4 per cent), together with the overall high average age, indicates a failure of membership renewal and highlights the problems of survival faced by the PCB even in the short term.

The PCB's Responses to Social Changes

Historically, the Belgian Communist Party took root mainly in the Walloon coal basins, which were densely populated by industrial workers, and in certain branches of the tertiary sector in Brussels. The economic crises which emerged in the 1970s severely hit these regions and devastated whole industrial sectors, such as iron and steel works, metallurgy, and mining. It was precisely in these sectors that the communists were best integrated. In addition to industrial decline, the actual organisation of work was subject to important changes. New working principles were developed on the basis of greater responsibility being given to the holders of specific posts. Furthermore, the very conception of the roles assumed by workers changed.

All these changes exerted a strong influence on the nature of class consciousness amongst the workforce. Indeed, within the space of a few years, the PCB lost its classical frame of reference. In common with a large part of the European labour movement, the PCB underestimated the scale and consequences of the economic, social and cultural transformations that were taking place. As demonstrated by its electoral results and fall in membership, the PCB failed to take into account the new realities which followed upon these developments. An analysis of the socio-professional origins of the party's membership provides further evidence of the ever-widening gap between the PCB's policies and changes in Belgian society. Ultimately, the PCB appeared unable to offer any response to these complex developments.

The results we have calculated must be interpreted with a certain amount of caution. In the first place, the occupational categorisation does not take into account the age of members. Consequently, we do not know whether the party members who were interviewed were still active at the time of the inquiry. Given the age profile of PCB members, this element should not be neglected as the source of potential distortions to certain of our extrapolations. A second warning should be added: the totals were obtained from information given by members on their membership counterfoil, which lists nine options. This may have led to certain inconsistencies, such as in cases where party members have had several different professions.

Even given these reservations, the massive representation of private-sector [blue-collar, manual] workers is a clearly established fact. Half of the Walloon members of the PCB (49.6 per cent) belong to this category. If public-sector workers, who amount to about 10 per cent, are added, then the total of [blue-collar, manual] workers reaches 60 per cent. This over-representation highlights the under-representation of other sectors, in particular professional employees (see Table 5.3).

Table 5.3   Socio-professional origins of PCB members in Wallonia

Private-sector employees	11.7%
Public-sector employees	10.0%
Teaching profession	6.7%
Para-medical profession	2.3%
Culture industry personnel	2.0%
Students	1.8%
Free professions	6.3%

Table 5.4   General election results since 1954

	National	Flanders	Wallonia	Brussels
1954	3.6	1.5	6.8	3.7
1958	1.9	1.0	4.5	2.7
1961	3.1	1.0	6.5	3.6
1965	4.6	1.7	9.8	4.1
1968	3.3	1.4	7.0	2.4
1971	3.1	1.6	5.9	2.8
1974	3.2	1.6	5.8	4.0
1977	2.7	1.0	5.3	2.7
1978	3.2	1.9	5.8	3.0
1981	2.3	1.3	4.2	2.1
1985	1.1	0.5	2.5	1.2
1987	0.9	0.5	1.6	1.0
1991	–	–	–	–

POLITICAL CHOICES AND THE DECLINE OF BELGIAN COMMUNISM

The downward curve of electoral results and the collapse of membership not only contributed to the crisis of the Belgian Communist Party, but also revealed the extent of the crisis. There are various objective factors, external to the party's organisation, which contributed to the PCB's decline: far-reaching socio-economic transformations which led to the effective disappearance of the working class as a class, and thereby deprived the party of its main source of electoral support; the large-scale settlement in the Brussels region of a Maghrebine population which showed little interest in the slogans and activities of the Communist Party; the increasingly negative image associated with the Soviet Union from 1975 onwards; new international tensions following the Soviet intervention in Afghanistan; and, finally, parallel crises in other Communist Parties in Western Europe which had a knock-on effect on the PCB.

Nevertheless, these factors cannot in themselves provide a full explanation of the PCB's collapse. Instead, emphasis must be placed on the essential role of political choices made by the party leadership. The most significant characteristic of the PCB's political practice has, undoubtedly, been the search for consensus and compromise between supporters of different political lines. The leadership kept manoeuvring under pressure from a strong pro-Soviet minority, only to end up paralysed by its internal divisions and personal quarrels which became all the more difficult to manage in that they revolved around a small number of people. Besides its impact on the whole organisation, the permanent search for compromise blocked the emergence of new leaders who might have been more sensitive to the claims of the new social classes. It is indicative that the PCB's president, Louis Van Geyt – a centrist upholder of consensus – assumed the party leadership in 1973 and remained in post into the early 1990s.

In regard to the PCB's political line, a permanent discrepancy existed between, on the one hand, ringing resolutions with an accent on innovation, and highly traditional practice on the other. Thus, in the matter of relations with the CPSU and the international communist movement, the Belgian communists often distanced themselves from Soviet policy during the great 'affairs' which shook the communist world, condemning, for example, the intervention of Warsaw Pact troops in Czecholosvakia, the trials against intellectuals in the USSR, the occupation of Afghanistan by the Soviet army, and the 'coup' in Poland. But the forms taken by these condemnations were compromises from the outset, difficult to achieve and reflective of the party's internal equilibria.

In August 1968 the PCB sent an open letter to the Communist Parties which had participated in the intervention in Prague. In it, the PCB declared that it was 'not able to approve the military intervention ... and underscores that in the present case [the intervening forces] have acted in such a way as to give the impression that the political changes which would enable the achievement of disarmament and the dismantling of military blocs cannot be made'.[4] After the 'Moscow accord', the Liège deputy, Marcel Levaux, reiterated 'to the Central Committee of the Communist Party of Czechoslovakia the solidarity of the Belgian communists with the normalisation [sic] of the situation and, more particularly, with the withdrawal of troops, and with the development and consolidation of socialist democracy and the defeat of reactionary forces'.[5] The term 'normalisation' was a most unhappy one given the connotation it was later to acquire. However, its use was not due to chance. Levaux represented the pro-Soviet tendency in the PCB and felt it necessary to evoke the 'reactionary forces' which political observers were still seeking among the main actors of the Czech drama more than twenty years after the Prague events.

After the Soviet invasion of Afghanistan, the Belgian communists were more cautious and offered an official reaction only on 7 January 1980, more than ten days after the first entry of Soviet troops. Moreover, the whole communiqué has to be read in order to discover the PCB's reprobation, wrapped up in attacks on the United States:

> after having inspired the NATO decision on the implementation of strategic missiles in Europe, the USA and some of its allies have found a pretext in the Soviet intervention in Afghanistan to give a new impulse to their Cold War policy.... The Communist Party of Belgium proclaims its solidarity with Afghan progressive forces [*sic*] which are struggling to free their country from underdevelopment and to ensure its stability in the context of full independence and national sovereignty..... It regrets that the Soviet Union has deemed it necessary to intervene in the internal affairs of the country up to the point of bringing into action an expeditionary corps.[6]

The formulae used were so tepid that they provoked internal polemics within the PCB. Step by step, however, the party began to show a more critical attitude towards the Soviet policy in Afghanistan, although it simultaneously refused to support any resistance movement.

Disapproval of the coup in Poland was more outright: 'the recourse to military power established in Poland on Sunday and the draconian measures it has taken are considered by the PCB as being incompatible with socialism in an advanced country. Consequently, the Political Bureau expresses its disapproval. It stresses the necessity of resuming urgently dialogue with *Solidarity* and the removal on both sides of all obstacles to such dialogue'.[7] The equivalence of 'both sides' provoked some internal discussions in the PCB, but the party's condemnation remained unequivocal.

In spite of slight differences, these three examples show that the positions adopted by the PCB have always involved the condemnation of repressive policies in the countries of Eastern Europe. However, 'regrets', 'disapproval' and 'condemnation' were never adopted as positions on more than just an occasional basis. In the course of debates over Soviet policy, the key concept which was repeatedly referred to was *'critical solidarity'.* Whether the first or second term of this expression carried greater weight depended on the partner in discussions. It should be added that such discussions, as well as the compromises reached, never fully penetrated the PCB rank and file, large parts of which remained blindly devoted to the USSR.

The analyses performed before Mikhail Gorbachev came to power implied that the USSR, in spite of all its duly denounced defects, was always seen by the party leadership and members as an indispensable counterweight to American imperialism. The PCB always refused to put both blocs on the same level, since they were regarded as being of a different nature. This kind of analysis left the persistent impression that, in spite of efforts to mark a distance, the PCB remained quite obliging towards Moscow. At any rate, positions taken on international relations were characterised by extreme caution, which made them look more and more like the diplomatic statements of a chancellery than the resolutions of a revolutionary party. Moreover, no thoroughgoing study was ever devoted to the nature of the socialist countries. The leadership preferred to avoid themes which could generate tensions inside the party.

Following the 1981 general elections, there could be no denying the crisis within the PCB. An open discussion began in the party newspaper, *Le Drapeau Rouge*, between what could be seen in somewhat schematic terms as two opposing tendencies. On the one hand, there were supporters of an *'ouvrièriste'* pro-Soviet line, in favour of Communist Party activity in factories. They were concerned primarily with issues of organisation and structure (democratic centralism, meetings of sections and cells, etc.), the functioning of the party as a whole and ways to improve it, and solidarity with the socialist countries. The Liège and Charleroi federations fell into this category. On the other hand, there were supporters of an autonomous policy towards Moscow being adopted, together with a new political practice oriented towards participation in the new social movements. Such an approach was favoured most clearly in Brussels and in the Flemish wing of the PCB.

Throughout the 1980s, the two opposing trends co-existed without either being able to establish a clear advantage. Even after the disappearance of the PCB from parliamentary life in 1985, and after the upheavals which occurred in the USSR that year and in Eastern Europe in 1989, the Belgian communists remained unable to escape the paralysing organisational logic within which they were caught. Only the theoretical review, *Cahiers Marxistes*, belatedly and rather timidly attempted to launch a debate. The Brussels federation and the Communist Youth also tried to move the party's positions towards greater critical independence from the socialist countries and sought a renovation in the PCB's political line. However, they were able to gain only minor concessions. Many militants seeking to reform the party from within were discouraged by the inertia of the leadership. Internal divergences consequently grew and intensified as it became more apparent that the Soviet bloc was suffering from severe sclerosis. It appeared by the mid-1980s that the PCB was in full social, political and electoral decline.

FROM GORBACHEV TO THE EVENTS OF 1989

The state of advanced decay in the PCB which preceded Gorbachev's coming to power explains to a large extent the party's silence and lack of reaction to the earthquake which *glasnost* and *perestroika* represented for the communist world. In fact, for the PCB it was already too late to expect any benefit from a 'Gorbachev effect' or to see, as occurred in other communist parties, an acceleration of transformations which had begun to take place.

The coming to power of Gorbachev hardly altered the course of events in the PCB. In spite of openly proclaimed support for the new secretary-general of the CPSU, and the 'justified' criticism of past errors, the PCB leadership felt no need to formulate any analysis which questioned its own past positions. Nevertheless, Soviet foreign policy became subject to such turnarounds that even those parties which had been 'critical' of the Brezhnev policy rapidly came to appear timid and even complacent when compared with the new positions being adopted by the CPSU. Once again in Communist Party history, major changes were initiated from Moscow.[8]

The Belgian leadership systematically expressed its satisfaction at the new Soviet initiatives and adopted them as its own, but without enacting any deep modifications in its political line or submitting its own past policies to critical examination. A complete silence was maintained on the numerous modifications entailed by the transformations in Soviet foreign policy.

Indeed, remaining silent was the main characteristic of the approach adopted by the Belgian communists during the events of 1989 The party carried on functioning 'normally'. This silence can be explained in the following terms. As has already been noted, the party's moribund state made it impossible to assemble a sufficiently large number of militants and diffuse the new slogans. Moreover, astonishment at the 1989 events was so great that it left many communists speechless. At the leadership level, to have underscored the revised analyses of the past would have necessitated a profound questioning of its own political actions and responsibilities – two practices which were rather unusual in the communist world. Many 'reformers' amongst the PCB membership were so disgusted at the leadership's 'conservatism' that they left the party.

At a moment when the entire basis of the communist world was being shaken and many leaders were being replaced, there was nobody in the PCB able to embody a credible leadership which might take up the torch. For all concerned, the easiest course of action consisted in carrying on as if nothing had happened. In November 1989, for instance, the PCB leadership decided to send an observer to the 14th Congress of the Romanian Communist Party, in spite of the contrary advice of a very strong minority. Its report contained no concessions:

The 14th Congress certainly has the right to adopt a triumphalist tone. However, we have no alternative but to record that in so doing it has been forced to sacrifice an essential aspect: its credibility. Indeed, how can we avoid being struck by the differences between the speeches which were given ... highly praising the merits of 'multilaterally developed socialism' and the trivial concrete reality experienced by the population which we can observe daily in shops and markets?[9]

Even when faced by the Ceaucescu regime, which was criticised privately by a number of leaders, the PCB leadership refused to break off relations with the Romanian Communist Party. For several years, the PCB president, Louis Van Geyt, refused to answer Ceaucescu's repeated invitations, but in the interests of diplomacy and in order not to create waves, the Political Bureau decided to send one observer. This most cautious diplomacy, which was often criticised within the party, was quite typical. Of course, these political gestures remained invisible to the outside world on account of the PCB's considerably reduced importance in Belgian politics.

After the fall of the Berlin Wall, the PCB held a Conference in March 1990 and a Congress in November of the same year. On neither occasion did it confront openly the changes taking place in the Soviet Union and the disappearance of the peoples' democracies. Surprisingly, the 1990 Congress resolution asserted that 'the critical and collective analysis of the history of real [*sic*] socialism and of our attitudes towards it will have to be pursued [*sic*] in the party organisation'.[10] Meanwhile, preparatory discussions for the March 1990 Conference revealed that the division between the two dominant trends in the party had been exacerbated and, for the first time, two different resolutions were presented to delegates. However, after two days of arduous discussions and negotiations, only one document was finally submitted to the Congress. This was another typical example of the famous *'compromis à la belge'*.

The content of the approved document was, to the say the least, rather fuzzy and it contained no specific commitments. In order not to displease anyone, it expressed as many grounds for satisfaction as for dissatisfaction. On the one hand, the document acknowledged that communist parties in their traditional form had ceased to exist and that their functioning – as classically defined by the principle of democratic centralism – had to be revised according to a new scheme of self-governing pluralism. On the other hand, however, the concrete implications of this analysis were never specified. The chapter on elections was similarly ambiguous, and left much room for interpretation: 'It is certainly essential to maintain a presence in the electoral field (through political campaigns, by depositing party lists, by means of cartels and more lasting alliances, or through other appropriate forms), but it is still more important to endeavour to help citizens and workers to take their destiny into their own hands'.[11]

Nevertheless, the March 1990 conference granted certain federations the right to pursue the establishment of 'Red/Green' fora. This initiative resulted from the efforts of Brussels militants to start a dialogue and, eventually, to conclude an electoral alliance with the ecology movement. However, the Green Party – faithful to its logic of 'neither left nor right' – refused any collaboration with a decaying party. Brussels communists decided, in response, to attempt to group together a range of militants involved in various associative movements, as well as individuals disappointed by traditional left-wing organisations. In spite of these efforts, though, the Red/Green Forum was unable to escape its own ghetto and failed to attract militants from new horizons. Instead, the Red/Green Forum appeared to be little more than a club for thinking and reflection.

Another original initiative entailed the transformation of the PCB daily newspaper, *Le Drapeau Rouge*. On 1 January 1991 it adopted the less overtly militant title of *Libertés*, intended to reflect the new pluralist approach of the left. However, the real extent of the change was open to doubt, since the editorial staff remained unchanged and the paper continued to be financed by the Communist Party and housed in their building. In fact, the experiment came to an end after just a few months. Faced with serious financial problems, the PCB decided to withdraw help for the new paper, even though it had begun to establish a basis of support which extended beyond the boundaries of the communist family. Subsequently, in December 1992, the PCB began to publish a new monthly review, *Avancées*, intended to open channels towards other progressive forces, but which failed to establish a readership of more than a thousand in the French-speaking part of the country. A new weekly, *Makrant*, was also launched in Dutch-speaking Belgium, but with a membership of no more than 150 the Flemish party had by then effectively ceased to exist.

In regard to the PCB's name, no debate ever really took place. In contrast to other communist parties (such as the Italian, British, Finnish and Swedish examples), and in spite of its being reduced to a very small group, the Belgian party decided to remain 'communist'. This decision was more than merely symbolic. The discrepancy between the manifest symptoms of an existential crisis within the PCB and the timidity of the choices it made, as well as the resolutions it adopted, offered a highly significant pointer to the likely future of the Belgian communists.

REACTIONS TO THE AUGUST 1991 COUP IN THE SOVIET UNION

The Belgian Communist Party reacted in two stages to the events which occurred in Moscow on 19 August 1991. The Bureau of the Union of Belgian Communists offered its initial response on 20 August, prior to the end of the attempted putsch, when it declared:

> The Belgian communists fully share the emotions and anxieties felt by all democratic and progressive opinion

.... It is not by putting recent freedoms and political pluralism into parenthesis, nor by restoring censorship, ...
that the new self-proclaimed leadership of the USSR will
solve the economic and social problems which *perestroika*
was unable to bring to an end.[12]

The lack of any explicit condemnation of the coup attempt
(which was never even described in such terms) was striking. In addition, the communiqué offered no support for
the restoration of Gorbachev to power. A second communiqué, dated 2 September, made explicit mention of the
'coup', and offered the judgement that

> through the implication of essential sectors of its appara-
> tus in the failed coup, the CPSU has ultimately demon-
> strated its inability to participate in the profound
> democratic changes which are desired by the Soviet
> Union's people.[13]

For the Belgian communists, the events of August 1991
carried numerous implications for left-wing political organisations. Primarily, the conditions under which progressive
forces would be able to develop their ideas and their strategies for action were profoundly modified, and future
progress would require a rapid and lucid response. The
shock caused by the attempted coup and by the indictment
of the CPSU induced at least the most open section of the
PCB, the Regional Bureau of the Brussels Federation, to
reflect on the party's past errors of analysis. The Brussels
Federation, which for years had been the most innovative
section of the PCB, issued a document which argued that
whereas numerous members believed that historical
'cousinship' with the international communist movement
was a burden, very few were really free of it. The document
set out four main errors of analysis committed 'even by the
most critical amongst us':

A. The surplus produced in eastern bloc countries has
been seized upon by the Nomenklatura.... We should

have discerned more clearly that it indeed constituted society's most dominant and exploitative pole.

B.   ... We have not understood concretely the real social
impact of dissidence, nor its links (even paradoxical
ones) with part of the Nomenklatura (technocratic,
modernist), nor the mass support enjoyed by a good
number of dissidents.

C.   By falling back on 'our' democratic way to socialism
we have either implicitly or explicitly considered that,
if democracy did not exist in eastern bloc countries,
then this was the result of their particular history,
which was different from ours. Except on a few
points, it was estimated that this [democratic way] was
neither a priority nor a necessity for an under-
developed country.

D.   ... We have not understood that the identification of
the party with the state has deprived the party of any
meaning and turned it into a caste of thrusters and
parvenus (if not mafiosi). What we must understand
today is that the dissolution of this state-gadget is the
necessary condition for the emergence of real
parties, of pluralism and of democracy ...[14]

Although this document expressed the sharpest criticism
ever formulated by Belgian communist leaders, it remained
isolated within the party and found little echo in the media.

FUTURE PERSPECTIVES

As far as elections are concerned, the PCB has continued its
long and slow agony. At the European elections of 1989, following a tight vote at the Brussels Congress, the Communist
Party decided not to present a list of candidates. In Brussels,
several leading PCB figures called on electors to vote for
Raymonde Dury, head of the Socialist list. In Wallonia,

Communists campaigned in favour of the Socialist candidate, José Happart, who represented the tough regionalist option. At the general elections of November 1991, most PCB federations decided not to put forward candidates. Only a few Walloon federations presented candidates in the districts of Mons, Charleroi, Soignies and Thuin. This amounted to what a preparatory document issued by the party called a 'strategy with variable geometry'. In reality, however, such a designation represented an attempt to conceal the profound divisions of opinion which still existed in the heart of the PCB over its future. Moreover, the same document admitted that 'another central question is whether at the present stage of our reflections we are together able to elaborate ... programmatic statements'.[15]

The few lists of candidates which were presented at the elections obtained results which varied between 1 and 1.5 per cent of the vote. In the entire French-speaking part of the country, the PCB obtained 5713 votes, a figure which is difficult to compare meaningfully with the 51,046 votes obtained in 1987 because of the very small number of lists presented.

Thus, it appears that with the disappearance of the USSR and also of its financial support, the PCB had reached a state of clinical death. Nothing appeared able to save it from disappearing completely. The little real estate which remained as part of its patrimony was likely to enable it to fulfil its social obligations towards its last remunerated permanent officials. However, without any short-term or long-term objectives, deprived of financial support, and emptied of all substance, the French-speaking wing of the PCB seemed to lack even the power to dissolve itself and sponsor the birth of an alternative political movement. Indeed, it is difficult to see what new arguments could have induced the last remaining die-hards to bring their struggle to an end, which implied that the PCB's death agony could be protracted.

On the other hand, the Brussels Federation did attempt – albeit without much success – to open itself to ecologists and other associative movements. Its Regional Bureau expressed the opinion that it should transform itself 'into something like a political foundation which, without any sense of shame, assumes its political references and first and foremost uses all available means to support projects aimed at reconstructing a force and a movement which carried ideals which were scoffed at, but which were and remain ours'.[16]

By early 1993, the PCB encountered difficulties in even organising a party conference. The preparation of the May 1993 Conference in Brussels, the first to be held since November 1990, was severely hindered by the party's effective collapse: some federations were not prepared to participate in what amounted to little more than a simulacrum. However, the conference did take place. Remarkably, in a short introductory report, three of its four pages were devoted to analysing the crisis of capitalism.[17] The conference concluded by calling for continued 'critical analysis' and consolidation of the party, in line with the direction established at the 1990 Conference (see Table 5.5).

Only the Brussels Federation sent a resolution calling for the Communist Party to be dissolved and proposing the foundation of a new, more loosely organised, structure. The idea behind the new structure would be to help participate in the reconstruction of the left in Belgium by fostering a

Table 5.5   Members of the Political Bureau, 1993

Pierre Beauvois (Centre), President. 48-year-old civil engineer.
Michel Godard (Brussels), 46-year old civil servant and director of the theoretical review *Les cahiers marxistes*.
Robert Houtain (Ourthe Amblève), 53-year-old teacher.
Pierre Lisens (Liège), 44-year-old technician.
Maurige Magis (Charleroi), 44-year-old director of the monthly review *Avancées*.
Jules Pirlot (Liège), 44-year-old teacher.
Jean-Claude Raillon (Charleroi), 48-year-old teacher.
Jean-Marie Simon (Borinage), 46-year-old professional.

Table 5.6   Parties of the left

In addition to the Communist Party, there are two other parties of the left in Belgium:

Parti ouvrier socialiste (Socialist Workers' Party, POS-SAP), a Trotskyist party which is a member of the Fourth International. Publishes a bi-monthly review, *La gauche.*

Parti du travail de Belgique (Belgian Labour Party, PTB-PvdA), a Maoist party. Publishes a weekly review, *Solidaire.*

---

new political culture, creating new networks, and developing and renewing Marxist analysis through *Les cahiers marxistes,* a theoretical review which had been closed to the PCB in the past.[18]

Meanwhile, pitched into a profound debate about the very future of their party, the Flemish communists appeared torn between straightforward dissolution and a 'transformation into an open political organisation with a Marxist imprint which, together with other progressive forces, will seek to elaborate an alternative policy and red-green movement' (see Table 5.6).[19]

CONCLUSIONS

It is obvious, after examining its electoral results and data on its internal functioning, that the PCB has been in deep crisis since the early 1980s. From its foundation, the PCB sought to articulate its action around certain poles of influence in Belgian society – notably, the great Walloon bastions of heavy industry which lay at the heart of Belgium's industrial growth and development. Since 1945, these political and trade union fiefdoms of the labour movement – mainly located in the regions of Hainaut and

Liège – have been in a slow decline which accelerated from the mid-1970s onwards until by the early 1990s they had almost disappeared.

The Communist Party sought to establish its influence in these sectors through both political and trade union activity. Faced by the accelerated decline of these traditional industrial sectors, the PCB was unable to provide any solution: the social basis upon which its influence was based effectively collapsed. The sharp fall in the party's membership (over 50 per cent in 15 years) reflects two key factors: the occupational background of its militants was strongly linked to the traditional blue-collar working class, with little penetration of the emerging professional classes, and the party's age profile was sharply skewed towards older members. The PCB's failure to make inroads into emerging social classes and its absence from new fields of political struggle was patently obvious.

However, these external factors are insufficient on their own to explain the parlous state of the PCB in the early 1990s. The party's consensual practice in internal as well as international politics led it into a state of permanent caution in regard to its political orientations. Balanced between a more *'ouvrièriste'* and pro-Soviet trend and a younger, more 'intellectual' current, the PCB refused to commit itself to the stances of either group. Neither the 1989 revolutions nor the events of August 1991 challenged the logic of this position. On the contrary, the PCB refused to initiate a genuine debate on the social and political nature of these events or on its own position in response to them. This new failure to respond to events represented perhaps the party's final opportunity, although by the time the 1989 events took place it was probably already too late to rescue the PCB. The absence of any reaction to the upheavals in Eastern Europe, together with a lack of renewal of its membership, led it down the road of slow disintegration, which took place in an atmosphere of complete indifference. By the early 1990s, virtually no one in Belgium knew or cared about the Communist Party.

NOTES

1. *Statuts du parti communiste de Belgique*, text adopted by the second session of the 24th Congress of the PCB, Brussels, 18 December 1982, p. 15.
2. The case of Brussels poses problems not just in regard to the PCB, but for the whole of Belgium. Brussels is the only bi-communal region in Belgium, and in consequence presents a difficult problem for a party which seeks to maintain a national leadership. To simplify matters, it should be remembered that the Brussels Federation intervenes simultaneously as a French-speaking component in the French-speaking federal organs, as a Dutch-speaking component in the Flemish federal organs, and as a region in its own right on all questions referring to the regions and regionalisation.
3. It should be stressed that these more favourable results often took place as a consequence of electoral alliances which were sometimes of a surprising nature. In Quaregnon in 1988 an alliance was set up between the PCB, the Liberal Party, and the Christian Democrats with the intention of overthrowing the Socialists' absolute majority.
4. 'Lettre ouverte du parti communiste de Belgique aux partis communistes URSS, de Bulgarie, de Hongrie, de Pologne, et de RDA', *Le Drapeau Rouge*, 23 August 1968.
5. Marcel Levaux, 'D'un mal peut sortir un bien?', *Le Drapeau Rouge*, 30 August 1968.
6. 'Communiqué de bureau politique', *Le Drapeau Rouge*, 8 January 1980.
7. 'Pologne: nette désapprobation du parti communiste de Belgique', *Le Drapeau Rouge*, 18 December 1981.
8. See José Gotovitch, Pascal Delwit and Jean-Michel De Waele, *L'Europe des communistes* (Brussels: Éditions Complexe, 1992).
9. Hubert Cambier, 'Souveraine... la Roumanie choisit l'isolement', *Le Drapeau Rouge*, 28 November 1989.
10. 'Quatrième Congrès du parti communiste, Montignies sur Sambre, 3–4 Novembre 1990', *Faits et arguments*, 95 (December 1990), p. 7.
11. Ibid., p. 2.
12. *Avancées démocratiques* (Communist Party bi-monthly periodical), no. 98 (September 1991), p. 15.
13. Ibid., p. 16.
14. PCB document, November 1991, pp. 2–3.
15. *Questions pour la campagne électorale*, Brussels, 8 July 1991.
16. Ibid., p. 3.
17. 'Note introductive', *Conférence francophone du 15 mai 1993 du parti communiste* (Brussels, 1993).
18. *Communication de la régionale de Bruxelles du PCB à la Conférence du 15 mai 1993* (Brussels, 1993).
19. Ibid., p. 4.

6 The British Road is Resurfaced for New Times: From the British Communist Party to the Democratic Left[1]

Nina Fishman

INTRODUCTION

The 41st Congress of the Britsh Communist Party (CPGB) was held at the end of November 1989 in the midst of the revolutions in Eastern Europe. The Congress proved to be fundamental to the party's political future. The party's very identity was subject to a major reappraisal, and the Congress led to the election of a new leader, Nina Temple, who subsequently transformed the CPGB into a non-communist party of the left, the Democratic Left (DL).

This chapter charts this transformation and attempts to explain its historical causes. It does so in the knowledge that there has been a tendency in the media to assume that the transformation of the CPGB into a non-communist party of the left can simply be put down to a knee-jerk reaction to the revolutions in Eastern Europe. This rather superficial conclusion is a product both of the party's perceived insignificance in British politics (the CPGB produced a mere two MPs who both lost their seats in 1950[2] and had only 50,000 members at its zenith in 1942–3) and, more importantly, of the lack of sustained academic analysis of the party (compared, say, with the French and Italian communist parties).[3] The domestic history of the party is far more

Table 6.1 Performance of British Communist Party candidates in general elections, 1945–1987

	No. of candidates	MPs elected	Deposits saved	Total vote	Average vote	Average % vote	Average % vote less exceptional results
1945	21	2	9	102,780	4,664	15.1	10.1
1950	100	–	3	91,765	917	2.0	1.6
1951	10	–	–	21,640	2,164	4.7	3.0
1955	17	–	2	33,144	1,950	4.9	3.5
1959	18	–	1	30,896	1,716	4.3	3.2
1964	36	–	–	46,442	1,290	3.5	3.0
1966	57	–	–	62,092	1,089	3.0	2.8
1970	58	–	–	37,970	655	1.8	1.7
1974 (Feb)	44	–	1	32,743	744	1.8	1.5
1974 (Oct)	29	–	–	17,426	601	1.6	1.4
1979	38	–	–	16,858			
1983	35	–	–	11,598			
1987	19	–	–	6,078			

Notes: British parliamentary elections are conducted under the 'first-past-the-post' system: in each constituency, the winning candidate is the one who receives the greatest number of votes. Each candidate who stands is required to pay a small deposit (£150 between 1945 and 1974) to the returning officer. The deposit is saved and returned to the candidate if he or she polls over one eighth (12.5%) of the vote in the constituency.

Exceptionally high votes were gained by Communists in West Fife, Rhondda East and Mile End/Stepney between 1945 and 1970 and in Dunbartonshire Central in the two 1974 elections. In 1945, Harry Pollitt missed winning in Rhondda East by a thousand votes.

Sources: For 1945–1974, Colin Ravden, 'Parliamentary Elections and the British Communist Party, a Historical Analysis 1920–1978', duplicated paper, London, June 1978. For 1979–87: Executive Committee Reports of CPGB to Party Congresses.

complex than such a conclusion permits. In particular, it overlooks the internal struggles which led to the party's 41st Congress. This chapter, after briefly outlining the CPGB's history between 1956 and the late 1970s, looks at the bitter conflict of the 1980s inside the party, and then at the effects of this conflict on the party in the late 1980s in terms of its eventual transformation.

THE CPGB: FROM 1956 TO THE LATE 1970s

The CPGB was traditionally characterised by 'revolutionary pragmatism', a product of the belief of the formative leaders (Harry Pollitt and Johnny Campbell) in the Communist International, and, at the same time, their successful anchoring of the party inside the trade union movement.[4] Revolutionary pragmatism incorporated a profound utopian faith in the inevitability of revolution. The belief that 'life itself' would bring about a revolutionary situation was a powerful factor in motivating the party's trade union activists, and ensured that largely thankless tasks (such as attending union meetings, recruiting union members and gaining routine concessions from management) were undertaken. Even if the utopianism and realism at the heart of revolutionary pragmatism were contradictory, there were few situations where they were patently exposed to be so, and activists regarded themselves as not guilty of reformism. This position became increasingly difficult for them to sustain as the party declined (see Table 6.1).

There is some dispute over exactly when the CPGB's decline began; but certainly, by 1956, when the party condoned the Soviet Union's action in defeating the Hungarian revolution, membership was contracting (see Table 6.2). The shrinkage sometimes proceeded at a slower pace, and there were even periods of considerable increase achieved by serious industrial and student recruiting (the

*Table 6.2   Membership of the Communist Party of Great Britain,
1945–91*

1945	(March)	45,435
1946	(April)	42,123
1947	(June)	38,759
1948	(April)	43,000
1950	(May)	38,853
1952	(March)	35,124
1953	(March)	35,054
1954	(April)	33,963
1955	(March)	32,681
1956	(February)	33,095
1957	(February)	26,742
1958	(February)	24,670
1959		25,313
1960		26,052
1961		27,541
1962	(May)	32,492
1963		33,008
1964	(February)	34,281
1965	(February)	33,734
1966	(February)	33,243
1967	(February)	32,916
1968	(June)	30,607
1969	(June)	28,803
1971	(June)	28,803
1973	(June)	29,943
1975	(June)	28,519
1977	(June)	25,293
1979	(June)	20,599
1981	(June)	18,458
1983	(June)	15,691
1985	(November)	12,711
1987	(July)	10,350
1988	(September)	8,546
1989	(June)	7,615

Table 6.2   continued

1991	(June)	4,742
1993	(June) (Democratic Left)	1,234

Sources: 1945–65: Kenneth Newton, *The Sociology of British Communism* (London: Allen Lane, 1969), p. 160; 1965–91: Reports of the CPGB Executive Committee to Party Congresses.

party had a beneficial fall-out from the political developments of the 1960s, including the Vietnam War and the May events of 1968). But the decline always resumed its apparently irresistible course.

The 1970s promised, for many in the party, something different as the eurocommunist movement swept through many West European Communist Parties. The CPGB did not remain unaffected. Indeed, *The British Road to Socialism* was revised in 1977 during the Callaghan Labour government when the general assumption was that corporatism and a strong trade union movement were permanent fixtures of British politics. The 35th Congress, which approved the 1977 *British Road,* represented the high point of the eurocommunist offensive inside the British party led by the young 'progressive' group who had been blooded both intellectually and politically in 1968. Martin Jacques, Jon Bloomfield, Dave Cook, Pat Devine and others persuaded Gordon McLennan, the party's untried and impressionable general-secretary, to pressurise his *apparat* and congress delegates to accept changes which were inspired by their Gramscian, creative Marxist perspective. But the Euro-*Road* did not set Britain alight. The youthful promise and unbounded ambition of the 'progressives' to make revolution in Britain were not fulfilled. Moreover, their attempt alienated the party's 'old guard' and laid the foundations for the party's most bitter conflict in the 1980s and for the exodus of a significant sector of the party. The nature, course and outcome of this conflict is fundamental to understanding the party's destiny in the late 1980s.

THE PARTY'S 'STAR WARS': THE 1980s

The conflict arose when, in the early 1980s, a 'conservative' group inside the *apparat* began to organise against the growing number of eurocommunists being appointed to full-time positions by the Executive. They objected to the new Euro-crat *apparat's* apparent willingness to reject party orthodoxy as laid down by the leaders of the heroic past, notably Harry Pollitt. The 'conservative' reaction was initially against new attitudes towards British domestic politics; but during the protracted bloodletting, each side's attitude to the Soviet Union and Eastern Europe became an important issue.

The 'conservative' opposition was mounted from the secure enclave of the management committee of the party's daily newspaper, the *Morning Star*. The *Star's* editor and deputy editor, Tony Chater and Dave Whitfield, pursued their 'progressive' quarry by factionalising in blatant disregard of perhaps the most sacred Marxist–Leninist canon of party organisation. The rich irony of defenders of the Stalinist faith committing mortal sins against it was lost on most observers, with the exception of avid spectators from Trotskyist sects who were initiates in the bolshevik catechism.

The *Star* camp's *casus belli* was an article which appeared in the September 1982 issue of *Marxism Today* written by Tony Lane, a party member lecturing at Liverpool Polytechnic whose father was a party industrial activist. Lane made some accurate comments about many shop stewards' low level of commitment and systematic abuses of union privileges. The *Morning Star* responded with a front-page headline denouncing Lane's article. The party's industrial organiser, Mick Costello, condemned it as a ' "cynical" and a gross slander on the labour movement'. He accused *Marxism Today* of forgetting that 'The shop stewards movement ... deserves only the wholesale backing of every progressive, in the spirit of repeated Communist Party Congress resolutions.'[5]

Because Chater and Costello had acted without making any reference to the party's Political Committee, the party Executive immediately censured them and Dave Whitfield for a serious breach of democratic centralism. But the Executive also concurred with most of the substance of Costello's attack. Jacques accepted the Executive's 'strong criticisms' and agreed 'that there should have been wider consultation before the article was published'.[6] Chater, Costello and Whitfield acquiesced in the Executive's censure, but escalated their public attacks on *Marxism Today* for betraying the party's proletarian legacy. Jacques and allies responded by protesting their own trade-union loyalism.

The *Star* camp had chosen its terrain well. The party's relationship to trade unions and to the shop steward movement in particular was shrouded in copious layers of official mythology originating from the early 1930s. The 'progressive' part of the *apparat* was initially caught off its guard by the incestuous challenge. It responded by reatreating. Jacques's continuing tenure as *Marxism Today*'s editor depended upon the support of McLennan and of the veteran former assistant general-secretary, George Matthews, and he evidently decided that these two would prefer him to yield political ground for the sake of maintaining the mythology untarnished and intact. Jacques and his eurocommunist colleagues declined to counter-attack by examining the heart of Chater's and Costello's argument, the need for British Communists' unconditional allegiance to the shop steward movement.

The struggle between the *Star* and *Marxism Today* continued for nearly three years, encompassing the 1984–5 miners' strike during which the two camps vied with each other to see which would exhibit the greater solidarity and mobilise the most support for the National Union of Mineworkers (NUM). Although *Marxism Today* had its differences with Arthur Scargill, leader of the NUM, they were expressed in muted tones and aesopian style, reminiscent of the Comintern's coded rhetoric. Jacques and the *Marxism Today* group followed a conciliatory strategy towards the *apparat*. Jacques took care above all to appease McLennan, for whom keeping up appearances was more important than the risky and uncertain business of facing political issues head on. Nevertheless, the *Star* 'conservatives' proved implacable. They were apparently bent on rooting out the *Marxism Today*/'Euro' element inside the party at all costs. McLennan belatedly and reluctantly accepted that his friend and comrade Chater had determined on rebellion and pledged himself to bring him and his confederates to book for their transgressions against democratic centralism.

The *Star* camp took advantage of the party's network of Soviet contacts to spread the message that the CPGB leadership had abandoned all pretence of being Marxist–Leninist. Their appeal for help was fruitful both morally and financially. The *Star* published a signed article from Victor Popov, the Soviet ambassador to the UK, celebrating the 60th anniversary of diplomatic relations between Britain and the USSR. The article was a clear sign of Moscow's approval of the *Star*'s stand against *Marxism Today*.[7] In Alex Mitchell's words,

> ...it became apparent that the *Morning Star* was brushing aside all restraint and becoming a more open mouthpiece of the Soviet bureaucracy and the Stalinist regimes of Eastern Europe.[8]

McLennan finally presided over the executive's expulsion of the *Star*'s editor, Tony Chater, assistant editor, Dave Whitfield, and leading members of the London District party in January 1985, and these were duly upheld at the 39th Special Congress of the CPGB in May 1985. When the Special Congress supported McLennan, there was intense jubilation and relief from the 'progressive' camp. The outcome had been genuinely hanging in the balance. However, the party *apparat* was unable to salvage the *Morning Star*, and the CPGB was without a daily paper for the first time since 1930. Most of the *Star*'s staff followed their expelled editor out of the party, along with many members of London district, the *Star*'s new printing press and its headquarters on a prime London site.[9]

THE *APPARAT*'S PYRRHIC VICTORY

The victory scored by McLennan and his youthful allies at the 39th Congress was indeed pyrrhic. They had won the battle without deploying substantive politics. The absence of serious and coherent political explanations from them meant that the large numbers of ordinary members who did not succumb to the *Star*'s emotional appeals and simplistic description of the conflict were flummoxed. They found the raging battle without meaning both distressing and perplexing. Accustomed to the British communist political culture of strong cohesion, they were further disorientated by fractious political conflict in their midst.

The decline in party membership accelerated (see Table 6.2). Some veteran members simply drifted out of the party by not renewing their party cards. Others seceded to join the *Star* stalwarts to form a new grouplet, the British Communist Party (as opposed to the tarnished Communist Party of Great Britain) in the autumn of 1985. By November 1985 the party's membership had fallen by over 5000 to 12,711. The rump of party members who remained were weary and confused. McLennan was also tired and spent after his formal triumph. There was a flurry of speculation and intense internal politicking amongst the victorious 'progressive' camp about possible successors to the general-secretaryship. McLennan would probably have been relieved to step down and hand over to someone who knew where they wanted to take the party. He had long admired Jacques and would probably have welcomed a bid from him.

In the event, none of the younger cohort made a decisive move. The *Marxism Today* group settled down into a routine but uneasy existence inside the party *apparat*. Their lassitude was matched by the party veterans, who had found it difficult to work up the energy and emotion required to expel people who had been old comrades and were saying many of the same things which they themselves had repeated for years. Like McLennan, their overwhelming emotion was fatigue, not renewed inspiration. They faced an unsettling situation in which they were no longer certain of their party's underlying political and intellectual rationale.

The *Marxism Today* group had more reason than their elders for feeling real triumph. From the inspiring formative moments of the May events in France and the Prague Spring in 1968, Jacques and his cohort of student intellectuals had committed themselves to pursuing an ambitious and revolutionary eurocommunist project inside the party in order that they could fashion a creative Marxist weapon with which to make a real revolution in Britain. They had apparently won the party to their side and should have been celebrating their triumph as the first stage towards the transformation of British society.

It is problematic, but important, to analyse the reasons for the *Marxism Today* group's demoralisation and ultimate fracture into a multitude of often conflicting approaches to politics and the real world. The most convincing explanation for the failure of the *Marxism Today* group to take advantage of their favourable opportunity in 1985 is that they had lost interest in the Marxist–Leninist project long before then. When the *Star* attacked, they had relied on a technical defence because they were outside the boundaries of even creative Marxism. They had fought because they had been challenged. They were actually uninterested in and practically indifferent to the *substance* of Costello's attack on Tony Lane.

In fact, the Eurocommunists' project forged in the white heat of 1968 and carried through with such determination up to 1977 had foundered soon after on the rocks of the

CPGB's deep-seated conservatism and centrist reflexes. In 1979 their proposals for democratising the party were rejected by the Executive and then the Party Congress. Subsequently they gained power and wielded influence inside the party; politically they were merely marking time. Their victory over the *Star* provided a fresh opportunity to transform the party. But they had lost sight of the reasons why they had joined the party in the first place and many now left, having recognised that their membership lacked any political purpose. They had ceased to think in Marxist–Leninist terms and were no longer sustained by revolutionary idealism.

The 'progressives' who remained inside the party certainly enjoyed greater freedom of action. Martin Jacques ceased to take any interest in the party and concentrated single-mindedly on making *Marxism Today* a force to be reckoned with inside mainstream British political culture. It became a rare event for *Marxism Today* to publish articles by party members or even 'fellow travellers'. Most of *Marxism Today*'s staff remained party members only in order to keep up appearances.[10] Jacques had vacated the hermetic realm of the international communist movement and retreated steadily through the dense native undergrowth of Anglo-Marxist/labour-movement culture. His gaze was directed resolutely outwards towards the wider arena of 'bourgeois' politics and post-modern culture.

But Jacques at least was reinvigorated. Under his revitalised editorship, *Marxism Today* attracted lavish praise from politicians of all hues, and communist party gatherings recorded its progress with unctuous satisfaction. To be accorded the status of a *Marxism Today* interview became a coveted cachet for more thoughtful Tory cabinet ministers and Labour frontbench spokespeople.[11] *Marxism Today*'s monthly appearance became an exciting event for intellectual political circles and those people inside trade unions who were trying to think their way out of their depressing situation. McLennan regularly remarked that the party would be nowhere without *Marxism Today*. Whenever he attended labour-movement functions, full-time union officials sang the praises of the thought-provoking material Jacques was publishing.

The effect of *Marxism Today* upon the left was interesting. It acted as a counter-irritant to divert the minds of tired left-wing intellectuals from their own failures. They found themselves experiencing a vicarious excitement at *Marxism Today's* analysis of Margaret Thatcher's crusading instinct and her inclination to attack vested interests. Ageing *enfants terribles* of the May events shared the resentment against the system nursed by their opposite numbers in right-wing think tanks. A perceptible fellow feeling developed as these comparatively mild British 'extremists' from the left and right felt a momentum for change building up at long last inside British politics. They each nursed principled griev-ances against the political establishment, including the cor-porate leadership of the trade union movement and the status quo over which it presided, and were elated at the prospect of being able to settle scores.

Many party members, including McLennan, remained ha-bitually uncertain of the political implications of *Marxism Today's* monthly message. Their bewilderment reflected the fact that the magazine had moved so far away from the tra-ditional terrain of British communism. There had always been a discrete but definite separation inside the British party between the intellectuals and the rank and file. But the intellectuals had operated within the discourse of Anglo-Marxist humanism, a rhetoric with which any inter-ested party members could acquaint themselves and even become conversant.

Though the eurocommunists had embraced feminism, gay liberation and black liberation and criticised the ossification of Marxism–Leninism, they had never attacked the traditional communist rhetoric with the intent of dis-placing it. The CPGB had always provided a spiritual um-brella for a surprisingly wide variety of utopian-minded individuals and movements, perhaps appropriately enough for a party whose founding members had included serious members of the Socialist Temperance Association. After 1985 *Marxism Today* abandoned the last vestiges of the party's intellectual and ideological edifice, that particular strain of Anglo-Marxist humanism so well cultivated by previous generations of party intellectuals. The magazine also left behind the new revolutionary discourses of the 1960s with which Jacques had emblazoned its columns upon his appointment as editor in 1977.

THE BIFURCATED PARTY

The divergence between the magazine and the party whose flagship it was supposed to be and upon which it relied financially can be gauged from the fact that *Marxism Today*'s circulation increased whilst the party's membership continued to decline.[12] There was an ominous haemorrhage of members after the 39th Congress in 1985. The rump who remained did so out of reflexive loyalty to the old party of Harry Pollitt. McLennan understood this older cohort because he was one of them and he had no wish to sully their vintage vision of a socialist society which Pollitt had so successfully propagated. Nevertheless, McLennan also continued to be strongly attracted by the pull of *Marxism Today*'s prestige and Jacques's ability to dazzle listeners with *Marxism Today*'s new rhetoric. There was nothing inside the party which could match *Marxism Today*'s energy, notoriety and boundless self-confidence: by the late 1980s Jacques had become McLennan's trusted and reassuring political mentor, and it was an initiative proposed by Jacques which was to deepen the party's internal divisions.

In March 1988, the party Executive, on Jacques's advice, appointed a group of eight party members with a 'completely free hand, [to work] on a discussion document as a preliminary to the actual redrafting of *The British Road to Socialism* next year'.[13] The composition of the group was mixed. Some were at the centre of the *Marxism Today* circle, including Beatrix Campbell and Charlie Leadbeater; there were other 'progressives' who remained true to the eurocommunist perspective and still other loyal members of the *apparat.* Jacques led the group with characteristic energy and flair and involved non-party intimates of *Marxism Today*, notably Stuart Hall and Robin Murray. After an intensive round of weekend seminars and meetings, a discussion document appeared as a supplement to the September 1988 issue of *Marxism Today*, largely written by Charlie Leadbeater, entitled 'Facing Up to the Future'. It 'received wide press and media coverage and great interest in the progressive movement'.[14]

To the surprise and dismay of most of the membership and the Executive, 'Facing Up to the Future' turned out to be an explicit rejection of the main corpus of the party's Marxist–Leninist past, including the 1977 Euro-*British Road*. Observant party veterans distrusted it for the same reasons that *Marxism Today*'s new loyal following heralded it. The document jettisoned the whole of their party's glorious traditions and previous orientation. It is hardly surprising that three members of the drafting group, Marian Darke, Monty Johnstone and Bill Innes, publicly dissociated themselves from it:

> we are critical of the document's failure to recognise the centrality of the class struggle in capitalist Britain today. ... Moreover, the democratic, pluralistic and self-managing socialism, for which we need to win conviction as a viable and desirable alternative to capitalism, is only treated in two brief paragraphs.[15]

Viewed in the context of the 'Star wars' and their pyrrhic aftermath, the public split which emerged within the drafting group of 'Facing Up to the Future' in October 1988 was wholly predictable. The CPGB had become a bifurcated institution. The three dissenters in the drafting group came from the fork of the traditional branch and district structure with its vastly depleted but loyal membership. Whilst many remained loyal they were also passive and demoralised. Those who were still functioning concentrated, as always, on campaigning, being active in their respective communities and upholding the burning current issues of world importance – peace, anti-imperialism, solidarity with Nicaragua, the European Campaign for Nuclear Disarmament, and so on.

The second fork was *Marxism Today*, whose *soi disants* had carved out their own niche inside the party and were interested in issues which appeared novel and often alien to the 'real party'. They were numerically much smaller than the rump of loyal members, but 'Facing Up to the Future' gave them a fresh sense of purpose, a political project inside the party which they had not possessed since 1979. Members whose first loyalty was to the party in its post-1977 Euro-incarnation, but who also regarded themselves as serious Marxist intellectuals, valiantly attempted to straddle both forks. These Euro-straddlers felt they owed an allegiance to *Marxism Today* even though its content had become irrelevant to their mundane political lives, which consisted of attending their party branch and campaigning. They felt the positive attraction of 'Facing Up to the Future', but were unable to connect its content to the other part of their political existence.

Ignoring the obvious disquiet inside the 'real party', McLennan induced the party Executive to appoint a commission of thirteen party members to produce a programme along the lines of 'Facing Up to the Future', even though this was a radical departure from the 40th Congress's decision merely to revise the *British Road*. He evidently decided that he had no alternative but to follow Jacques wherever he might lead the party. It was McLennan's intellectual and political dependence upon the *Marxism Today* fork of the party which determined the course of events up to and including the 41st Congress in November 1989.

The commission included Jacques, Leadbeater, Rodrigues, and Campbell and Marian Darke from the initial drafting group. However, care was taken to include a cross-section of members representing the *apparat* and the various different shades of politics beginning to emerge from this fractured party. They delivered their report at the end of March 1989, and it was issued as the *Manifesto for New Times*. In June

1989 *Marxism Today* published a bound-on 'New Times Supplement' featuring a marginally different version.

Whilst the commission worked on their report, the *Marxism Today* fork experienced a fresh resurgence of interest in the party which they had mostly abandoned to its own devices. Now, it seemed that this party was about to set out on a new, exciting and seriously revolutionary trajectory. Their mounting anticipation was satisfied when the *Manifesto for New Times* explicitly cut the umbilical cord with Marxism–Leninism. Acknowledging that the Russian Revolution in October 1917 had 'usher[ed] ... in a historic phase in world development', the *Manifesto* nevertheless declared that,

> the revolution also bequeathed a tarnished socialism, in which the individual and civil society were subordinated to the state and the party ... regimes [which] sought to justify their authoritarian and repressive nature by developing rigid and dogmatic ideology which borrowed the language of Marxism, while distorting its essence.[16]

The *Manifesto* re-dedicated the party to pursue utopian revolutionary aims which were situated primarily on the terrains of greening, sexuality and ethnicity rather than class. The central pledge to combat poverty appeared within the context of empowerment for all the world's people. The industrial proletariat did not have a unique role in either making the revolution or enjoying its fruits. The potential for feminising society was assigned an equal, if not greater, weight in the struggle to make the revolution.

AUTUMN 1989: THE BEGINNING OF THE END

The feeling that the British party was approaching a crossroads was palpable throughout the autumn of 1989. Within a bifurcated party the impact of the unexpected revolutions in Eastern Europe was predictably split. The rump of loyal members were disorientated and shocked by the spectacle of 'the people' rising up in revolt against 'people's democracies'. For *Marxism Today* supporters and the Euro-straddlers the revolutions provided a potent injection of fervent and febrile enthusiasm. The *Manifesto*'s vision of an approaching new revolutionary epoch seemed suddenly to be vindicated and in the most fitting of places, the heartland of the old Marxist–Leninist orthodoxy.

The *Manifesto* was circulated to the membership in good time, sixteen weeks before the 41st Party Congress at the end of November 1989. But it was hardly read by the rank and file. Members were deterred by both its excessive length and its radical substance. The Euro-straddlers read it, but its content failed to dispel their fears roused by 'Facing Up to the Future'. The *Manifesto* undermined the very fabric of branch and district life which they had been earnestly Euro-ising. It eschewed their beacons and signposts, and their cherished aspirations for a creative Marxist party had somehow been forgotten along the way.

The most political veterans pragmatically laid aside their principled objection that the *Manifesto* was not a revision of the *British Road*. They recognised that the Executive had no intention of withdrawing it and there was insufficient independent spirit inside the party rump to force them to do so. They concentrated on organising amendments to dilute the *Manifesto's* post-modern heterodox content and restore their 'real party' traditions. There was a flurry of activity inside the core of highly political party members as they busily formulated amendments for their branches and districts to submit to the 41st Congress. The most significant aimed to reinstate the corpus of Marxism–Leninism, restating the catechism that the prospects for revolution and socialism depended upon the Communist Party and the working class. The veterans looked to McLennan to assert himself on behalf of the 'real party'. In addition to their internal politicking, they organised public pressure on him to defend Pollitt's legacy.[17]

The 41st British Party Congress was held from 25 to 28 November, over the same weekend that Alexander Dubcek first reappeared in public in Prague. Dubcek received a tumultuous reception from an enormous crowd of enthusiastic people in Wenceslas Square, who braved the extreme cold to hear him. These Czech events infused *Marxism Today* supporters and the Euro-straddlers at the British Congress with a huge draught of adrenalin. Dubcek and the Prague Spring of 1968 had been particularly important in their political formation. They were profoundly moved by this fresh sign of the times reverberating so strongly with their youthful past. Every news report over that weekend provided a potent stimulant to alter their mood. The emergency resolution adopted by Congress on Eastern Europe reflected their euphoric high. It could be accurately described as radical Gorbachevist:

> Congress welcomes the process of reform and democratisation in the European socialist countries. The changes in Eastern Europe have come about through mass demonstrations in which people have pressed for an end to one party rule, economic reform, respect for human rights, democracy. ... Socialism must mean the fullest expansion of an active participatory democracy.[18]

Everyone at the British Congress was a Gorbachev supporter. There were only differences of degree and gradation about what his changes meant for the Soviet party's practice. Veterans still believed stout-heartedly that the USSR was socialist and preferable to capitalist states. Even Jacques had been prepared to concede that 'Lenin was a brilliant pragmatist, seeking to make and defend a revolution under the most difficult conditions.'[19]

The *Manifesto* praised Gorbachev's *perestroika* for taking the 'creative risks' necessary for 'radical renewal'. 'It is creating the first opportunity in a generation for communists and socialists across the world to talk the same language, to heal the disastrous rifts and estrangements caused by Stalinism, the cold war and later the period of stagnation under Brezhnev.'[20] The principal amendments to this section came from a centrist Gorbachevist position. They harked back to the post-1956 perspective of the British leadership which was broadly committed to the socialist Soviet Union and its revolutionary tradition, but which had been nuanced, expediently hedged and even openly critical at times, such as when the Soviet tanks had rolled into Prague in 1968. Thus the amendment from the Surrey District Committee condemned 'the criminal excesses of the Stalin period' whilst intoning the homily that the socialist revolutions were 'events of world-historic importance of a fundamentally democratic and progressive nature'.[21]

In another radical departure from communist tradition, it was not McLennan but Jacques who gave the political report to Congress.[22] He was unrepentantly triumphant in introducing the *Manifesto for New Times* as a break with Communist/Marxist pasts:

> The British Road to Socialism was conceived in the era of the politics of the social-democratic consensus, of Fordism and its culture. ... But the truth is that the changes of the last decade lie like the San Andreas fault between us and those times. That old world in many senses is dead or in decline. ... The concept of nation which is characteristic of all modern forms of socialism is in rapid decline. The socialist form of society as manifest in the communist world has run its course. ... And the state, which has been the pivotal institution for socialists, can no longer be seen in such a way.[23]

However, McLennan intervened to dilute Jacques's vision. In the heat of the congress atmosphere, he faced up to the real possibility that delegates would desert the platform unless he acted to preserve the appearance of the old faith. In an effort to prove its commitment to democracy rather than democratic centralism, the Executive had refrained for the first time from giving formal advice to delegates on how they should vote on *Manifesto* amendments and resolutions.[24] Nevertheless, McLennan could still wield effective moral pressure. Kate Hudson, one of the younger defenders of the old faith at the Congress, summed up the congress horsetrading:

> Believing that unity around the *manifesto* could still save the party, McLennan pressed for the inclusion of certain incompatible phrases, about class being central and the importance of the Communist party's role. Such an approach by the General Secretary secured a narrow victory for the leadership.[25]

McLennan's fudge was just sufficient to push the Congress behind the *Manifesto*. The decisive vote was on a motion which welcomed the *Manifesto* and the wide debate it had initiated, but only as a discussion document. The *British Road* would survive intact as the party's programme. The motion was defeated by 112 to 86 with 3 abstentions, an uncomfortably small majority of 26 for the British party Executive, accustomed to habitual and un-reflexive loyalty from its congress delegates.[26] Moreover, delegates passed two resolutions which were 'critical of *Marxism Today* for being insufficiently aligned to the party'. The former treasurer revealed that she had resigned her position in part because her proposal to reduce the subsidy to *Marxism Today* had been thwarted.[27] Delegates from the 'real party' who had bent to McLennan's persuasion over the *Manifesto* were evidently determined to record their strong views about the party's other fork.

AFTER THE FALSE DAWN

The heat and light which the Eastern European revolutions had lent to the *Manifesto for New Times* were soon dissipated. Nina Temple was elected general-secretary of the CPGB by the incoming party Executive soon after the 41st Congress (see Table 6.3). Almost immediately she was faced with the very real prospect that the bifurcated party would divide into two. Her election seemed strange to outside observers

Table 6.3   General-Secretaries of the CPGB, 1945–91

1945–May 1956	Harry Pollitt
May 1956–March 1975	John Gollan
March 1975–November 1989	Gordon McLennan
December 1989–December 1991	Nina Temple

and to party members not privy to the internal dynamics of the party *apparat*. She appeared to be a novice whose skills and abilities were largely untried, and she was a woman.

Temple certainly succeeded McLennan against his will and despite his attempts to persuade two other men to do the job. His most earnest wish had been for Jacques to inherit the mantle. After Jacques's intentions not to stand were revealed to McLennan, he had plumped for Ian McKay, the National Organiser who was very much in McLennan's own mould, having served loyally in the Scottish *apparat* for years. McKay would probably have won the Executive's approval if he had been willing to stand for the job. But he declined to stand against Temple once she declared her intention to be a candidate.

Nina Temple's decision to stand for general-secretary had its own political logic, drawn from her own trajectory, first as a Young Communist League (YCL) activist in London and then as a full-time party worker swiftly rising inside the *apparat*. In the early 1970s the CPGB general-secretary Johnny Gollan had noted her precocity and his interest may have contributed to her progress inside the party (his own adolescent prominence in the Scottish party had been due to YCL activism).

Temple's evident political abilities had led to her election first as general-secretary of the YCL, and consequently to the party Executive in 1979, and then to the party's inner cabinet, the Political Committee, in January 1982. She had been Jacques's only supporter on the Committee when the *Morning Star* had fired the first shots in the war against Tony

Lane's *Marxism Today* article. She succeeded Tony Chater as head of the Press and Publicity Committee in January 1983 following the first engagement in the party's conflict with the *Morning Star*.

From this leading position she played an important part in the conflict: supporting both McLennan and Jacques; tendering shrewd advice about the next manoeuvres; and often superintending their execution personally. She witnessed the damaging political vacuum which set in after the conflict from the comparative objectivity of two periods of maternity leave. During the second period of leave she decided to return to work full-time for the party in order to stand for the general-secretaryship which everyone knew McLennan wished to vacate. She felt the party organisation crumbling underneath her and felt she had to be willing to become general-secretary in order to redress the situation.

Having taken this decision, she insisted upon being appointed by the Executive to the commission preparing the *Manifesto for New Times*. She wanted to have a significant input into a document which would determine the terms of the next general-secretary's political stewardship. She attended its first meetings with her baby in arms, much to the amusement of some of its members. When she returned to full-time work, she openly declared her intention to stand for general-secretary in what was regarded as a startling breach of British party tradition. Previous general-secretaries had emerged rather like the Pope from a murky conclave of political elders and, at least in Pollitt's instance, due to the Comintern's intervention.

The Executive chose Temple at their first meeting after the 41st Congress because she was the only person inside the *apparat* who was committed to renewing and transforming the party along the lines agreed by the Congress, and willing to take on the strains and demands of the job. The only other potential candidate, Ian McKay, recognised and deferred to her clear political vision. If the party had been in good health, he might have claimed his birthright to a post which had previously been held by two other Scottish working-class men. He knew well enough that the times

were out of joint and evidently was content to leave what
had become a difficult and troubled post to someone who
really wanted it.

The 41st Congress had stopped short of removing any
mention of Marxism–Leninism from the party's rules, a
move strongly supported by radical *Marxism Today* supporters. Nevertheless, the pressure applied by the radicals
showed no sign of abating. The in-coming Executive was
committed to instituting an internal debate about the
party's future. However, it seemed that the party rump and
the *Marxism Today* radicals would embark on a collision
course instead, because there was insufficient common
ground between them even for debate. Temple's urgent
task was to restore equilibrium to a party whose collective
sense of balance had gone badly awry.

THE BEGINNING OF THE END OR THE BEGINNING?

It is a measure of Temple's achievement that she constructed a middle way between the two forks of the party
which had substantial political credibility. Radicals on the
Marxism Today wing considered that she stalled the debate
and denied them the advantage of the momentum built up
with the *Manifesto*. This was probably an accurate description of her tactics. She was concerned to pour oil on the
troubled waters inside the branch and district structure.
Nevertheless, she did not baulk discussion of the really
difficult issues. Her perspective was a commitment to translating the abstract positions contained in the *Manifesto for
New Times* into political practice combined with a belief in
the positive value of the institution whose guardianship she
had accepted.

Unforeseen assistance to her project was provided by
Martin Jacques' abrupt disengagement from all party
matters some three months after she assumed office. He evidently judged the probability of the 'association' option suc-
ceeding to be minimal and sought to limit the damage to

his own position at *Marxism Today* by moving himself and the magazine further away from the party's sphere. He probably also judged his chances negligible of being able to mould Temple's actions to fit his needs, as he had done so expertly with the malleable McLennan. Whatever his calculations, he abandoned the *Manifesto for New Times* to its fate and instead began to cast around for means of independently financing *Marxism Today*, sanitised of its Marxism. Deprived of Jacques's tactical finesse and single-minded pursuit of the *Marxism Today* agenda, the *Marxism Today* radicals floundered and got bogged down inside the arcane ways and by-ways of the party.

At the end of 1990, delegates to the 42nd Special Congress of the party were presented with three options. The first, proposed by the radical wing of the *Marxism Today* group, was for the party to dissolve and become an 'association' of loosely connected individuals. The party's considerable assets would be vested in a trust which would bestow them on worthy campaigns and intellectual ventures.[28] The second, for 'renewal', was proposed by members of Straight Left, a politically ineffectual but aesthetically correct faction, the only serious organised faction to emerge in the course of the CPGB's history.[29] They stood for a renewed commitment to the anachronism of Anglo-Marxist humanism and a resumption of rank-and-file activity inside the debilitated and decomposing trade union movement.

Nina Temple placed the third, 'twin track', option into the ring. This called for 'a revised version of the new formation alongside a transformed CP, putting the emphasis on local, regional and national initiatives'. She argued that this blend was not only possible but desirable. Not surprisingly, it was her 'twin track' centrist option which was adopted by the 42nd Special Party Congress in December 1990 by a two-to-one margin on a show of hands.[30] The reflex of delegates supporting their general-secretary at Party Congress was still strong. Moreover, this new general-secretary appeared to know very firmly where she was going.

Because of a last-minute legal hitch, the 42nd Congress was unable to vote to disavow the title 'Communist' even though Temple was now firmly committed to abandoning it. Congress delegates had decided to 'transform' the party, but its name, new shape, and precise political substance still hung in the balance. However, Temple had already made her mark on the party and she had good reason to be sanguine about the hurdles ahead. She had not only survived a year in office but was entering 1991 with a stronger hold on the party *apparat* and her vision of a positive future undimmed.

There was the example of the Italian Communist Party transforming itself into the Party of the Democratic Left to inspire her. She had already begun the process of weeding out the politically unreconstructed and/or personally obstreperous officeholders. In their places she appointed activists with energy and flair who were committed to bringing the 'twin track' option to fruition, notably the new editor of the party newspaper *Changes*, Mike Power, and the assistant secretary, Joe Marshall.

Temple and her team made imaginative use of timely opportunities in the year before the 43rd Congress, which would finally decide the CPGB's destiny. The British party immediately denounced the attempted coup in the Soviet Union in August 1991. A party delegation to the Soviet Embassy was accompanied by Gordon McLennan lending the imprimatur of the past to their support for the democratic forces led by Boris Yeltsin.[31] In September, *Changes* carried revelations from George Matthews of how Stalin himself had been actively involved in the conception and detailed formulation of the first *British Road to Socialism*. In November, Mike Power outscooped The *Sunday Times* when *Changes* revealed details of the substantial amounts of money which the Soviet Communist Party had paid the CPGB between 1956 and 1979.[32]

These *démarches* had the effect of isolating the remaining members of the Straight Left faction and disorienting the veterans inside the 'real party' who still hankered after the glorious past. After the coup it seemed that the only course left was to mourn its passing. After the news about Stalin's hand on the *British Road* and the laundered pound notes being passed to the CPGB's Reuben Falber, it seemed that there was no longer a glorious past to mourn although many veterans remained unapologetic and upbeat about both revelations.

When the 43rd Congress assembled on 22 November 1991, Temple had set an ambitious agenda. There was a proposal to sever all connections with the international communist movement and Marxism–Leninism and to change the CPGB's name, shedding the denomination 'party', to 'Democratic Left', which 'exists in order to enable its members to contribute to the development of a popular movement for a socialism which is democratic, humane and green'.[33] This voluntary euthanasia and immediate rebirth *sans* party was accepted by a majority of nearly two to one. Despite the last-minute politicking in which proponents of the three main options had engaged, the result had never really been in doubt. Temple was a consummate tactician and she knew her party.

Temple's valedictory speech as a Communist made more than a token obeisance to 'the best in our tradition ... our daily struggle against injustice and the belief that people, through the power of their ideas and actions, can effect change'.[34] Her strong commitment to the best in her inherited past, that strong utopian streak and continuing efforts to translate it into reality, has sustained her in office as secretary of Democratic Left (DL) through difficult times since December 1991.

DL's membership has remained much smaller than its predecessor; the active membership in June 1993 was a mere 1234. (see Table 6.4).[35] The initial shrinkage from the CPGB was partially voluntary. DL officers had no desire to build up numbers with paper members from the CPGB's past who did not agree with the non-party's new approach. DL's very slow growth has reflected the general disillusion in British civil society and in particular the real alienation towards politics felt by the current student generation. The other barrier to growth is DL's determination not to engage in indiscriminate recruiting. Temple has refused to compete in the market already served by the Trotskyist sects

Table 6.4   Age profile of Democratic Left membership

Age in years	Percentage
0–19	1.1
20–29	10.0
30–39	15.7
40–49	17.1
50–59	11.6
60–69	17.6
70+	26.1

There were 1331 members of Democratic Left at the end of February 1992. This was 28 per cent of the CPGB's membership on 1 September 1991. In June 1993 there were 1648 members of Democratic Left. However, 414 were three months' in arrears with their subscriptions, leaving 1234 active members. The average age of Democratic Left members is 56 years and 3 months; 44.4 per cent are aged over 60, 44.4 per cent between 30 and 60 and 11.2 per cent are under 30. This profile is inherited from the CPGB membership. The trend of the average age is downwards, and the trend of the 20–29 age range is rising at a rate of 1/5 per cent per month through 'new' members; 13.2 per cent (177) of the membership is new, i.e. were not members of the CPGB. There is a starkly different profile between the two groups (previous and new). A worrying sign is a falling percentage of the 30–39 age group despite the 'new' members. The number of older members demonstrates that the commitment to the transformation spreads across all generations. The average age of new members is 37.4 years compared with 56.9 years for previous members. The profile is very much younger, with the largest age group being 20–29 year olds (33.9 per cent). There is also a large number of 30–39 year olds, in contrast with the declining trend overall.

Source: Democratic Left Membership Report, 1 December–29 February 1992; *Democratic Left Conference Report,* June 1993.

on the basis that recruits gained through messianic promises and sloganising do not stay and are often politically burnt-out within a year.

The CPGB had literally nothing left to lose at its dissolution. It had no MPs, no trade union base, no popular support and only a tiny handful of local councillors. Its membership had been falling steadily for nearly thirty years, a decline which accelerated to the point of collapse in its last decade. Ex-members still mourning the passing of British Marxism–Leninism are grieving for the past, not the present. The grouplets which lay claim to the inheritance of Pollitt and Lenin call themselves Communist parties. But they have few members. Nor are they making connections inside civil society to enable them to exploit the simmering and unredressed grievances which have accumulated during fourteen years of Conservative governments. They remain locked inside an antiquated political outlook which they refuse to adapt to take current circumstances into account. DL, on the other hand, is trying to re-establish itself in a pivotal position between civil society and the political establishment. It is a bold ambition, given the current fragmentation of left-wing politics and the disorientated mood besetting most of its practitioners.

NOTES

1. I have benefited greatly from interviews with Jack Adams, Martin Jacques, Joe Marshall, Mark Perryman, Mike Power and Nina Temple, who were active participants in the British Communist Party's internal affairs. I discussed the CPGB of the 1970s with Chris Hill and Geoff Roberts, and the Party of the 1960s with Dick Pountain. I am grateful to Geoff Andrews, Donald Sassoon and Professor Eric Hobsbawm for reading and commenting on the chapter in draft. The views expressed are, of course, my own.

2. Willie Gallacher (West Fife 1935–1950) and Phil Piratin (Stepney 1945–50). Each owed their victories to energetic electioneering

and exceptional circumstances which created a temporary hole in their working-class voters' normal allegiance to Labour.

3. The publicly available material on British Communism consists largely of minimal superficial narrative from academics, hagiographic anecdote and witness statements from veteran Communist heroes and dogmatic denunciations and impassioned *mea culpas* from ex-members who had seen the anti-communist light. An early account is Henry Pelling, *The British Communist Party, A Historical Profile* (London: Adam and Charles Black, 1958) (the 1975 edition was republished without revision, but contained a short introduction commenting on developments since 1958). The two serious scholarly works on the Party's early history are L. J. Macfarlane, *The British Communist Party, Its Origin and Development until 1929* (London: Macgibbon and Kee, 1966) and Roderick Martin, *Communism and the British Trade Unions, 1924–1933: A Study of the National Minority Movement* (Oxford: Clarendon Press, 1969). Kevin Morgan, *Against Fascism and War: Ruptures and Continuities in British Communist Politics, 1935–41* (Manchester: Manchester University Press, 1989) contains research on the response of CPGB members to the Party's change of line on the Second World War. His life of the CPGB general secretary, *Harry Pollitt* (Manchester: Manchester University Press, 1993) is a good introduction to CPGB history up to 1956. John Callaghan has a chapter on the CPGB in *The Far Left in British Politics* (Oxford: Basil Blackwell, 1987) and a life of R. Palme Dutt, the CPGB's premier intellectual *Rajuni Palme Dutt: A Study in British Stalinism* (London: Lawrence & Wishart, 1993). J. R. Campbell, chief theorist and propagandist for trade union activity and domestic economics, has been neglected probably because Party mythology assigns him only a subsidiary place. The official party histories are James Klugmann, *History of the Communist Party of Great Britain*, vol. I, *1919–1924*, vol. II *1925–6* (London: Lawrence & Wishart, 1968 and 1969) and Noreen Branson, *History of the Communist Party of Great Britain 1927–1941* (Lawrence & Wishart, 1985). A further volume by Noreen Branson extending into the post-war period is expected. Willie Thompson, a younger historian who was also in the CPGB, published a history of the entire span of the CPGB, *The Good Old Cause* (London: Pluto Press, 1992). It is more critical than Branson but still shares most of the mythologic conventions of the Communist historians' group, now rechristened the Socialist History Group.

4. Nina Fishman, *The British Communist Party and the Trade Unions, 1933–45* (London: Scholar Press, 1994).

5. Alex Mitchell, *Behind the Crisis in British Stalinism* (London: New Park Publications, June 1984) pp. 8–9. Mitchell is an investigative journalist for *News Line*, the Workers' Revolutionary Party's daily paper. His account remains the most thorough examination of the dispute, albeit from the viewpoint of the purest Trotskyist sect.

6. Ibid., p. 10.
7. Ibid., p. 126.
8. Ibid., p. 114. The Soviet Union's large order for the daily newspaper represented an important subsidy for the paper. Mitchell reported that just over half of the paper's print run was sent to the USSR and Eastern Europe. At the beginning of 1984, the paper's price was increased by 20 per cent, yielding an extra £4500 per week (p. 121).
9. Mick Costello escaped expulsion because he had ceased to occupy any official position inside the party and had not committed any technical infringement of the party's rules. The ownership of the *Morning Star* was vested in a cooperative, the People's Press Printing Society (PPPS), dating from 1945 when the party leadership had cherished hopes of involving non-party progressive forces in a drive to make Britain a people's democracy. Its shareholders included many ex-members and trade union 'fellow travellers'. In the course of the conflict, the party *apparat* expended huge amounts of time and energy in fruitless attempts to mobilise sufficient numbers of PPPS shareholders to vote Chater and Whitfield off the *Star*'s management committee at AGMs and emergency AGMs.
10. Interview with Mark Perryman by the author.
11. The interest was furthered by the interviews it [*Marxism Today*] ran with political and cultural celebrities, as often as not vehemently anti-socialist ones. Extracts from its material often appeared as features in the *Guardian* or *Independent*. It was commented upon favourably by Neil Kinnock and Roy Hattersley (Thompson, *The Good Old Cause*, p. 198).
12. *Marxism Today*'s circulation increased from 11,000 in 1983 to 15,600 in the last half of 1988, whilst CPGB Party membership fell from 15,691 to 8546. Figures from Executive Committee Reports for the 40th Congress (1987) pp. 8 and 17, and 41st Congress (1989) pp. 8 and 18.
13. 'Facing Up to the Future', *Marxism Today*, September 1988, p. 1.
14. Executive Report for the 41st Party Congress, August 1987–July 1989, p. 4. 'Facing Up to the Future' was greeted by a surge of interest from *Marxism Today*'s Labour left-wing and academic habitués.
15. *Marxism Today*, October 1988, p. 40.
16. *Manifesto for New Times: A Strategy for the 1990s* (The Communist Party: London, 1990), pp. 13–14. In a signed *Marxism Today* leader in October 1989, Jacques was more outspoken: 'The stalinist system has finally floundered. It has reached the point of no return. But it is not simply the end of stalinism. In an important sense it is the end of leninism' (p. 3).
17. A typical example was the debate between Jim Mortimer and McLennan on the *Manifesto*, on 26 October 1989 (*News and Views*, issue 51, November 1989).

18. *News and Views,* issue 52 (December 1989), p. 2.
19. *Marxism Today,* October 1989, p. 3.
20. *Manifesto,* p. 14.
21. Amendment 68. Similar amendments appeared from Leeds University staff (Yorkshire); Aire Valley (Yorkshire); Wanstead and Woodford (Eastern); Granby (Merseyside and Cheshire). 41st Congress, *Manifesto for New Times, Amendments* (n.d.), pp. 10–12.
22. Thompson, *The Good Old Cause,* p. 203.
23. *News and Views,* issue 52 (December 1989) Centre, pp. ii–vi.
24. Thompson, *The Good Old Cause,* p. 203.
25. Kate Hudson, 'Post-communism: the Impact in Britain: Decline and Demise of the Communist Party of Great Britain', Occasional Papers, Number 1 (Politics Division, South Bank University, London: June 1993), p. 9. Nina Temple concurred with Hudson's description (interview with the author).
26. *News and Views,* issue 52 (December 1989), p. 1.
27. Thompson, *The Good Old Cause,* p. 203. Thompson cites £50,000 as the regular yearly subsidy given by the party Executive to *Marxism Today* (p. 207). However, Martin Jacques pointed out that the party's loss on *Marxism Today* had been very small during the first decade of his tenure, 1977–87, and had not increased in real terms. (Separate accounting procedures for *Marxism Today* began in 1984–5 on Jacques's initiative. Previously it had been impossible to discover the true costs of the magazine for the party.) He estimated that *Marxism Today* lost approximately £15,000–17,000 per annum during the mid-1980s. This was substantially less than the money spent on press and publicity and also less than the losses incurred by other party magazines. He felt that *Marxism Today* had not become a financial liability for the party until the late 1980s. *Marxism Today* was redesigned and relaunched in October 1986 in a much more ambitious form. Thereafter, the party sustained yearly losses of £35,000–50,000 on *Marxism Today.*
28. The CPGB had realised substantial profits from the successive sales of their King Street headquarters in Covent Garden and then their St John Street headquarters in Smithfield. Thompson cites their assets as being around £3 million in 1990, *The Good Old Cause,* p. 206.
29. Straight Left members objected to euro-communism from 1977 onwards. However, they were so devoutly loyal to the Pollitt/Lenin observance that the prospect of leaving the party to join the seceding Marxist–Leninists in the New Communist Party in 1977 or the British Communist Party in 1985 was evidently unthinkable. Thompson charts their twists and turns in *The Good Old Cause,* pp. 181–2, 186–7, 189, 205–6.
30. *Changes,* 22 December 1990–18 January 1991, p. 1. There were actually five alternative positions which were discussed. The 'association' position had two marginally different permutations: one

containing 'Communist', the other omitting it and substituting 'New Times'. The fifth position was a minimal spoiling option which sought to omit all reference to association/formation in the draft resolution.

31. For the CPGB's response to the coup, see *Changes*, issue 22, 31 August–13 September 1991, pp. 1–2.
32. George Matthews wrote his story in *Changes*, Issue 23, 14–27 September 1991. The Moscow gold revelations appeared in *Changes*, Issue 28, 16–29 November 1991. The CPGB Political Committee issued its own statement on the news on 11 November.
33. *Draft Constitution of Democratic Left* (1991), p. 1.
34. Her speech is reprinted in *New Times*, journal of the Democratic Left, no. 1, 30 November 1991, pp. 6–8.
35. See Table 6.2.

7 German Communism, the PDS, and the Reunification of Germany

Günter Minnerup

The histories of Germany and of communism have been inextricably linked. Without Marx and Engels, and without the war between Imperial Germany and Tsarist Russia, there would not have been an October Revolution and Union of Soviet Socialist Republics. The extension of the communist revolution into Germany was the chief strategic aim of the Bolsheviks, and had it been achieved during the turbulent period of 1918–23, Russia might have been spared the two great nightmares of Stalinism and the Nazi aggression. Victory over Hitler and the conquest of Eastern Germany finally elevated Soviet Russia to the status of a world power. It is fitting, therefore, that the final phase of the demise of Soviet communism should have been ushered in by the fall of the Berlin Wall and German reunification.

The German Democratic Republic which collapsed in 1989–90 may have been a result of Soviet occupation, but that is only one half of its story. It was also, in however distorted a fashion, the culmination of decades of struggle by the German communist movement. There may not have been a genuine popular revolution after 1945, but the construction of the GDR would not have been possible without the active participation of the German communists. In this sense, the division of Germany was also the geographical consolidation of the latent civil war that had characterised pre-war German society. The communist left was identified, for better or for worse, with East Germany, and virtually eliminated from the domestic political spectrum of the Western state.

From the 1890s to the 1930s, Marxism had inspired the majority of the German labour movement – including the majority of the social-democratic SPD – and shaped its political thought and traditions. The KPD (*Kommunistische Partei Deutschlands*, German Communist Party), after its emergence from the left wing of the SPD (*Sozialdemokratische Partei Deutschlands*, German Socialist Party) in the aftermath of the First World War, was by far the largest Communist Party in Central and Western Europe.[1] By the 1950s, however, in the Western part of divided Germany, communism had ceased to be a significant element in the political culture even before the Constitutional Court formally proscribed the KPD in 1956.

THE WEST GERMAN COMMUNIST PARTY (KPD/DKP)

No West European communist party was as badly affected by the Cold War as the West German one. The once powerful KPD had already been decimated by Nazi persecution up to 1945 and widespread popular Russophobia immediately afterwards, but still achieved respectable results in various post-war regional elections, gaining representation at many levels including, in 1949, the first parliament of the Federal Republic (see Table 7.1). The East German workers' uprising of June 1953, however, worsened the already hostile Cold War climate to such an extent that the 1956 ban proclaimed by the Federal Constitutional Court hit an isolated organisation incapable of rallying much opposition against its proscription. Operating underground and through legal front organisations such as the pacifist DFU (*Deutsche Friedensunion*, German Peace Union) and the VVN (*Vereinigung der Verfolgten des Naziregimes*, Association of those Persecuted by the Nazi Regime), its members being subjected to frequent police harassment and legal persecution, it became even more dependent on East Germany, where its organisational centre was now located. In 1969, the

Table 7.1   Election results in the post-war period (percentage of votes cast)

	KPD	DFU	DKP	PDS
(1932)	16.9			
(1946) British zone	10.5			
(1946) US zone	8.0			
1949	5.7			
1953	2.2			
1957	–			
1961		1.9		
1965		1.3		
1969		–		
1972			0.3	
1976			0.3	
1990 (W)				0.3
1990 (E)				11.1

Brandt government permitted the reconstitution of a legal communist party under the slightly different name of DKP (*Deutsche Kommunistische Partei*), largely to facilitate the establishment of better relations with East Germany and the countries of Soviet-dominated Eastern Europe, but the 1956 ban remained in force, hanging like a Damocles' sword over not only the DKP itself but also the smaller communist (Maoist and Trotskyist) parties which had emerged from the 1968 student movement.

The DKP never achieved any significant electoral success or parliamentary representation, apart from a few dozen local councillors, but was able on occasion to play an influential role in extra-parliamentary politics because of its considerable press and publicity apparatus, its recruitment of many student activists through the MSB Spartakus, and a certain residual strength in the trade unions, especially at full-time official and enterprise-council level. High points of its political influence were the campaign to ratify the Basic Treaty between the two German states, the campaign against the *Berufsverbot* (the ban on the employment of political radicals in the extensive German public sector), the Vietnam solidarity campaign and the Peace Movement. The membership of the DKP reached its high point in the mid-1970s with 42,453 according to the executive report to the IV Party Congress in 1976.[2] The student organisation MSB Spartakus claimed 5300 members, the youth organisation SDAJ 33,000.[3]

Despite its considerable base among students and intellectuals, the DKP remained a monolithic, pro-Moscow and pro-GDR party which tolerated no internal dissent and distanced itself aggressively from 'Eurocommunism'. After 1985, when it followed its East German sponsors in resisting Gorbachev's *glasnost* and *perestroika*, the first significant fissures emerged in the party organisation, with a current of 'renovators' supporting the Soviet line. The tensions came to a head some nine months before the fall of the Honecker regime in the GDR, when the DKP's January 1989 Congress in Frankfurt saw the reformers split the party.[4] Most of them have since joined the PDS or formed various splinter groups, leaving the tiny unreconstructed remnant threatening to stand candidates against the PDS on its East German home ground.

The full extent of the DKP's dependence on the financial support of the GDR was only revealed when the subsidies dried up after October 1989. Almost overnight, the publications ceased to appear, offices were closed, and full-time officials lost their employment.[5] Throughout its existence, the DKP had been little more than a lavishly funded public-relations agency for the East German leadership, its purpose to influence sections of West German public opinion rather than to win elections or gain political power for itself.

THE PDS – HEIR TO THE RULING EAST GERMAN COMMUNISTS

Contrary to some initial expectations, the former ruling parties of communist Eastern Europe have not simply vanished without trace following the overthrow of their regimes but have attracted a substantial minority following in free elections and show signs of augmenting that support by rallying some of the social discontent of the many victims of hasty and socially disastrous privatisation. If such resilience was surprising in the case of, say, the Polish and Czechoslovak CPs, it was perhaps most unexpected from the heirs of the East German regime. The PDS (*Partei des Demokratischen Sozialismus*, Party of Democratic Socialism; the successor to the SED, *Sozialistische Einheitspartei Deutschlands*, Socialist Unity Party of Germany), however, has survived as a significant political and electoral force on the territory of the former GDR despite the incorporation of the East German state into the Federal Republic and the enormous pressures brought to bear upon it by the conquering West German establishment. In six of the eight electoral districts of East Berlin, for example, it remains the strongest single party, polling 29.7 per cent overall in the 1992 local council elections in the former capital city of the German Democratic Republic; even more significantly, this represented a substantial increase over the 23.6 per cent polled in the 1990 elections to the Berlin Parliament. Over ten thousand local and regional representatives, as well as seventeen members of the Federal Parliament, have been elected as PDS candidates since 1990.

Thus the principal threat to its continued presence in the national parliament beyond the 1994 general elections stems not so much from a loss of support in the East but from its weakness on the territory of the 'old' Federal Republic. It has failed entirely to expand its electoral and membership base westwards after reunification, polling a derisory 0.3 per cent (as compared with 11.1 per cent in the East) in the 1990 post-reunification general elections on the territory of the former West Germany, and counting only a few hundred members in the West.[6] As was the case throughout the Cold War era, therefore, German communism remains essentially an East German phenomenon, even after reunification.

But is the survival, for the time being, of relatively vigorous remnants of the old ruling communist parties in both Germany and Eastern Europe more than just a transitory phenomenon? And, even if they do survive in the longer term both organisationally and electorally, what will they stand for programmatically? In countries such as Poland and the Czech and Slovak republics, the ex-CPs have restyled themselves as 'social-democratic' parties, embracing parliamentary democracy and the capitalist market in principle but defending social security and public ownership. In the former GDR, however, the transition has taken a completely different form. Here, the old social and economic infrastructures have all but disappeared following incorporation into the FRG, and along with the Western capital and Western institutions has come a 'real' social-democratic party, the SPD.

THE ABSENCE OF A REFORM-COMMUNIST WING IN THE SED

Perhaps the most striking difference between the political history of East Germany and that of its immediate East European neighbours Poland and Czechoslovakia (but also Hungary and, indeed, the Soviet Union itself) is its very continuity, the absence of any sudden and dramatic changes of course and leadership. There had never been an organised reform-communist or national-communist wing challenging the ascendancy of the Moscow-oriented, orthodox Stalinist leadership, so that the terminal crisis of Soviet-style communism hit a party without any established culture of inner-party debate and factionalisation. While the existence of such traditions would probably not have made any real difference to the course of events in 1989, their absence left the PDS with a party cadre steeped in a monolithic immobilism that was unusual even by East European standards. It had no prominent figure with sound reformist credentials to be presented as Erich Honecker's successor in October 1989, and even by 1994, the bulk of the rank-and-file membership remained largely passive and uninvolved in programmatic reform debates which continued to be dominated by a thin layer of party intellectuals.

The reasons for this monolithism are not difficult to appreciate. It had its roots in the extreme pressures brought to bear on the East German state by the powerful and rich capitalist neighbour in the West, producing a 'siege mentality' in the leadership and ranks of the party, so that even dissenters were prepared to close ranks in public lest a weakening of party unity brought about the collapse of the fragile structures of the 'first German workers' and peasants' state'. The precarious position of the GDR as a frontline state in the Cold War, exposed to the daily corrosive influence of the West German media and cross-border family ties, led even the critics of the party leadership to accept the Soviet Union as the only real guarantor of the stability and existence of the GDR, and hence the only 'safe' road to political change in the GDR as leading through Moscow. The challenges of the 1950s to the then General Secretary Walter Ulbricht were conducted entirely through lobbying of the CPSU leadership, and after Mikhail Gorbachev's accession to office in 1985 the reform-inclined elements in the SED confined themselves to jockeying for positions in anticipation of a Moscow-initiated change, brought about perhaps by the successor to the ageing and ailing Erich Honecker (as had happened so often in the communist world, not least with Gorbachev's takeover after the death of Konstantin Chernenko). Nationalism, elsewhere in Eastern Europe a most powerful motor of communist deviation from the Moscow path, was too dangerous a toy to play with in divided Germany.

However, the fact that the GDR was largely a state imposed on East Germany by the outcome and aftermath of the Second World War, in particular the Cold War, and that therefore the real share of the German communists in its creation and maintenance was always subordinate to the dominant interests of the Soviet Union, can also be seen, if somewhat paradoxically, as a kind of 'historical alibi' for the heirs of German communism organised in the PDS today. For if they really only played a supporting role on the German Cold War stage after 1945, if the 'first German workers' and peasants' state' was never truly theirs, then their responsibility for its crimes, shortcomings and failures must also be considered a limited one. This consideration no doubt offers significant psychological comfort to the depleted ranks of the German communist movement today. Significantly, the chief ideologist of the 'new' PDS, deputy chairman André Brie, placed heavy emphasis on the Asiatic roots of 'Marxism–Leninism' when attempting to answer the question of why Soviet-style communism had failed.[7]

THE SED'S RESPONSE TO THE UPHEAVALS OF 1989

There was some evidence of widespread disaffection in the ranks of the party in the run-up to the 40th anniversary celebrations of the founding of the GDR in October 1989, especially in the unusually high number of members lost through resignation or expulsion.[8] Educated in the slogan 'To learn from the Soviet Union is to learn to be victorious' (*Von der Sowjetunion lernen heißt siegen lernen*), many SED cadres were disoriented by the failure of their party leaders to emulate Moscow's turn to *perestroika* and *glasnost*, and confused when the German edition of the Soviet journal *Sputnik* – previously required reading for every functionary – was effectively removed from circulation in the GDR in November 1988.[9] The party leadership, in close alliance with its similarly neo-stalinist Czechoslovak counterpart, remained aloof from the new reformist spirit sweeping the Soviet Union and Eastern Europe. Indeed, there were heavy hints that at least sections of it entertained the possibility of regaining the initiative by adopting the 'Chinese solution' of clamping down hard on all forms of dissent.[10] Given the degree to which awareness of the Soviet reforms, the daily confrontation of the activists with popular discontent, and

the propaganda of the West German media had already cor-
roded party discipline and morale, it is unlikely, however,
that any recourse to massive repression could have worked –
East Germany simply was not China. Indeed, one of the
most striking aspects of the events of autumn 1989 is the
weakness of the resistance from the party and security apparatus: with the (conscript) army and the police probably as
split and demoralised as the party itself, the only reliable repressive instruments at the disposal of the hardliners were
the special units of the State Security (*Stasi*). By October
1989, the hostile reaction of the party membership to Egon
Krenz as Honecker's successor, and the largely tolerant behaviour of the People's Police during the continuing
demonstrations, indicated that the mood had already swung
decisively towards sweeping reform and democratisation.

It is clear now that long before the open eruption of the
autumn 1989 crisis there had already existed divisions
within the Politburo and Central Committee about how to
respond to the changes in the Soviet Union. These were not
reported at the time, but have since been revealed in a
series of memoirs by, and interviews with, key party leaders
and members of the Politburo.[11] Honecker's successor,
Krenz, for example, claims that as early as 1988 a group of
Politburo members intended to challenge the general secretary because 'the course pursued by the Politburo was
bound to fail in view of the developments in the Soviet
Union'. According to Krenz, the key figure in this incipient
plot was Werner Felfe, Agriculture Secretary of the Central
Committee, whose sudden death prevented this initiative
from ever being properly launched. Krenz also names Willi
Stoph, Erich Mielke, Werner Krolikowski, Gerhard Schürer
and Werner Jarowinsky among those who were critical of
Honecker's opposition to Gorbachev.[12]

Essentially, the policy of the SED leadership in the run-up
to the 40th anniversary of the GDR consisted of playing for
time, in the hope that the conservative forces in the Soviet
Union would reign in Gorbachev and that the close symbiosis with the Federal Republic, which provided credit at exceptionally favourable terms and ready access to Western

export markets, would allow it to see out the mounting economic difficulties.

Once the growing pressure of the streets had forced the IX Central Committee plenum to replace Honecker with Krenz on 18 October 1989, the response of the SED leadership consisted essentially of demonstrative declarations of support for Gorbachev and pragmatic, often panic-stricken concessions and retreats – the most decisive of which, of course, was the opening of the Berlin Wall on 9 November. It soon became clear that the Politburo had lost all authority and it resigned en bloc at the Extraordinary Party Congress of 8/9 December, to be replaced by an executive headed by the lawyer Gregor Gysi, who had extensive experience as defence counsel for prominent political dissidents. A week later, the party was renamed SED–PDS.

The October revolt posed the SED with several intractable problems. The first and most immediate of these was one of personnel, of finding post-Honecker leadership figures who could credibly represent a new, reformist orientation. Hans Modrow, the party secretary in Dresden, and Wolfgang Berghofer, mayor of the same city, were the only communist leaders associated in the public mind with reformist leanings, but both lacked not only a real power base in the party outside their localities but also any clearly defined programme for change. Of the senior Politburo members, only Günter Schabowski, party secretary for Berlin, appeared to have the personal courage to confront the people and the flexibility to adapt to new circumstances, but his failure to speak out before Honecker's resignation saddled him with the aura of opportunism, and caused him to be received with hostility when he addressed the big demonstration in Berlin's Alexanderplatz on 4 November. Certainly, the newly elected party leader Egon Krenz, for many years Honecker's successor-designate, leader of the Free German Youth (FDJ) organisation, and only recently dispatched to Beijing to congratulate the Chinese leadership on their bloody suppression of the Tian-an-men Square revolt, was a most unlikely figure to lead the SED into the new era of democratisation.

Secondly, the SED had the programmatic problem of defining just what a reformed East German socialism would look like. The key issue, both for the party leadership itself and for the democratic opposition outside the SED–PDS, was whether or not the 'turn' (*Wende*) proclaimed after the toppling of Honecker would preserve the 'leading role of the party'. This was not just a formal constitutional issue – the relevant clause was struck out of the GDR Constitution by the *Volkskammer* on 1 December 1989 – but one that went right to the heart of the nature of the democratisation and reform process: would it remain a partial reform and democratisation granted, under pressure from below, by what would remain the 'natural party of government' in a socialist state, or could democratisation lead to the challenging of the state power of the SED–PDS and its replacement by new forces?

By January 1990, the question of the relationship between party and state focused on one central 'hot issue': that of the continued existence of the detested State Security. The Modrow government, but also the Gysi leadership of the SED–PDS, embarked on an offensive to reorganise the Ministry for State Security (MfS, or, as it was more popularly known, the '*Stasi*') as a new 'Office for the Protection of the Constitution'. The suggested parallel with the West German *Verfassungsschutz* convinced nobody, nor did the intensive propaganda campaign of the still communist-dominated media against a supposed 'fascist danger'.[13] This episode became the final nail in the coffin of the Modrow government: faced with widespread anger in the streets and the opposition's threat to terminate cooperation through the institutions of the 'Round Tables', Modrow was forced to form an all-party caretaker government to see out the remainder of his period of office. The *Volkskammer* elections were hastily brought forward from their original date in May to 18 March 1990.

Thirdly, even if the SED had been capable of finding credible leadership figures and formulating a coherent programme for change, there was the question of the ability of the rank and file successfully to implement such a programme and to gain public support for it. For the post-October SED was a demoralised and isolated party whose internal discipline was rapidly breaking down. One of the first problems faced by the new chairman, Gregor Gysi, was to fend off growing rank-and-file demands for the voluntary self-dissolution of the party.

FROM STATE PARTY TO OPPOSITION PARTY

It is perhaps ironical that a party which, after 1956, had identified Stalinism as 'the cult of the personality' was now saved from the final collapse of the Stalinist system by its almost total identification with one person, Gregor Gysi. Gysi had not been a member of the old leadership, and his activities as a defence lawyer for dissidents gave him considerable credibility as the 'new face' of the PDS (see Table 7.2). He set about his task of recasting the party's image with a fine sense for Western-style political show business, exemplified by his appearance in a television election commercial on a motorbike, clad in black leather, to the tune of the rock song 'Born to be Wild'. With his witty repartee and sharp polemical tongue, Gysi soon became a star of the talk shows and a figure of almost charismatic attraction to the young left, particularly in the West. Although replaced as party chairman by the less colourful Lothar Bisky in early 1993, he remained the leader of the PDS in Parliament and its best known 'public face'.

Table 7.2   Leaders in the post-war period (SED–PDS)

Walter Ulbricht (1945–1971)
Erich Honecker (1971–1989)
Egon Krenz (Oct–Dec 1989)
Gregor Gysi (1989–1993)
Lothar Bisky (1993–?)

But despite this new, trendy image given to the SED's successor by the new chairman and the band of young reformist intellectuals grouped around him in the party leadership, the 'new' party found it difficult to shed the legacy of the past, especially as the logic of organisational survival dictated that even Gysi had to be careful not to alienate the former SED members and functionaries who still made up the overwhelming majority of its organisation. He soon found himself involved in a difficult balancing act of promoting the new while defending and protecting the old. The most damaging aspects of the past related to the close symbiosis that had existed between the East German state and its ruling party, and two issues in particular that were to haunt Gysi's PDS: its connections with the hated State Security (*Stasi*), and its inheritance of the property and finances of the SED.

The PDS was, of course, not the only party to be affected by revelations about *Stasi* activities on the part of its leading representatives. Given the omnipresence of the *Stasi* and its task of gathering information about non-conformist political activities, it is not surprising that its tentacles reached deep into the non-communist parties, the Churches and even the dissident underground.[14] For such parties and organisations, however, revelations about individuals could be explained away as the result of hostile infiltration, while the PDS was the successor to the party of which the *Stasi*, according to its own motto, was to be 'sword and shield'. There can be no doubt that a significant percentage of the PDS membership had been working for the State Security[15] and any attempt by the party leadership to cleanse the organisation of all *Stasi* links would be a hopeless undertaking. It is doubtful, in any case, if such a purge would have significantly altered the public perception of the PDS as the heir to the SED, *Stasi* and all. On the other hand, however, it was of vital importance to the leadership to demonstrate the credibility of its own break with that past. The allegations that Gysi himself was collaborating with the *Stasi* behind the back of, and against the interests of, his dissident clients when working as a lawyer under the Honecker regime were potentially disastrous for the party's fortunes. First published by the news magazine *Der Spiegel*,[16] the allegations had not, by late 1993, been conclusively proved and Gysi was able up to that stage to limit the damage to his reputation. His deputy and intellectual driving force behind the programmatic reorientation of the PDS, André Brie, however, admitted his *Stasi* involvement and was obliged to resign.

After forty years of continuous monopoly rule by the SED, the boundaries between party and state had inevitably become heavily blurred and both individual members and the party organisation enjoyed substantial material privileges derived from the tenure of political power. This close material symbiosis proved most intractable in the area of real-estate property, where original ownership was often difficult to prove.[17] The post-Krenz leadership was undoubtedly caught in a difficult conflict of interests: on the one hand, it was essential that the new, reformed party was seen to have cleansed itself of organised corruption by disposing of anything in its inheritance which could not be directly proved to have been legitimately acquired from the legacy of the KPD or through the voluntary contributions of its (now severely reduced) membership; on the other, however, it was only natural that it would seek to secure its continued existence and competitiveness with the wealthy West German parties. It also had financial responsibility for the livelihoods of the large number of full-time functionaries and other employees bequeathed to it by the old state party, with their substantial wage and old-age pension entitlements.

Even where no *Stasi* links or issues of material corruption are involved, however, the legacy of the old SED continues to rest heavily upon the PDS in terms of the social–psychological outlook and political habits of the older generation of party members, which continues to dominate in the organisation. This is one of the main obstacles to the recruitment and retention of new, younger members, as the statements of many who have resigned from the PDS in despair testify.[18]

It is not surprising, therefore, that the abortive Soviet coup in August 1991 met with considerable sympathy in the ranks of the PDS (as well as, of course, the Stalinist rump of the West German DKP). Reflecting these pressures, both the party presidium and its newspaper *Neues Deutschland* published highly ambiguous statements expressing the desire that the Emergency Committee headed by Yanayev would 'prevent the country drowning in violence, chaos, hunger and lawlessness' (presidium) and 'stem the undeniable and, up to now, seemingly inexorable disintegration of state power and death of the economy'.[19] The pro-Gorbachev wing of the leadership did not publicly reassert itself until the Moscow coup had collapsed.

SOCIAL COMPOSITION

The official statistics of the old SED concerning the social composition of its membership have always been notoriously unreliable because the precise criteria used to determine such key social categories as 'intelligentsia' and 'working class' were unknown and probably not applied consistently over the years. Taken at face value, the official figures suggest that the working-class component declined sharply during the 1950s – probably as a result of the post-1953 purges and disillusionment, especially among former social democrats – and rose again sharply in the 1970s as a result of Honecker's turn away from Ulbricht's 'socialist community' (*sozialistische Menschengemeinschaft*) and renewed emphasis on the party's proletarian character. After October 1989, however, there was a rapid exodus of working-class members from the SED–PDS: between then and January 1990, 460,000 of the 900,000 working-class members deserted the SED–PDS.[20] By June 1991, only 26 per cent of the membership were said to be working-class, with 45 per cent salaried employees and 3 per cent self-employed, of a total remaining membership of 242,000 (see Table 7.3). Many of these, moreover, were unemployed or

Table 7.3 Social composition of party membership

	1947	1957	1961	1976	Oct. 1989
Workers	48.1	33.8	33.8	56.1	52.0
Farmers	9.4	5.0	6.2	5.2	4.4
Intelligentsia	22.0	42.3	41.3	20.0	21.9
Others	20.5	18.9	18.7	18.7	21.6

Source: *DDR-Handbuch,* p. 950; for October 1989: Siegfried Suckut and Dietrich Staritz, 'Alte Heimat oder neue Linke? Das SED-Erbe und die PDS-Erben', *Deutschland Archiv*, 10/1991, p. 1039.

pensioners: no less than 59.7 per cent had no secure employment, 47.9 per cent were aged 61 or over. Only 10.5 per cent were younger than 30.[21]

However, while the statistics paint a picture of a party of pensioners and former SED functionaries, there is also the apparently contradictory, youthful image presented by the party in its electioneering, and the fact that its public events and rallies are dominated by the young generation. In a sense, there are two versions of the PDS: that of the conservative old cadres nostalgic for the old GDR, which dominates the life of most local PDS branches and of its main organisational apparatus, and that of Gysi, his young intellectual backers, the projected public image and the activists in the party's special-interest groups such as the *AG Junger GenossInnen* and the *Linke Sozialistische Frauenarbeitsgemeinschaft*. These have a life of their own, sometimes with only tenuous links to the mainstream party structures, but play a disproportionately influential part in its debates and provide a significant element of the canvassers and propagandists which give the PDS its public profile.

IDEOLOGICAL SELF-CRITICISM AND PROGRAMMATIC RENEWAL

According to a poll conducted by the East Berlin Institute for Social Data Analysis, 21 per cent of East Germans expect 'socialism to return in a better form one day'. Among supporters of the PDS, the figure was 75 per cent.[22] For much of the ageing PDS membership, however, such loyalty to the idea of socialism tended to articulate itself in terms of a nostalgia for the GDR rather than a readiness to face up to the challenge of the new situation of capitalist reunification, and in stubborn resistance to any radical self-criticism. The programmatic refurbishment initiated by the Gysi leadership, by contrast, consisted primarily of a wholesale dumping of the old ideological baggage of 'Marxism–Leninism' in favour of a rapid adoption of what can only be characterised as an eclectic mix of classic social-democratic positions with contemporary Green and feminist ideas.

The ideological debate in the PDS has been subject to a variety of intense and often conflicting pressures: the need for some ideological continuity, to retain the loyalty of the bulk of the SED's old membership, versus the need to appeal to the concerns of a younger generation radicalised in the environmental, peace, women's and civil rights movements; the need to differentiate itself from the SPD by a more resolute anti-capitalist stance versus the pressures to adapt to the overwhelmingly pro-market consensus in East German popular opinion; the need to maintain an identification with the 'positive achievements' of the GDR versus the inevitability of embracing reunification. This attempt to straddle opposing positions is sometimes reminiscent of the pre-1914 debates in the SPD. Gysi summed up the two poles of opinion in the party in his speech to the 2nd Party Congress in December 1991 as follows:

> On the one side there is the perspective of fighting for new social majorities, for the emergence of democratic countervailing powers, and to change society gradually in this way, to break the dominance of capital accumulation,

the profit motive and the market in order to eventually overcome society's capitalist nature.

On the other, we have the view that capitalist society cannot be changed socially, ecologically and democratically but that all reformist potentials are being channelled by the capitalist system and that therefore such changes only lead to the prolongation of the capitalist rule which today is ruining humanity and nature in unprecedented fashion. A culture of resistance and counter society are seen as the main road towards creating system-transforming (*systemüberwindende*) forces.[23]

Another necessary debate hampered by the weight of the backward-looking majority of older party members is that about the question of where 'actually existing socialism' went wrong and what precisely the nature of the SED regime was. Without such an answer, all programmatic adaptations to 'modernity' must remain patchwork. The prevailing tendency so far has been to emphasise the moral decline of the party during the Honecker years in comparison with the idealism of the early years of 'building socialism', but this, if anything, tends to idealise the brutal Stalinism of the Ulbricht years against the comparative 'liberalism' of the Honecker period, presumably as a concession to the pride of the older generation of party members and functionaries in the achievements of the difficult years of post-war reconstruction.

THE PDS IN ALL-GERMAN POLITICS

As soon as it became clear that the collapse of the old GDR regime had opened up an inexorable dynamic towards German reunification – as was the case from early 1990, at the latest – the PDS leadership recognised that to secure its long-term survival, it had to sink roots into West German soil and become a genuinely nationwide political party. This was not just a question of electoral arithmetic: only a successful expansion of the party organisation into the West would decisively shift the balance against the conservative GDR nostalgia so dominant among the Eastern membership. The problem was that while this isolation persisted, it was also that much harder to attract new allies on the West German left. The attempts of the Gysi leadership to square this particular circle fell into three distinct phases.

Before the *Volkskammer* elections of 18 March 1990, and while perhaps not the question of unification itself, but at least that of its modalities was still open, the PDS attempted to forge a broad alliance of all those who opposed unification in the form of an unconditional *Anschluß*. It was well known that resistance to a simple surrender to the Deutschmark extended deep into the Christian Democrat camp, and was particularly strong among many of those in the 'Citizens' Movements' (*Neues Forum, Initiative Demokratie und Menschenrechte, Demokratie Jetzt*) who had been in the forefront of the anti-Honecker opposition. The latter's misgivings against Bonn's reunification drive were, however, outweighed by their hostility to the ex-SED, leaving the PDS isolated except for occasional alliances with various smaller left-wing splinter groups.

Following the decisive victory of the Right in the March elections and the subsequent rush towards monetary union and political unification, priority was given to the attempt to build West German branches in preparation for the first all-German parliamentary elections scheduled for December 1990. Carefully avoiding too close an identification with the West German Communist Party and skilfully exploiting the charismatic appeal of Gregor Gysi, these efforts were targeted chiefly at the left wing of a faction-ridden Green Party and the many smaller left-wing and pacifist groups. Although it achieved some initial success in building the PDS/Linke Liste electoral alliance, this success was limited because of the overwhelming sympathy of most of the West German left with the anti-PDS citizens' movements, and it was also drawn into the factional warfare which characterised relations between the rival Green and Trotskyist groups involved in the project. The poor showing of the

Linke Liste in the December 1990 elections and the hostility of the East German rank and file to the Western left-wingers promoted into the party leadership soon persuaded the PDS again to switch their priorities back to a consolidation of its position in the former GDR.

Here, disillusionment with the social and economic consequences of unification has led to a rapid fall in the popularity of the newly elected CDU governments, and left the SPD and PDS to compete for the role of principal representative of the fast-growing discontent. Relations with the SPD are particularly fraught, both for historical and more recent reasons. Many Social Democrats remember the fratricidal conflict between the two wings of the workers' movement during the Weimar Republic, the forced merger of their party into the SED in 1946, and the persecution and denunciation of social democrats and social democracy throughout the history of the GDR. But the SPD is caught in a dilemma: the largest left-of-centre force electorally, it has still not succeeded in re-implanting itself into its traditional working-class milieu: it has only around 26,000 members in the ex-GDR (compared with 900,000 in West Germany), with a mere 6000 in industrial Saxony, where there were 137,000 at the end of the Weimar Republic.[24] A party of 'priests, engineers and the middle classes' according to former SPD general secretary Peter Glotz,[25] it must identify itself more strongly with the social discontent over the consequences of marketisation if it is to rebuild its former working-class base, but in doing so will inevitably share a common political territory with the PDS and be forced into at least partial collaboration with the former communists. Already the leaders of the SPD are quietly encouraging the Eastern organisation to relax its hostility to the recruitment of individuals with an SED past or a PDS membership card, but resistance to this remains strong.[26] A similar dilemma for the social democrats is posed by the continuing ability of the PDS to attract sufficient votes in local elections to force other left-of-centre parties – the SPD as well as the *Bündnis 90* – to choose between an arrangement with the ex-SED and entering a Grand Coalition with the CDU to be able to form workable administrations. The latter choice, of course, makes it even more difficult for the SPD to develop its own profile and thus aids the PDS in consolidating its position as the main force on the left opposing the social consequences of free-market economics. Yet, wherever good working relations between the two parties of the left do develop at a local level, it is by no means the PDS which reaps the benefits: over half of the 300 or so *Bürgermeister* (executive mayors) gained by the PDS in the May 1990 local council elections are reported to have resigned from the party since then,[27] either defecting to the SPD or preferring to further their local government careers without the encumbrance of PDS membership.

PROSPECTS

It appears almost inevitable that the next federal elections will see the end of PDS representation in the Bundestag, given the 5 per cent clause and the PDS's nationwide opinion-poll standing of around 2 per cent. Unless, that is, the party's campaign to persuade the Federal Constitutional Court to extend its suspension of the all-German 5 per cent clause for the 1990 elections to the forthcoming one is successful, or it gains direct seats in some East German (East Berlin) constituencies on a first-past-the-post basis.[28] Although it is far from certain that elimination from the Federal Parliament would affect the continued survival of the PDS as a political–parliamentary force at regional and local level in the territory of the former GDR, it would probably spell an end to the party's ambitions of establishing itself as a nationwide force to the left of the SPD and the Greens.

The long-term fate of German communism – or what remains of it – cannot, however, be divorced from that of its historic twin, social democracy. Social democracy and communism, after all, share a common ideological and sociological source: Marxism and the workers' movement. They continue to compete for the same social constituencies and to promote broadly common values, those of an egalitarian, free, just, 'classless' society. Contrary to what ideologists on either side of the divide have written and said at times, the lines of demarcation between them have been far from fixed: the social democrats have not always been more democratic than the communists, nor have the communists always been to the left of the social democrats. The only reasonably stable difference has been that, by and large, the social democrats have been more closely identified with the existing order, promoting a gradual change of the status quo, while the communists have represented an alternative model to the status quo, that of the Soviet Union. The precise content of communist policy has always depended on the political nature of the Soviet Union: from the revolutionary internationalism of the Leninist era to the reformist co-existentialism of Khrushchev and his successors.

This alternative model has now ceased to exist, at least in Europe, and to that extent the European communist parties have finally lost their raison *d'être*. No longer able to promote an alternative 'actually existing socialism', their only means of differentiating themselves from social democracy, and maintaining an independent organisational and electoral base, is to advance an alternative strategy to that of social democracy in the struggle for a more egalitarian society. Will they be able to do this in a sustained and coherent fashion? All the evidence, in Germany and elsewhere in Europe, points to the conclusion that they will not.

In terms of the immediate prospects, therefore, all the pressures on the party-political remnants of the communist camp are in the direction of further, rapid social-democratisation and, as a consequence of the blurring of ideological frontiers, an increasing trend towards organisational absorption by social democracy in the medium and longer term. In a historical perspective, however, this would only confirm the end of an era which began with the Bolshevik Revolution and ended with the collapse of the Soviet Union – the era of open, party-political confrontation and competition between two currents in the organised labour movement which had coexisted within a common organisational framework before 1917. It would not necessarily preclude the reappearance of the old schism between reform and revolution in a new form at some point in the future. The increasing pressures exerted on social democracy by a worsening social and economic crisis as well as an uncertain future for Germany in a more volatile, post-Cold War Europe may well produce new internal differentiations in which the left-wing traditions embodied – in however contradictory and deformed a fashion – by the present-day PDS and its membership could yet play a significant part.

NOTES

1. The membership of the KPD at the beginning of 1921 was 359,613. Cf. Hermann Weber (ed.), *Völker hört die Signale. Der deutsche Kommunismus, 1916–1966* (Munich, 1967), p. 369.
2. Cf. Betrifft, *Verfassungsschutz '76* (published by the West German Ministry of the Interior, Bonn, 1977), p. 69.
3. Betrifft, *Verfassungsschutz '76*, pp. 74–5.
4. Cf. Peter Schütte, 'Die Musik bestimmt, wer bezahlt', *Deutschland Archiv*, 11/1990, p. 1725.
5. Ibid., p. 1724.
6. The stark contrast between the electoral strength of the PDS in East and West applies even to Berlin, where the 29.7 per cent polled in the 1992 local elections in the Eastern districts was complemented by a mere 0.9 per cent in West Berlin. Cf. *Der Spiegel*, 23/1992, p. 34.
7. Cf. 'Gibts es eine moderne sozialistische Alternative?', in *PDS-Pressedienst*, 12/7/1990.
8. From January to October 1989, the party lost 66,000 members, and the reports back from the local organisations often emphasised the widespread disaffection and demoralisation in the ranks. For some examples of such reports, see Manfred Behrend and Helmut Meier (eds), *Der schwere Weg der Erneuerung: Von der SED zur PDS* (Berlin, 1991), pp. 104–14 and *passim*.
9. For documentation of the widespread negative reaction to this step inside the party ranks, see Behrend and Meier, *Der schwere Weg der Erneuerung*, pp. 48–53.
10. Cf. Behrend and Meir, *Der schwere Weg der Erneuerung*, pp. 83–94.
11. Egon Krenz, *Wenn Mauern fallen. Die Friedliche Revolution: Vorgeschichte – Ablauf – Auswirkungen* (Vienna, 1990); Günter Mittag, *Um jeden Preis. Im Spannungsfeld zweier Systeme* (Berlin and Weimar 1991); Hans Modrow, *Aufbruch und Ende* (Hamburg 1991); Günter Schabowski, *Der Absturz* (Berlin, 1991); Reinhold

Andert and Wolfgang Herzberg, *Der Sturz: Erich Honecker im Kreuzverhör* (Berlin: Weimar, 1990). See also, among many others: 'Ich sterbe in diesem Kasten', interview with Erich Mielke, in *Der Spiegel*, 36/1992, pp. 38–53.

12. Egon Krenz, *Wenn Mauern fallen*, pp. 23–5.
13. The daubing of right-wing slogans onto the Soviet War Memorial in Treptow (East Berlin) – the perpetrators were never found – was used as a pretext for a near-hysterical campaign by the party leadership against a spurious neo-fascist threat. While successful in mobilising and uniting the hard core of party activists, it only served to isolate the SED–PDS (as it was then known) further from the population.
14. Among the more prominent figures in East Germany's public life who had to resign because of *Stasi* accusations were Wolfgang Schnur, co-founder of the *Demokratischer Aufbruch;* Lothar de Maizière, leader of the East German CDU, deputy leader of the all-German CDU, and the GDR's only freely elected Prime Minister, and Ibrahim Boehme, co-founder and leader of the East German SPD. Manfred Stolpe, a prominent figure in the East German Protestant Church and later SPD prime minister of Brandenburg, has also been accused of having been an 'informal informant' of the Ministry for State Security.
15. According to the chairman of the PDS in the East Berlin Marzahn district, Klaus Wiezorek, 'less than 20 per cent' of its 6200 members were former employees of the MfS. Quoted in *Der Spiegel*, 46/1990, p. 33.
16. Cf. *Der Spiegel*, 8/1992, pp. 30–3.
17. For an overview of these problems, cf. Johannes L. Kuppe, 'Die PDS-Finanzen – eine Skandalgeschichte', *Deutschland Archiv*, 12/1990, pp. 1821–4.
18. Cf. *PDS-Pressedienst*, 35/1991; also *Der Spiegel*, 50/1991, p. 70.
19. Cf. *Der Spiegel*, 35/1991, pp. 28–9.
20. Cf. Siegfried Suckut and Dietrich Staritz, 'Alte Heimat oder neue Linke? Das SED-Erbe und die PDS-Erben', *Deutschland Archiv*, 10/1991, p. 1046.
21. Ibid., p. 1050; also Johannes Kuppe and Thomas Ammer, *Von der SED zur PDS* (Bonn, 1991), pp. 4–15.
22. Quoted in *Der Spiegel*, 50/1991, p. 71.
23. Speech to the 3rd Session of the 2nd Party Congress, 14/15 December 1991, *Pressedienst. Presse-und Informationsdienst des Parteivorstandes*, 51/91, 20 December 1991, p. 2.
24. Figures from *Der Spiegel*, 43/1991, p. 66.
25. Ibid.
26. See 'Sehr reserviert', ibid., where it is estimated that only about 3 per cent of the current East German SPD membership are former communists (p. 68).
27. Cf. *Der Spiegel*, 18/1992.

28.   For the 1990 elections, the Constitutional Court accepted the argument that the very different living conditions in the five new Länder justified the separate counting of the votes towards the 5 per cent clause, thus allowing the PDS, the Bündnis 90 and the DSU representation in the *Bundestag*.

8 The West European Communist Movement: Past, Present and Future[1]

Martin J. Bull

What is the current state of the West European communist movement? How has it been affected by the East European Revolutions of 1989? What are the prospects for the movement in the late twentieth century? An assessment of the movement's *present* state and *future* prospects is not possible without first evaluating the movement's *past*: what *was* the West European Communist movement before 1989 and what condition, domestically and internationally, was it in? This conclusion, therefore, in drawing out the common themes which emerge from the studies in this book, is divided into three parts: the past, the present, the future.

THE PAST: AMBIGUITY, DECLINE AND FRAGMENTATION

The West European Communist Identity

Evidently, when reference is made to a West European communist *movement* it is to a particular 'set' of political parties, this book having examined seven such cases. Yet, beyond a common label, what were the factors binding these parties together which allowed them to constitute a common family and a grouping in the European Parliament, and which made them unacceptable as coalition partners to most other parties?

Historically, the common factor was indisputable. These parties were products of the 1917 Russian Revolution. In the pre-Second World War (and part of the post-war) period this was translated in terms of abject loyalty to the Soviet Union's dictates. In the latter part of the post-war period, abject loyalty was gradually replaced by a privileged link with Moscow based on a shared recognition of the Russian Revolution and communist rule. Two other binding factors followed from this privileged link: these parties' teleological nature (i.e. their commitment to building a society different from the capitalist one) and their internal organisational principle, democratic centralism, which ensured appointment through co-option and suppressed internal dissent.

Yet, it would be wrong to reduce the West European communist movement to a set of parties having been based on these binding factors as distinguishing characteristics. On the one hand, as is evident from the chapters in this book, the strength and persistence of these factors varied between and inside parties and changed over time. On the other hand – and inseparable from the first point – many, if not most, of the parties (at least from 1956 onwards) wished to distinguish themselves not only from other Western parties (which the above factors successfully did) but also from the Soviet Communist Party (CPSU) and communist parties in Eastern Europe. They did this through claiming that, whatever the nature of their goals for reshaping society in a socialist direction, they would none the less respect those rights and privileges normally associated with 'bourgeois democracy': parliamentary institutions, civil liberties, pluralism of political parties and interest groups etc. As with the first set of factors, however, the degree of commitment to these principles varied between and inside parties and over time.

Broadly speaking, then, the West European communist objective was to carve out an identity which was distinguishable from Western parties (liberal democratic and social democratic) on the one hand, and orthodox communist parties on the other, and since this exercise involved borrowing from both traditions, the result was a high level of ambiguity which aroused suspicion about the parties in both the West and the East. In short, the West European communist movement is best seen as having been located on an 'ambiguity continuum' ranging from 'more orthodox' parties – such as the French (PCF), Portuguese (PCP), Greek (KKE), German (DKP), and Belgian (PCB) – to 'more liberalised' parties – such as the Italian (PCI), Spanish (PCE), British (CPGB), Swedish (VKP), Finnish (SKP) and Dutch (CPN) – the continuum also having been latently present inside the parties in the form of internal party debate. The closer the parties came to the centre of the continuum the more ambiguous their nature. The ambiguity was perhaps best symbolised in the notion of the 'third way' (which constituted the heart of eurocommunism): that Western communist parties would build socialism whilst upholding those rights and traditions associated with the Western democratic tradition. Real change, however, in the direction of liberalisation (i.e. in the sense of a transformation into non-communist parties of the left) was ultimately constrained by the mechanics of democratic centralism. Yet, as will be argued below, this issue crept up the political agenda in the 1980s.

The State of the Movement: the Domestic Context

The eurocommunist period of the mid-1970s was seen at the time as a 'golden era' which held out the promise of government for several of the parties. From hindsight it was a peak from which began an inexorable decline and a crisis of multi-dimensional proportions. Although the parties refused to see this as a crisis of the movement, there were common factors at work: long-term socio-economic changes which had resulted in a decline in the traditional working class (the bedrock of these parties' support) and class-related voting behaviour; the rise of the 'new politics' and concomitant decline in salience of economic issues (on which communist parties essentially relied); the rise of the 'new right' and an 'anti-state' consensus in the 1980s (when these parties' programmes were traditionally predicated on state intervention to restructure society); and the total discrediting of the Soviet model (the historical association with which was an indelible mark on these parties' nature). The crisis did not affect all of the parties to the same degree, and their varying fortunes depended much on their abilities to adapt to the changes and to exploit the peculiarities of party political competition in their respective countries. Nevertheless, for all of the parties, the crisis was multidimensional and common trends were visible.[2]

Electorally, all the parties analysed in this volume (and one can add the Greek, Finnish, Dutch, Danish, Norwegian, Swiss and Swedish parties) suffered a decline (in some cases a sharp drop) in their levels of support in the 1980s (whether at the national, sub-national or supra-national levels). At the *organisational* level too, most of these parties suffered a decline in membership (although obtaining reliable membership figures is notoriously difficult), and a concomitant decline in activism as the class cohesion of their electorates and memberships dwindled. *Socially*, the parties suffered increasing isolation through their declining influence in the trade union movement (and the crisis of the trade union movement itself) and a declining 'presence' in their respective societies, perhaps best reflected in the decline in sales of party newspapers.[3] At the *intellectual* level, the parties suffered in the 1980s from the onslaught of the 'new right' and the loss of intellectuals essential to responding theoretically to that challenge. *Strategically*, many of the parties reached an impasse as the prospect of achieving office as part of a government whose goal would be the restructuring of society became more remote. Many appeared, by the late 1980s, to have exhausted all strategic alternatives, and the experience of the PCF in the early 1980s confirmed the hazards for communist parties seeking office.

Finally, at the *internal* level, as the intensity of the crisis increased so the pressure of dissent inside the parties became greater in the 1980s. In many of the parties, and particularly those where liberalisation had already begun, debate over strategic alternatives was gradually overshadowed by a debate about these parties' very identities. If there was a common fundamental division in this debate it was between those who felt that the putative 'distinctiveness' of West European communist parties had become an albatross which should be jettisoned and those who believed that the root of the crisis lay in deradicalisation and the *de facto* reduction of objectives to monitoring or overseeing capitalist development *à la* Mitterrand–González–Craxi. In short, the 'ambiguity continuum' (noted above) along which Western communist parties could be located gained more and more prominence inside the parties themselves. The leadership position in this debate was invariably either 'centrist' (attempting to mediate between the extremes, while proceeding with some liberalisation) or 'orthodox' (resisting any moves in this direction). Common to both positions was a preference for debate to focus on external strategic issues rather than on internal issues concerned with the parties' identities.

The State of the Movement: the International Context

The international context in the 1980s compounded the West European communist movement's domestic problems.[4] The post-1956 history of international communism was characterised by a consistent decline in the control exercised by the CPSU over the international movement and a growing diversity in the relationship of Western communist parties to Moscow as a consequence of the degeneration of the Soviet Union's image abroad. Eurocommunism in the 1970s was predicated on the rejection of the Soviet Union as a universal model of socialism. Eurocommunism's demise in the late 1970s simply confirmed that a uniform relationship of non-ruling communist parties to Moscow – whether based on autonomy or dependence – was unlikely to occur again. The 1980s consequently witnessed a fragmentation of the parties in their relationship to Moscow. Some parties, such as the PCF, PCP and the KKE, reaffirmed the validity of their link with Moscow. Others, such as the PCI and PCE, continued to distance themselves. Indeed, the PCI went as far as to enact a definitive 'rip' (*strappo*) with Moscow over Jaruselski's seizure of power in Poland in 1981. The international issue increased the intensity of divisions inside the parties.

In this context, the appointment of Mikhail Gorbachev as general-secretary of the CPSU in 1985 and the beginning of *perestroika* had a paradoxical effect in changing the nature of the debate over the Western communist parties' relationship to Moscow. On the one hand, being 'pro-Soviet' no longer meant 'pro-Stalinism' but 'pro-reform'. 'Pro-reform', moreover, did not entail abandoning socialism. It is important to remember that the declared goal of *perestroika* was to reform socialism, *not* destroy it. Whatever lay behind the rhetoric, the hopes engendered by this possibility gave Western communist parties a new focus, for if Gorbachev were to be successful it offered a new and more convincing model of development to which these parties could aspire and which could provide a possible solution to their domestic decline. Consequently, West European communist parties were led, willy nilly, into a convergence of positions based on support for *perestroika* (and a type of support that differed from that given by other non-communist parties in the West). Even the PCI, which (as noted above), having apparently made an 'irrevocable' break with the Soviet Union over Poland, re-established a privileged relationship with the CPSU in the form of the so-called 'new internationalism', and in January 1989 the *strappo*, by mutual consent, was buried as a break with a ruling group which had abandoned the goals of socialism.

On the other hand, despite an apparent convergence of positions *in support* of *perestroika*, divisions deepened in the West European communist movement over the implications of the reform programme for the parties themselves. *Perestroika* allowed some parties, such as the PCI, to pursue internal liberalisation more vehemently, while placing others, such as the PCF and PCP, under increasing pressure to begin internal reform. The latter's refusal (despite growing internal pressures) to respond to these pressures enhanced the existing division in the West European communist movement at the same time as modifying its exact nature: it was now a matter of 'pro-Soviets' versus 'pro-Stalinists'. The latter's support of *perestroika* was increasingly viewed as no more than paying lip service to the concept. The most vivid illustration of the changed nature of the division was the decision of the PCI and PCE, after the 1989 European elections, to leave the existing communist group in the European Parliament and create a new formation, 'For a United Left'. In fact, deputies elected on communist lists were from then on enrolled in no less than four separate groups.

In short, the appointment of Gorbachev exacerbated the fragmentation of the West European communist movement, but not in the direction in which it had been heading before the beginning of *perestroika*. Before 1985 liberalisation had gone hand in hand with detachment from Moscow; after 1985 it drew on the example and support of Moscow. This new (or re-)attachment made the impact of the revolutions of 1989 on the West European communist movement greater than it might otherwise have been, in as far as those revolutions involved a rejection of *perestroika* as a means of reform because of its evolutionary nature. There is an evident paradox here in that without Gorbachev the dramatic changes in Eastern Europe would not have occurred. Yet, it can none the less be argued that had West European communist parties not been seduced back into a 'special relationship' with Moscow in the period after 1985, they might not have found themselves quite so bewildered and overtaken by events in the summer and autumn of 1989.

THE PRESENT: THE IMPACT OF THE 1989
REVOLUTIONS

For the West European communist movement the immediate significance of the revolutions of 1989 lay in their qualitative difference from existing developments in the Soviet Union. As already noted, the declared goal of *perestroika* was to 'reform socialism'. Whatever the actual meaning of this, it meant that change was limited and evolutionary in character. The changes in Eastern Europe, however, took on a radically different dimension: they were concerned with throwing out not only Stalinism but socialism altogether. The unexpected nature and speed with which the events occurred, coupled with the erstwhile optimism in Gorbachev's reform programme, caught the West European communist movement unprepared and the remarkable situation arose of communist parties in Eastern Europe – beginning with the Hungarian – shedding their names and heritage while parties in the West continued to hold on to theirs. The Western parties were thrown into turmoil as they confronted a common dilemma: should they abandon their principles, names and heritage wholesale or, if not, how could they dissociate themselves from the failure of their Eastern counterparts while maintaining those principles intact and a degree of political relevance in their respective countries? The central issue, then, for the West European communist movement shifted almost overnight from one concerned with whether and how to adapt themselves to reverse long-term decline to an issue focused fundamentally on whether and how to transform themselves in order to survive. Four years after the revolutions, that issue remained at the heart of the movement, even though several parties had gone a long way to attempting to resolve it definitively. The impact was to intensify divisions both *between* and *inside* the parties.

The divisions existing *between* West European communist parties were intensified to the point at which it became difficult in the early 1990s to view them any longer as a 'family' of political parties. The 'ambiguity continuum' was stretched to breaking point. Broadly speaking, the parties can be seen as having divided into three groups in their (leadership) responses to the revolutions.[5] First, some rejected the idea that the changes in Eastern Europe required any changes to the parties themselves. These orthodox

Marxists and pro-Soviets continued to believe in the viability of the international communist movement and the relevance of the communist goal, as traditionally understood. The PCP, PCF, PCB and DKP fell into this category, although three of these (the PCF, PCP and PCB) may be headed in the direction of the second category (outlined below), the PCF and PCP under new leaders in 1993. Secondly, some parties argued that the failure of communism in Eastern Europe represented a failure of a degenerated model of socialism (Stalinism) and not socialism *per se*. Indeed, with the final collapse of this model, it was argued, new opportunities opened up for Western communist parties, no longer constrained or tainted by its presence, to develop the original principles of Marxism in the context of the changes brought about in advanced capitalist society. The PCE, KKE and *Rifondazione comunista* fell into this category, with the possibility of other parties joining them from the first category (mentioned above). Thirdly, some parties concluded that the collapse of communism in Eastern Europe represented a failure of communism itself, requiring the shedding of the name, symbols and heritage of WECPs and their transformation into non-communist parties of the left. This road was followed by the PCI, CPGB, CPN, VKP and SKP.

In the four years since the collapse of the Berlin Wall the West European communist movement has disintegrated through the different responses of the individual parties. Their erstwhile fragmentation has become separation and, in the future, it will no longer be possible to generalise about these parties as a 'family', nor fruitful to study them within the same analytical framework. Asking why the parties reacted so differently is, to a large extent, misguided. Had the parties all reacted *in the same way* then it would have been pertinent to have asked why. As argued earlier, the differentiation between communist parties before the revolutions of 1989 was considerable and the movement was undergoing further fragmentation. By the late 1980s the only thing which really united these parties was support for the attempt to reform, and therefore save, socialism in the Soviet Union. Yet, even this, at the same time, divided the parties further because of its implications for their own internal reform. The failure of that attempt and the collapse of the 'socialist motherland' removed the last vestiges of possible unity, and the parties quickly divided in the paths they followed. What it confirmed was what students of West European communism have long argued: that, despite their identification under a common label, parties such as the PCI and PCF were always very different political animals.

Paralleling the divide between the parties have been divisions *inside* the parties themselves. Indeed, it is possible to detect elements of all three categories of response (outlined above) present inside most of the parties. The intensity of division inside each party has obviously varied, as the chapters in this volume document. In general, those whose leadership responses place them in the third category have suffered greater inner turmoil. This is not only because their choices involved finally crossing the Rubicon, but also because the parties which responded in this manner were those which had already undergone a degree of liberalisation. These parties, therefore, had already become more open and democratic in their internal operation, thus providing more orthodox elements inside the parties with the opportunity to oppose openly the leaderships' proposals. The PCI provides the best example here. Its internal reform programme began almost a year before the revolutions in Eastern Europe, and at its 18th Congress in March 1989 the party effectively dismantled democratic centralism as an organising principle. Consequently, when the leader Occhetto launched his proposal to transform the party into a non-communist party of the left he had already lost the mechanisms of control and suppression of dissent which democratic centralism provided, and the party was thrown instantly into its worst crisis. The leaderships of the more orthodox parties such as the PCF, on the other hand, were able more effectively to control opposition to their position through the traditional party structures (although this is not to suggest that they remained free from increasing pressure).

Shorn of their status and mutual support as part of an international movement and deeply divided amongst and inside themselves, the West European communist parties, unsurprisingly, failed, in the four years after the revolutions, to resolve their domestic crises. Although the East European revolutions swept away an entire political order they did not attenuate the domestic problems which lay at the heart of the decline of the communist movement in the West. Those problems remained – and remain – in place and the parties still need to address them. With the exception of the PCE (as part of a coalition of the left in Spain), elections in the four-year period since the collapse of the Berlin Wall have confirmed the continuing decline and growing political isolation of parties either carrying, or until recently carrying, the communist label.[6] This introduces the question of the future of the West European communist movement.

THE FUTURE: THE PROSPECTS FOR WEST EUROPEAN COMMUNISM

The West European communist movement as we have known it is dead. This is not to suggest that communist parties will no longer exist in the West, but those which remain cannot be the same as before. However firm their refusal to countenance change, they have to face the fact that the collapse of international communism embodies a change in their own nature. West European communism in the post-war period was the product of a specific mix of factors which emanated from a mistaken optimism in the Soviet Union and a painstaking, but incomplete, attempt to gain independence from that country. The ambiguous identity which resulted constituted the heart of the West European communist tradition, and it is that tradition which has disappeared. What, then, are the prospects for the West European communist movement? Are the parties all destined to follow the Italian, British, Swedish, Finnish and Dutch examples in seeking a non-communist identity or is there a future for communism in Europe? Broadly speaking, one can identify three possible scenarios or avenues for parties of the old West European communist tradition: first, remaining an unchanged 'more orthodox' communist party; second, becoming a 'refounded' communist party; and third, changing into a non-communist party of the left.

Remaining an Unchanged 'More Orthodox' Communist Party

It is evident that even if – as the PCI experience admirably demonstrates – embarking on the transition to non-communist status is an arduous and risky business (the outcome of which is far from clear) *not* doing so constitutes, in many ways, as much of a challenge. This is not just because of the collapse of the international communist movement but is also due to the turning of the liberalisation process in Eastern Europe against everything these parties have stood for. Germany's unique case is symptomatic here. The SED (the East German Communist Party), in quickly changing its name to the PDS, would have no truck with the hard-line party in the West (the DKP) because the latter's Stalinist credentials were regarded as an impediment to attracting new sectors of the German vote. In short, the Western communist parties which have refused to countenance change have been left gaping into a void, linked to what is universally regarded as a failed experiment and to a label under which there is increasingly little to sell.

The argument against this scenario is that the massive dislocation and economic hardship caused by the regime transitions and the consequent disillusionment with the entire process might work to these parties' advantage. Parties such as the PCF, for example, were quick to criticise the effects produced by the attempt to introduce capitalism in Eastern Europe. Yet, despite popular disillusionment with the changes in Eastern Europe, the driving force of opposition to these changes has come from hard-line communist

elements willing to consider violence to gain their objectives, something which suggests that if a revival of 'communism' were to occur it would be in the form of a military
coup. The attempted coup in the Soviet Union in 1991 and
the military show-down between Yeltsin and hard-line elements of the Russian Parliament in 1993 were significant in
revealing the sort of allies with which unchanged Western
communist parties could become associated. Significantly,
the PCF, after the resignation of its leader Georges Marchais
in 1993, decided to drop internationalism and reorganise
the party, effectively abandoning democratic centralism.

Seen in this context, the domestic prospects for unchanged Western communist parties are to remain hard-line
parties of protest which represent the most disadvantaged
sectors of society. However, this role – which parties such as
the PCF used to play effectively – has changed as a result of
the decline and fragmentation of the working class. Protest
parties now represent an inter-class mix of those most disillusioned with advanced capitalism, and communist parties may
find themselves competing on the same terrain as extremist
parties and movements from the other end of the political
spectrum: hardly a scenario dear to Marx or Lenin.

Becoming a 'Refounded' Communist Party

How far can a West European communist party modernise
itself without 'crossing the ford'? *Rifondazione comunista* –
which was born out of a split from the PCI shortly after the
crucial vote to transform the party into the PDS – can claim
to be the only real 'new' communist party. With 5.6 per cent
of the vote (in 1992) it is a small party, although its achievement is greater than its percentage suggests when viewed in
the context of the Italian party system. Yet, the party is in-
delibly associated with the CPSU because of the previous
pro-Soviet location inside the PCI of its leading personnel
(such as Armando Cossutta). Indeed, some critics would
argue that it is an unchanged 'more orthodox' communist
party which stayed behind when the PCI took its leap
forwards.

The party's name ('Communist Refoundation'), however, does sum up aptly the key question: can communism be refounded? This is an issue which goes beyond the parties' responses because it concerns more profound theoretical issues. There is a clear division on these issues between East and West (besides the obvious divisions in the West itself). Many Western Marxists were slow to recognise that the 1989 revolutions involved not only the overthrow of Stalinism but of socialism *per se*. Because the revolutions were made possible by Gorbachev's reform experiment it had been too easy to assume that this accelerated form of liberalisation would retain Gorbachevian (i.e. socialist) objectives.[7] That the reality was so different was first confirmed for Western Marxists in late 1989 at a meeting between members of the British New Left and erstwhile East European dissidents, then in the mainstream of their countries' revolutions. The latter rejected the former's continued commitment to socialism, insisting that their peoples had rejected socialism altogether and that what was returning in Eastern Europe was 'the concept of Western civilisation' or 'the idea of the West'. David Warszawski, a Solidarity journalist, for example, stated that 'the Polish people have rejected socialism as such', and that 'you people speak a language we no longer understand'.[8] Indeed, David Selbourne's analysis of the attitudes and beliefs of East Europeans during the period of the revolutions found that many of them admired Margaret Thatcher and aspired to a form of hybrid Toryism.[9] The first elections after the revolutions (in countries such as Hungary and East Germany), where conservative parties proved most popular, confirmed these trends. Moreover, as already noted, those who, since then, have become disillusioned with the transition to capitalism have turned to orthodox extremism rather than the promise of a reconstituted Marxism.

The left in the West has not been so quick to consign Marxism to the historical dustbin. True, awareness of the almost universal rejection of the doctrine in Eastern Europe has caused considerable despondency; but there are various theorists who – and parties and party factions which –

remain committed to Marxism as an ideal (while unequivocally denouncing Stalinism). Their primary objective now is
to investigate Marxism's new potential in the aftermath of
the collapse of the communist regimes.[10] The possible
appeal of this attempt should not be too readily written off.
The victorious gloating which characterised some immediate responses to the collapse of communism (perhaps best
symbolised, rightly or wrongly, in Francis Fukuyama's *The
End of History and the Last Man*[11]) has given way to more
sober and realistic assessments of the future of Europe.
These have been influenced by the deep problems experienced by the countries of Eastern Europe since the collapse
of communism, showing that a transition to capitalism is
neither smooth nor inevitable. They have also been influenced by the problems which have beset Western Europe
since the collapse of communism, in the form of rising extremism and nationalism of the far right, which have revealed that capitalism's erstwhile strength and unity was, at
least in part, due to the existence (and threat) of the communist monolith.

It is possible, therefore, that, if the dangers of destabilisation and extremism were to continue in the long term,
Western parties acting as vehicles for a rejuvenated form of
communism might find some popular appeal. Yet, that
would depend on their own ability to unite around a
common set of principles and action. The experience of
Rifondazione comunista in this attempt is significant. Having
started life in an optimistic and united spirit, the party has
already been wracked by a leadership crisis over its political
line, which resulted in the resignation of the leader, Sergio
Garavini, in 1993.

In the short to medium term, the success of Western communist parties will probably depend less on their ability to
'refound' communism than on the nature of domestic political competition, the strength and image of the existing socialist parties and the relationship the communist parties
have with them. In Spain, for example, the relative success
of the PCE-led United Left (IU) was made possible by
public disillusionment with the governing Socialist Party's

apparent abandonment of its socialist ideas. This type of support, for obvious reasons, may prove to be ephemeral. Nor is it clear that retaining a specifically 'communist' label is essential to exploiting political competition of this kind, because the electoral support may amount to little more than a warning to the socialist party that it has moved too far towards the centre (the New Left party in Sweden, for example, continued to play this role despite its abandonment of communism). Indeed, being 'too communist' can undermine the ability of a left-wing party to play this role, as the failure of the PCF to gain at the expense of the French Socialist Party shows. There is, in short, a long and difficult road ahead for those parties committed to 'refounding communism'. But, difficult as it is, these parties will be aware from the third scenario (below) that renouncing the attempt will not necessarily solve their problems. This awareness, more than anything else, may ensure the persistence of communist parties in Western Europe.

Changing into a Non-Communist Party of the Left

The five parties which have made the transition to the status of 'non-communism' (the PCI, CPGB, VKP, SKP and CPN) have shown it to be a process fraught with difficulties and uncertainties, the political effects of which (in the short term, at least) have been far from beneficial. None of the parties has managed to arrest the continued electoral and organisational decline. On the contrary, in the two cases analysed in this volume, the decline has steepened. The PCI–PDS transformation has cost the Italian party 10.5 per cent of its vote (between 1987 and 1992) and 330,240 members (between 1990 and 1991, a figure over three times as high as the 1989–90 loss and eight times as high as the 1988–9 loss), part of this decline being due to *Rifondazione comunista*. Similarly, the CPGB–Democratic Left transformation has cost the British party two-thirds of its membership (down from 4742 in 1991 to 1234 in 1993). The internal turmoil generated by the transition process, moreover, has not abated. There remain substantial remnants of opposition inside the parties to their very existence as non-communist parties. Preferring to continue the struggle from within, these members' objective is to radicalise the party and its line (or, at a minimum, prevent its further deradicalisation). In the Italian PDS, for example, the opposition has labelled itself the 'Democratic Communists', an indication of the direction in which they would take the party if they gained control.

What, then, does the future hold for ex-communist parties which have chosen this road? The most profound problem they face concerns the political movement they are entering. They have – albeit with difficulties – successfully left one political movement: a threshold has been crossed and now separates the ex-communist parties from those still carrying the label. In renouncing their communist identities these parties are, whether purposefully or by sheer action of the political tide, entering a new political movement: that of 'social democracy', of the non-communist left. This is perhaps most vividly expressed in the Italian PDS's decision to leave the 'United Left' Group in the European Parliament and to apply to join (and subsequently be accepted by) the Socialist Federation and the Socialist International. In leaving one political movement for another, the simple question arises: what is the state of the political movement the ex-communist parties are entering? The answer is that it is also a movement long in crisis. Under whatever labels they have been campaigning ('social democratic', 'democratic socialist', 'socialist', 'Labour'), the parties of the non-communist left have, in the 1980s, been grappling with many problems which are analogous to those facing Western communist parties: electoral and organisational decline, an identity crisis and the need to find a new programme of policies.[12] Small wonder, then, that the parties which have made the transition to non-communist status have chosen to avoid any reference to 'democratic socialism' or 'social democracy' in deciding their new names, opting instead for names such as 'New Left', 'Democratic Left', 'Green Left', 'Leftist Alliance' and 'Democratic Party of the Left'. Besides reflecting compromises forged inside the parties between different factions, these names amount to an implicit recognition that if the political movement the parties have just left is in crisis the one they are entering is not in much better shape.

The new party names also amount to a statement that ex-communist parties are in search of something different from the known traditions of the non-communist left. This search for a different identity within the non-communist left is not something new. Indeed, the 'social democratic tradition' has always contained within it considerable diversity.[13] Most notable, perhaps, was the emergence of Southern European socialism in the 1970s and 1980s, which differed in many respects from Western social democracy of the 1950s and 1960s. Yet, that experience is perhaps indicative of the task facing a 'new democratic left' of ex-communist parties. The expectations generated by the coming to power of the French, Spanish and Greek socialist parties – which claimed not to have been deradicalised like the more traditional social democratic parties – quickly turned to disillusionment as the socialist governments failed to achieve any restructuring of society. Most damning, however, was the apparent willingness of some of them – despite their radical rhetoric – to abandon their democratic socialist principles and adopt state-patronage policies typical of their predecessors. After this experience the arrival of another 'new breed' of democratic socialist parties coming from yet another historical tradition is hardly likely to generate confidence amongst potential members and voters. Significantly, at the moment when, theoretically speaking, there is no longer any historical reason for socialist and communist parties to be split, the fragmentation of the socialist–communist area is greater than ever before: communist parties have divided amongst themselves, one (the PCI) has split in two, and no communist and socialist parties have managed to reunite. The idea of a 'new democratic left', then, more than anything else, seems to symbolise the fact that ultimately the problems faced by both political worlds ('refounded' communism and the non-communist left) amount to the same thing: the crisis of the democratic-socialist project itself. In this sense, the passing of the post-war Western communist tradition does not solve anything for the left in Europe; rather, it simply exposes the depth of its current plight.

NOTES

1. The author thanks, for their comments, the participants in the seminar on Comparative Political Parties run by Maurizio Cotta at the European University Institute, 1992–3 (where an early draft of the chapter was presented), and Paul Heywood.
2. For a detailed analysis of the decline of the parties in the 1980s, see Marc Lazar, 'Communism in Western Europe in the 1980s', *Journal of Communist Studies*, 4(3), September 1988.
3. The significance of the party press should not be underestimated, as the chapter on the CPGB shows, where the internal dispute inside the party in the 1970s and early 1980s took on a form of warfare between the party's two newspapers, the *Morning Star* and *Marxism Today*.
4   The following argument draws partly on Martin J. Bull, 'A New Era for the Non-Rulers Too: West European Communist Parties, *Perestroika* and the Revolutions in Eastern Europe', *Politics*, 11(1), 1991, pp. 17–19.
5. These groups were first tentatively outlined in ibid., p. 19. The relevance of Albert Hirschman, *Exit, Voice and Loyalty: Responses to Decline in Firms, Organisations and States* (Cambridge, MA: Harvard University Press, 1970) to the dilemma facing WECPs and the leadership responses to it should be noted (something which is also apparent in the section on 'The Future' below). The three groups do not exhaust the possible responses. Jürgen Habermas, for example, in his analysis of the consequences of the collapse of communism for the theoretical traditions of the West European left, identifies six interpretations: 'Stalinist', 'Leninist', 'reform-communist', 'postmodern', 'anti-communist' and 'liberal' ('What Does Socialism Mean Today? The Rectifying Revolution and the Need for New Thinking on the Left', *New Left Review*, **183**, September/October 1990). One can find traces of all these interpretations in the debate inside the parties, but they are not particularly helpful in identifying the actual path which the parties followed. The three groups could obviously be sub-divided further according to other nuances, but this would detract from the aim here which is to provide a relatively simple analytical categorisation by which the responses detailed in this volume can be differentiated.

6. It is possible that, in the future, the Italian PDS may prove to be another exception in so far as support for the traditional ruling parties in Italy has collapsed; however, as will be noted below, its decline thus far has actually steepened.

7. A point aptly made by Frederic Jameson, 'Conversations on the New World Order', in Robin Blackburn (ed.), *After the Fall: The Failure of Communism and the Future of Socialism* (London: Verso, 1991), p. 256.

8. David Selbourne, 'Apologists Must Apologize', *The Times*, 6 November 1989.

9. David Selbourne, *Death of the Dark Hero: Eastern Europe, 1987–1990* (London: Cape, 1990).

10. For a flavour of some of the contributions to the debate see, for example, Blackburn (ed.), *After the Fall*, Christiane Lemke and Gary Marks (eds), *The Crisis of Socialism in Europe* (London: Duke University Press, 1992), and L. Karvonen and J. Sundberg (eds), *Social Democracy in Transition: Northern, Southern and Eastern Europe* (Aldershot: Dartmouth, 1991).

11. Francis Fukuyama, *The End of History and the Last Man* (London: Hamish Hamilton, 1992).

12. For a recent summary, see Martin J. Bull, 'The Crisis of European Socialism: Searching for A (Really) Big Idea', Review Article, *West European Politics*, vol. 16(3), July 1993.

13. Stephen Padgett and William E. Paterson, *A History of Social Democracy in Postwar Europe* (London: Longman, 1991).

Index

Numbers marked in **bold type** denote a chapter devoted to the subject. 'n' denotes a footnote; 't' denotes a table

and transformation of CPGB,
145, 168–70, 171
see also CPGB
Thatcher, Margaret, xvii, 157, 216
'third way', 101
Thorez, Maurice, 33, 35, 47
Tiersky, Ronald, 52, 54
Togliatti, Palmiro, xviii, 10, 15
Tortorella, Aldo, 11, 12, 14, 17,
22

UCD (Union of the Democratic
Centre) (Sp.), 61, 64, 87–8n
UDP (Popular Democratic Union)
(Port.), 109, 110
UGT (General Workers' Union)
(Port.), 108
UGT (General Workers' Union)
(Sp.), 70, 74
Ulbricht, Walter, 184, 192, 195
Union of the Democratic Centre
(UCD), 61, 64, 87–8n
United Left, *see* IU

Van Geyt, Louis, 129, 135; *see also*
PCB
Villalonga, Isabel, 74
VKP (Swedish Communist Party),
205, 211, 218
VVN (Association of those
Persecuted by the Nazi
Regime), 179

Wallonia, 122, 124, 125, 139–40
Warszawski, David, 216
West European Communist
Movement, **203–21**
ambiguity of, 205, 210

electoral decline, 206
identity, 203–5
impact of 1989 revolutions, 56,
209–13
division between parties in
response to, 210–12
division inside parties in
response to, 212–13
internal dissent within parties
of, 206–7
international context, 207–9
isolation, 206, 213
membership decline, 206
objective of, 204–5
prospects for, 213–21
changing to non-
communism, xix,
218–20
refoundation of, xix,
215–18
remaining unchanged,
xix–xviii, 214–15
reasons for crisis in, xvii–xviii,
205–7
and Soviet Union
effect of collapse, 56, 199;
see also Soviet Union
and *perestroika, see perestroika*
relations with, *see* CPSU
see also eurocommunism;
individual parties
West German Communist Party,
see DKP; KPD
Whitfield, Dave, 151, 152, 153

Yeltsin, Boris, xx, 46, 51, 112, 215

Zamora, Pedro, 76